# THE POST-BOOM IN SPANISH AMERICAN FICTION

SUNY Series in Latin American and Iberian Thought and Culture
Jorge J. E. Gracia, Editor

# THE POST-BOOM IN SPANISH AMERICAN FICTION

DONALD L. SHAW

State University
of New York
Press

Published by
State University of New York Press, Albany

© 1998  State University of New York

Production by Susan Geraghty
Marketing by Patrick Durocher

Printed in the United States of America

For information, address State University of New York
Press, State University Plaza, Albany, N.Y., 12246

**Library of Congress Cataloging-in-Publication Data**

Shaw, Donald Leslie, 1930–
    The post-boom in Spanish American fiction / by Donald L. Shaw.
        p.     cm. — (SUNY series in Latin American and Iberian thought
and culture)
    Includes bibliographical references and index.
    ISBN 0-7914-3825-2 (hc : alk. paper). — ISBN 0-7914-3826-0 (pb :
alk. paper)
    1. Spanish American fiction—20th century—History and criticism.
I. Title.  II. Series.
PQ7082.N7S515  1998
863—dc21                                                                   97-34102
                                                                                    CIP

10  9  8  7  6  5  4  3  2  1

# CONTENTS

# PART 1

# *The Post-Boom*

# CHAPTER 1

# *The Post-Boom*

To write about the Post-Boom in the contemporary Spanish American novel is in reality to risk a few generalizations, based on selective evidence, for fellow critics to modify and refine, if they notice them, from the standpoint of their own expertise. The field is vast and evolving, the required materials are hardly to be found under one roof, and there is no consensus at present about relevant authors, periodization, or methodology. Nonetheless, it seems increasingly clear that something began to change significantly in Spanish American fiction during the mid-1970s, and a lapse of twenty years should be enough to make possible some tentative remarks. Indeed there is already a growing body of material on the Post-Boom[1] with useful indications about how to proceed.

Inevitably the first step is to try to characterize the Boom in such a way as to facilitate the task of showing how the Post-Boom is different. This is no easy task, for the Boom itself was a very complex phenomenon with a number of contradictory creative patterns existing within it. To complicate matters further, some of the major Boom writers, including García Márquez, Fuentes, Donoso, and Vargas Llosa, have undergone an evolution that has brought them on occasion to some extent into line with what are often perceived to be major features of Post-Boom writing. In the case of Cortázar we even have a 1978 essay on contemporary literature that advocates an approach that, in its support for sociopolitical commitment and emphasis on specifically American preoccupations, reads like a Post-Boom manifesto.[2] In addition, it is clear that factors shaping the Post-Boom became evident quite early in the Boom period itself, so that if we take the view that Puig and Sarduy (especially) illustrate the transition from the Boom to the Post-Boom, as seems correct, we have to see a certain overlap developing even during what appear to be the peak years of the earlier movement, that is, the 1960s. Finally, as D. W. Foster has reminded us,[3] alongside the Boom writers there were always others, like David Viñas and Mario Benedetti, who in retrospect represent a kind of prolongation of the broadly realistic, pre-Boom pattern of writing, linking it to certain aspects of the Post-Boom.

Despite the attendant problems, however, it is not unreasonable to characterize the Boom more or less in the terms which I, Duncan, and Sklodowska have at different times proposed. Attempting to sum up the conclusions of my *Nueva narrativa hispanoamericana* in 1981, I postulated the following as characteristics of the Boom:

1. La desaparición de la vieja novela "criollista" o "telúrica," de tema rural, y la emergencia del neoindigenismo de Asturias y Arguedas.

2. La desaparición de la novela "comprometida" y la emergencia de la novela "metafísica."

3. La tendencia a subordinar la observación a la fantasía creadora y la mitificación de la realidad.

4. La tendencia a enfatizar los aspectos ambiguos, irracionales y misteriosos de la realidad y de la personalidad, desembocando a veces en lo absurdo como metáfora de la existencia humana.

5. La tendencia a desconfiar del concepto de amor como soporte existencial y de enfatizar, en cambio, la incomunicación y la soledad del individuo. Anti-romanticismo.

6. La tendencia a quitar valor al concepto de la muerte en un mundo que es ya de por sí infernal.

7. La rebelión contra toda forma de tabúes morales, sobre todo los relacionados con la religión y la sexualidad. La tendencia paralela a explorar la tenebrosa magnitud de nuestra vida secreta.

8. Un mayor empleo de elementos eróticos y humorísticos.

9. La tendencia a abandonar la estructura lineal, ordenada y lógica, típica de la novela tradicional (y que reflejaba un mundo concebido como más o menos ordenado y comprensible), reemplazándola con otra estructura basada en la evolución espiritual del protagonista, o bien con estructuras experimentales que reflejan la multiplicidad de lo real.

10. La tendencia a subvertir el concepto del tiempo cronológico lineal.

11. La tendencia a abandonar los escenarios realistas de la novela tradicional, reemplazándolos con espacios imaginarios.

12. La tendencia a reemplazar al narrador omnisciente en tercera persona con narradores múltiples o ambiguos.

13. Un mayor empleo de elementos simbólicos.[4]

If at that time I had read Jitrik's *El no-existente caballero*,[5] I should have added a reference to the shift in the methods of presentation of fictional characters that he mentions.

In 1986 J. Ann Duncan basically agreed, while reducing the list to seven outstanding features.[6] Finally in 1991, Sklodowska picked out thirteen characteristic features of the new novel in Spanish America as a whole.[7] While many of them are similar to those identified by Duncan and myself, others are more applicable to the work of writers in the period following the Boom. Still, the common features of these lists seem to be based on one fundamental assumption, that what above all characterizes the Boom writers is their radical questioning of

a. reality
b. the writer's task

This questioning is seen as having led to the rejection of old-style realism, with its simple assumptions about time and cause and effect, and to its replacement, on the one hand, by a heightened sense of the mystery and ambiguity of things and, on the other, by a greater reliance on fantasy and the creative imagination. In addition, new areas of reality, both social and individual, came to be explored. To express this shifting vision, new, experimental narrative strategies had to be developed. These included deliberate abandonment of linear, chronological narrative, of conventional character-presentation and of obtrusive authorial authority, a much more sophisticated view than previously of the role of language in fiction, and, as a general consequence a greater tendency toward "writerly" rather than reader-friendly fiction, often with the inclusion of a certain challenge to the reader. Fuentes attempted to sum it all up in three key-words: "mito, lenguaje y estructura."[8] Among the overall effects is believed to be that of lifting Spanish American fiction to a new level of universality.

We should notice, however, at this point, that what seemed to many non-Spanish American critics to be a move away from the overt *americanismo* of the dominant type of pre-Boom novel, recently reinterpreted by Carlos Alonso and Roberto González-Echevarría,[9] to others was no such thing. Angel Rama, for instance, insisted that for many Spanish American readers the Boom continued at a deeper and more sophisticated level the search for a continental identity which had been at the heart of *criollismo*.[10] In this he was followed by no less a Boom writer than Cortázar.[11] Similarly, García Márquez, in his Nobel Prize speech, said, "La interpretación de nuestra realidad con esquemas ajenos sólo contribuye a hacernos cada vez más desconocidos."[12] Thus, in contrast to what was alluded to above and has commonly been taken for granted, namely, the cosmopolitanization of Spanish American fiction in the Boom period, it is possible for a more ethnocentric critic like Inca Rumold to assert that, "La búsqueda de una identidad nacional había llegado a ser, pues, la clave de la nueva literatura latinoamericana,"[13] and to seek to relate the "writerly" innovations of the Boom novelists to "un esfuerzo consciente por parte de los escritores para llegar a una imagen nacional" (p. 22). How far one would go along with this view is a moot point. But the fact that it forms part of the ongoing discussion of the Boom indicates that the "return" to the interpretation of the here and now of Spanish America, thought to be one of the defining elements of Post-Boom writing, might be less of a return than it seems. It follows that, in discussing the new movement, caution must be exercised in perceiving in it too radical a break with the immediate past. Rather, we should perhaps envisage a gradual intensification of certain tendencies which were always present in some degree in the Boom, but which in the high Boom period were overshadowed: a change of emphasis rather than a new departure.

Nevertheless, the most generally held view seems to be that which postulates a deliberate reaction against certain aspects of the Boom novels and argues that the Post-Boom partly defines itself in terms of what it rejects. For clearly defined ideological reasons, Alejo Carpentier was among the first to call for a halt to technical innovation and for a return to a simpler concept of fiction. A highly professional novelist, he was fully cognizant of the novelties which the Boom writers had introduced and which have at times been seen as the main factor which produced the famous *salto de calidad* between their work and that and that of novelists of an earlier generation. He himself had been a contributor to the trend, notably in "Viaje a la semilla" and other stories in *Guerra del tiempo* (1958). But near the end of his life, and partly as a consequence of his return to Castro's Cuba, where he came under pressure to accommodate his theory of the novel to the new political realities there, he radically modified his stance. In "Problemática del tiempo y del idioma en la moderna novela latinoamericana" (1975) and more bluntly in "La novela latinoamericana en vísperas de un nuevo siglo" (1979), he insisted that the contemporary novel was in crisis, but that happily, in Latin America at least, the way forward was clear: "la nueva novela latinoamericana tiende hacia lo épico y para responder a las aspiraciones de un tiempo épico habrá de ser épica," that is to say "de acción grande y pública." It also must be strongly socially orientated: "debe tener al individuo siempre relacionado con la masa que lo circunda, con el mundo en gestación que lo esculpe." Implicitly, it should deal above all with social upheaval.[14] There is nothing particularly unfamiliar about this, coming as it does from a writer who by now had declared his adherence to Marxism. But Carpentier went on to mention five characteristics that it seemed to him in the late 1970s (i.e., at the end of the Boom) that the next phase of of the novel in Latin America should incorporate. These are: melodrama, manicheism, political involvement, urban settings, and finally "la aceptación de giros sintácticos y de modismos esencialmente latinoamericanos."[15] The thrust of his argument is plain: there is a need to return to more popular and socially orientated novels.

Interestingly, at approximately the same time, a much younger novelist from the other end of the continent, the Chilean Antonio Skármeta, who has been described by his Argentinian fellow-novelist Mempo Giardinelli as "quizá el más representativo autor del posboom,"[16] was also discussing characteristics of the Post-Boom as he saw them emerging in his own generation (he was born in 1940). If one were to attempt to date the birth of the new movement specifically, an appropriate date might be 1975, the date of the Boom's last great blockbuster and perhaps its swan song, Fuentes's *Terra Nostra*, but more especially of Skármeta's *Soñé que la nieve ardía*. The story deals with the last phase of the Allende government in Chile and the *pinochetazo* which brought it to an end. It is not irrelevant to notice that the novel was finished in exile and thus belongs, in one sense, to a significant sector of Post-Boom fiction, the novel of exile. Holding a degree from New York's Columbia University, Skármeta is a teacher of Spanish American literature as well as a writer and movie maker. It is possible to argue that partly because of his scholarly formation, he is the most self-aware of the Post-Boom novelists and that his relevant critical writings provide us with some of the most reliable insights into the movement from Boom to Post-Boom. I am comforted to find that Gutiérrez Mouat concurs in this view.[17]

Of key importance for our present concerns are Skármeta's essays "Tendencias en la más nueva narrativa hispanoamericana" (1975), "La novísima generación: varias características y un límite" (1976), and especially his crucial "Al fin y al cabo es su propia vida la cosa más cercana que cada escritor tiene para echar mano" (1979).[18] In the first of these he analyzes critically the refusal of the Boom writers to accept "el rostro convencional de la realidad" (p. 758) and their avoidance of plot-centered novels, overt political commitment and proletarian characters and settings. Using Vargas Llosa's Zavalita (from *Conversación en La Catedral*, 1969) as an archetypal fictional figure of the Boom, he attacks his older contemporaries for their obsession with passive, bourgeois figures who were unable to transform their dissatisfaction with life and society into efforts directed at changing and renovating the surrounding system. In the second article he takes issue even more openly with what, as he points out, Fernando Alegría had already called "el circo de la supertécnica," characteristic of the Boom, in which "la obra queda espejándose en su propia estética" (p. 11).

Underlying many of Skármeta's comments is his acute consciousness of the proximity of the Boom and an explicit desire to distance himself from it. He is not an aggressively "parricidal" figure, but it is clear that he felt the pressure of his older contemporaries and, at the end of the 1970s, wished to avoid being regarded as holding on to their coattails. Speaking of the formative period of writers of his age group in Chile, he declared in "Al fin y al cabo":

> "Ya es hora que afirme de que nuestra vinculación con la narrativa latinoamericana en aquella época inicial . . . del ingenioso premio Seix-Barral, la rayuelización del universo por Sudamericana, era prácticamente nula. Cuando estas obras llegan . . . nosotros hemos avanzado ya en una dirección que en algunos casos entronca con la obra de ellos [i.e., the Boom novelists], en otros difiere, y en otros acepta la vertiginosa influencia de su éxito. Pero en nuestros inicios, los tratos con la literatura van, en el caso de la narrativa, por senderos muy alejados de los latinoamericanos. Al contrario, huíamos de ellos. (p.134)

They fled even faster from the *criollismo* and regionalism of the pre-Boom novel. In which direction they fled is not made completely clear, though Skármeta does specifically mention Camus, Kerouac and the films of Jean-Luc Godard. But he is careful to explain that this does not mean that his generation surrendered passively to the cultural imperialism of Europe and North America.

Skármeta provided a list of Post-Boom characteristics in the generation to which he saw himself as belonging. Although his list was rather longer than the comparable one offered by Carpentier, in one or two respects he echoed the older novelist, especially with regard to urban settings: "Aquí está el punto de arranque de nuestra literatura: la urbe latinoamericana—ya no la aldea, la pampa, la selva, la provincia—caótica, turbulenta, contradictoria, plagada de pícaros, de masas emigrantes de los predios rurales traídas por la nueva industrialización. Todo esto con unas ganas enormes de vivir, amar, aventurear, contribuir a cambiar la sociedad" (p. 135). The last phrase is noteworthy. It is their lack of social commitment as well as their ingrained tendency to subvert what Skármeta calls "esta realidad que por comodidad llamamos realidad"[19] that primarily motivates his attack on the Boom writers. As late as 1984, in an article on Rulfo, he writes, apropos of them and their work:

> "se trata en estos autores de mostrar lo conocido, de conocer más al mundo ya escrito que ellos reescriben. De eso se trata en la narrativa de esta generación. No de cambiarlo. Semejante ausencia lleva necesariamente a un recorte de la realidad: los personajes de todas esas obras carecen de peso social, de clase, son cifras para ilustrar mitos."[20]

These words proclaim the social commitment that Carpentier had also advocated. Indeed Skármeta noted: "Nuestra generación entró de lleno a participar en la vida social, y en numerosos casos lo hizo en la forma más explícita de la militancia partidaria" ("Al fin y al cabo" p. 134). If we were to ask for an example of the kind of "epic" novel, with the novelist in the role of a modern-day *Cronista de Indias* dealing with dramatic public events, which Carpentier had envisaged, one could hardly find a better example than Skármeta's *La insurrección* (1981), with its story of an entire Nicaraguan community united heroically against the oppression of the Somoza regime.

Let us review the remaining characteristics of the novel in his generation which Skármeta mentioned in 1979. They are:

1. Sexuality: "La sexualidad y su ejercicio pasará a ser un tema privilegiado de la generación: suprimidas las causas traumáticas, se entrega a una desenfrenada exploración del erotismo" (p. 132)

2. Exuberance: "vida y más vida en su comunicable fiebre"; "la afirmación de la vida frente a sus limitaciones" (p. 135)

3. Spontaneity: "desconfianza ante todo lo que coartara la espontaneidad" (p. 135)

4. *Cotidianeidad*: "nosotros nos acercamos a la cotidianeidad con la obsesión de un miope" (p. 138)

5. Fantasy: "la aceptación de la cotidianeidad como punto de arranque para la fantasía" (p. 136)

6. Colloquiality: "la coloquialidad era asumida sin escrúpulos . . . encontramos en el lenguaje coloquial la herramienta adecuada para trabajar la realidad" (p. 136)

and, oddly enough,

7. Intranscendence: "Lo que en Cortázar es una dramática y regocijada búsqueda de la trascendencia . . . es en los más jóvenes una desproblematizada asunción de la humilde cotidianeidad como fuente autoabastecedora de vida e inspiración. En este sentido, nuestra actitud primordial es intranscendente" (p. 138)

Summing up his comments on his generation's work, as he saw it in 1979, Skármeta concludes: "La narrativa más joven . . . es vocacionalmente antipretenciosa, pragmáticamente anti-cultural, sensible a lo banal, y más que reordenadora del mundo . . . es simplemente presentadora de él" (p. 139). He continues: "La más nueva narrativa se debate en este proceso que se podría caracterizar como infrarreal en motivos y personajes, *pop* en actitud y realista-lírico en su lenguaje" (p. 140). Apart from writers of his own generation in Chile, Skármeta named as relevant: José Agustín, Gustavo Sainz, and Jorge Aguilar Mora (Mexico); Luis Rafael Sánchez (Puerto Rico); Manuel Puig and Eduardo Gudiño Kieffer (Argentina); Reinaldo Arenas and Miguel Barnet (Cuba), Oscar Collazos (Colombia); and Sergio Ramírez (Nicaragua).

These remarks by Skármeta offer one of the best currently available approaches to the Post-Boom. They remind us that the assumptions made by the Boom writers—whether about reality, the human condition, and society or about narrative techniques and the relationship of language to any possible exterior referent—were to be in some cases directly contradicted in the next generation. We find Skármeta's views generally confirmed, if not actually repeated, by other writers. Mempo Giardinelli, an Argentinian novelist, for example, in the article already referred to, also postulates a return to "realismo poético" and to colloquialism. In addition, he indicates the experience of exile (whether interior or exterior) as a major influence on many recent novelists. But most of all, he emphasizes a change of tone: "en la literatura del posboom no hay resignación ni pesimismo." In the light of the extreme pessimism characteristic of large areas of Boom fiction, this seems to be an important shift.[21]

Indeed it was recognized as such by another leading Post-Boom writer, Isabel Allende. In an interview, she observes that despite differences and geographical separation, writers in the Post-Boom stay in touch with each other's work: "leemos lo que cada uno publica. Y hay puntos comunes . . . pertenecemos a una generación que ha experimentado más o menos las mismas cosas, y tal vez por eso hay puntos comunes en lo que contamos . . . [somos] voces divididas que conforman un coro más o menos armónico de acuerdo a una época."[22] Which are, in her view the points in common? There are two in particular: a return to the love-ideal as part of the means of coming to terms with existence, and a greater degree of optimism than before. "Somos gente más esperanzada," she asserts. "Este es un punto bien importante de lo que ha marcado a nuestra ola de literatura. Por ejemplo en la actitud frente al amor somos más optimistas, no estamos marcados por ese pesimismo sartreano, existencialista, propio de la posguerra. Hay una especie de renovación—yo diría de romanticismo, del amor, de los sentimientos, de la alegría de vivir, de la sensualidad. Y una posición mucho más optimista frente al futuro y vida" (p. 76). In Boom novels, we recall, love is almost never treated as a significant element in the way characters confront the existential situation in the hope of finding a harmonious and fulfilling solution to its dilemmas.

Like Skármeta's, Allende's affirmations run almost completely counter to what we have come to expect from writers in the high Boom period. We discern, alongside the reevaluation of love and the sense of optimism, unrepentant ethnocentricity and radical commitment: "Siento que soy latina, que represento lo latino y si mi obra puede dar voz a esa mayoría silenciada habré cumplido con una pequeña misión porque la gran tarea está en el plano político."[23] "Mi trabajo [es] un aporte al esfuerzo común por la causa de la libertad, la justicia y la fraternidad, en la cual creo," she proclaimed in 1985.[24] Thus, in contrast to many of the Boom writers, she does not see her books primarily as pure literary artefacts, verbal creations: "Un libro," she declares, "no es un fin en sí mismo, es un medio para alcanzar a otra persona, darle una mano, contarle aquello que para mí es importante y, si es posible, sacudir a mi lector, emocionarlo, ganarlo para las causas que son mías."[25] By the same token, she accepts that her writing breaks with two of the basic "writerly" values of the Boom: "I am not detached or ironical."[26] And, again in genuine Post-Boom fashion: "El testimonio de primera mano me parece fundamental."[27] In this sense, one of the contributions of Allende to our understanding of the Post-Boom is her emphasis on its political radicalism, at least initially. As we shall see in the next chapter, both Benedetti and Viñas, as well as certain critics, attack the Boom writers for their lack of radicalism, their tendency to embrace a "liberal" solution that masks their acceptance, as a middle-class group, of the culture of dependency. Up to a point, the Post-Boom incorporates, in works such as Allende's *De amor y de sombra*, Skármeta's *La insurrección* or Poniatowska's *La noche de Tlatelolco*, a more radical response. At an extreme stands a figure such as the Nicaraguan—Sandenista—writer Sergio Ramírez, who asserted uncompromisingly in 1987:

> "como un acto profético la literatura no puede servirse sino de una realidad total. Política, ideología, represiones, heroísmo, masacres, fracasos, traiciones, luchas, frustraciones, esperanzas, son aun materia novelable en Latinoamérica y seguirán siéndolo porque la realidad no se agota; el novelista toma el papel de intérprete entre otros muchos que se arroga y quiere hablar en nombre de un inconsciente colectivo largamente silenciado y soterrado bajo un cúmulo de retórica falsa y pervertida. Y en esto el escritor no pude dejar de cumplir un acto político, porque la realidad es política."[28]

However, such a view requires qualification. For meanwhile, with greater hindsight, Giardinelli, for example, had changed his mind after his 1986 article. If, as has been suggested, for example, by Jaime Mejía Duque,[29] that an important event triggering Boom fiction was the triumph of the Cuban Revolution in 1959, it is no less evident that behind much Post-Boom writing lie the dictatorial regimes of the 1970s, especially in the Southern Cone of Latin America. Indeed this perhaps helps to explain why the Post-Boom seems to manifest itself more in

Argentina, Chile, and Uruguay than, for instance, in Mexico. Both Skármeta and Giardinelli recognized that in regimes a setback for the agendas of the progressive middle-class intelligentsia had occurred that stimulated a revision of ideas. The former, in 1981, affirmed à propos of his situation and that of fellow–exile writers:

> Cuando nos enfrentamos a otros mundos, relativizamos nuestros conceptos, cuestionamos nuestras creencias como una manera de acceder a la cultura y la política. Por ejemplo: uno de los grandes problemas que hemos tenido en el fracaso de nuestras experiencias pro socialistas o pro democráticas en general, ha sido el sectarismo evidente, la incomprensión que hemos tenido para saber detectar quienes serían nuestros aliados eventuales, y cierto veneno retórico . . . descubrimos que nuestra retórica es ridícula.[30]

For his part, Giardinelli declared in 1988: "Nosotros fuimos derrotados. Hoy mi visión no tiene el optimismo que tenía hace quince años."[31] Two years later, speaking specifically of the Post-Boom, Giardinelli reiterated his conviction that it was not an optimistic movement. Relevant to its origins, he argued, were: "el fiasco del 68, de Vietnam, de la perdida revolución social latinoamericana y la llamada 'muerte de las utopías.'"[32] In consequence, he went on, among the features of the Post-Boom were rebelliousness and pain: "esta escritura contiene una elevada carga de frustración, de dolor y de tristeza por todo lo que nos pasó en los 70s y 80s, una carga de desazón, rabia y rebeldía" (p. 31). For the rest, his account of Post-Boom characteristics is familiar. He mentions a change of tone and style compared with the Boom, the impact of exile, humor, a greater degree of political moderation, a more reader-friendly technique, signs of the influence of the media, the emergence of an important group of women writers, and a certain tendency to deal with disagreeable subject matter (pp. 31–32).

Without fully accepting Giardinelli's simplistic identification of Post-Boom and postmodernism, we can see that his comments partly accord with and partly contradict others reported above. His ideas underline the "pluralist," complex nature of the Post-Boom and the fact that professional writers who comment on it have their own work primarily in view. But, as always in discussions of the Post-Boom, what emerges as central is the return to confidence in the writer's ability to handle reality. In an interview also published in 1990, Giardinelli reiterated his belief that fiction inevitably reflects the social and political reality in which the writer operates: "Me nutrí y me nutro de lo que se llama 'realidad' y creo que mi deber como escritor es dar cuenta de ella."[33]

Whether this produced a certain sceptical pessimism, as in his case, or a strengthened allegiance to libertarian ideals, as in the case of

Allende, what contact with the reality of authoritarian regimes helped to reawaken among Post-Boom writers was the sense of a different relationship between fiction and its sociopolitical context. Teresa Porzecanski, who lived through the terror in Uruguay, called it "la desidealización del mundo."[34] In the Boom, as we saw in Oscar Collazos's somewhat notorious *Literatura en la revolución y revolución en la literatura*,[35] writers tended to be content to believe that innovative works or art in themselves operate against the status quo and have a social effect. Hence the writer's first duty was to revolutionize writing. The Post-Boom writers seem increasingly to have perceived that this was a myth. Under the tragic impact of events in Argentina, Chile, Uruguay and Central America, they tended to return, therefore, to fiction with greater emphasis on content, directness of impact, denunciation, documentality, or protest.

Turning briefly from the views of Boom writers to those of critics, we can see two relevant tendencies. One, which was also present in the remarks of Skármeta and Giardinelli, is to draw attention to what are regarded as major shortcomings in the outlook and work of the Boom writers, shortcomings that justify the change of course undertaken by their younger contemporaries. The other is to attempt to characterize the Post-Boom as such. While the second critical tendency is more productive, the first should not be overlooked. Probably its most vocal representative is Hernán Vidal in his *Literatura hispanoamericana e ideología liberal: surgimiento y crisis*,[36] especially chapter 3, "Narrativa del Boom." Vidal vehemently rejects the view of some of the Boom writers that to revolutionize literature was a step towards revolutionizing society. On the contrary, he asserts: "Dando un mentís a sus afirmaciones revolucionarias a través de su propia práctica literaria, su crítica tiene procedencia intraliberal, a partir de actitudes ideológicas, complejos temáticos y simbólicos, además de concepciones de la función social del escritor que más bien tienden a reforzar el orden social que critican" (p. 68). He sees the Boom as the literary equivalent of the internationalization of Latin American industry by the multinational companies during the fifties and sixties. The Boom writers' "universalization" of fiction brought with it "una creciente alienación de la realidad nacional" (p. 73) and a sense of indifference toward social problems. "La obra literaria fue concebida como mundo ficticio heterónomo, cuyas leyes tienen sólo validez interna; el escritor construía 'artefactos' literarios condicionados por sus 'demonios personales' . . . Es decir, debemos entender las teorizaciones literarias de los escritores del *boom* dentro del marco ideológico del desarrollismo burgués en su época de auge" (p. 86). The Boom, in other words, was the literary manifestation of "dependency" on the part of Spanish American middle-class intellectuals as a social group. Their view of reality, Vidal asserts, was both limited and distorted; their mythification of reality was an attempt to escape from the process of history and their major characters were devitalized and excentric: "de trasfondo cultural diferente a la norma" (p. 104), marginal and degraded. In brief, the Boom represents a "callejón ideológico sin salida" (p. 109). This is not the place to discuss the obvious reductivism of Vidal's approach or its derivation from Viñas's *De Sarmiento a Cortázar*. What is more important is the way in which his essay clearly illustrates a reaction to the Boom that leaves abundant room for a change in direction.

Hardly less extreme in his approach is Juan Manuel Marcos, especially in his *De García Márquez al Post-Boom*.[37] Earlier, in *Roa Bastos, precursor del Post-Boom*,[38] he had begun to feel his way toward a concept of Post-Boom writing based essentially on *Yo, el Supremo* (1974), seen both as a parodic demythification of Paraguayan history and a remythification of certain aspects of it in the interests of the masses (esp. pp. 93–94). The book suffers from the author's failure to create a clear distinction between Boom and Post-Boom, but in his second book on the topic he is much more explicit, arguing that the Boom writers were essentially the lackeys of the sociopolitical establishment in Spanish America and produced elitist, cosmopolitan fiction which was at once thematically abstract and ideologically confused. By contrast:

> Autores de la nueva generación, desmantelando la tradición borgiana, socavando el narcisismo pequeño burgués, parodiando el discurso establecido, carnevalizando la palabra hegemónica . . . se encuentran hoy a la vanguardia de lo que provisoriamente se podía llamar el "postboom. . . ." Estos nuevos autores comparten el compromiso por mostrar con un realismo sin simplificaciones, basado en el arte compilatorio del habla coloquial, ya la revolución antisomocista como ha hecho Antonio Skármeta, ya el callejón sin salida de la plutocracia bogotana que ha descrito Helena Araújo, ya la crisis interna del típico exiliado de los sesenta que ha confesado con fuego y deslumbrante poesía callejera Mempo Giardinelli. (p. 11)

Later he affirms

> Los relatos del "postboom" despliegan un discurso que, lejos de reclamar la admiración del lector por la orfebrería individual del poeta, configuran un trama de situaciones y tipos que se iluminan y complementan para establecer una imagen dialéctica del conflicto social y lingüístico . . . Esta nueva escritura invierte el código tradicional con que la crítica canónica del "boom" ha evaluado el género. Estas breves narraciones radican su valor en aquello que no tienen, de que se han despojado, de que se han sabido desnudar. (pp. 18–19)

The key phrase here is "un realismo sin simplificaciones," while the crux of the approach is the affirmation that the representative writers are Skármeta, Giardinelli and Araújo. Marcos's approach raises two basic problems. One is that the return to (a new form of) realism and social preoccupation is only one of the strands that make up Post-Boom writing, albeit probably the central one. The other, and much more difficult problem, which Marcos ignores, is concerned with how it is possible to return to any form of realism after the Boom's radical criticism of both our ability to perceive reality and the capacity of language to express it. Leenhardt comments:

> La novela realista, como forma épica problemática, admite los antagonismos en la sociedad y les da forma. Sin embargo, no sobrevivirá más que el tiempo en que el antagonismo permanezca fundado sobre una concepción de la realidad compartida por los adversarios. Tan pronto como, por el contrario, las reglas del juego social dejan de ser respetadas por uno de los protagonistas, o surja una duda al respeto, toda figuración clásica se tornará imposible. Mientras la cuestión de las acciones no sea abordada, el significado de las palabras se constituirá en un problema. O [*sic*] en razón de que la narración realista está indisolublemente ligada a la figuración de las acciones—lo que Lukács denomina la *Gestaltung*—esta última se hace imposible pues se halla sujeta a incertidumbre de orden epistemológico o semántico.[39]

This hits the nail on the head. To the extent that they advocate a return to any conventional form of realism, in other words to a "principle of intelligibility," writers and critics in the Post-Boom find themselves, willy-nilly, open to the objection that their whole approach is based on unjustified assumptions about the nature both of reality and language.

This objection has so far not been pressed home. Instead what has emerged as central to the discussion of the Post-Boom as a purely literary phenomenon is the issue of narrative experimentation versus some form of neorealism, the epistemological and semantic basis for which is simply taken for granted. Much criticism of the Boom writers has been in one guise or another "political" criticism from writers and critics with left-wing sympathies, for example, Skármeta, Vidal, and Marcos. It immediately tempts us to identify the Boom with modernism, which, as Huyssen has pointed out was also "chided by the left as the elitist, arrogant and mystifying master-code of bourgeois culture."[40] They tend to oppose radical forms of experimentation not so much in themselves as because they are alleged to encourage elitism and to distract the reader from what is seen as the really appropriate strategy: that of concentrating attention on themes of social injustice, authoritarianism, the will to revolution, and so on. However, a slightly different strand of criticism, one less developed than the other, takes issue with the Boom writers' exploitation of new fictional techniques on the grounds that it has been pushed too far. In the discussion at the 1979 symposium that led to the publication of *Más allá del Boom*, Luis Rafael Sánchez is reported as having asserted that "la gran trampa del *boom* había sido crear la expectativa de que cada nueva novela sería un acto sobre la cuerda floja más osado aún. Lo estridente había venido a ser el criterio por el cual un autor era juzgado excepcional" (p. 298). To date, the critic who has reacted most strongly against Boom experimentalism as a literary rather than a political aberration is Peter Earle. In a rather intemperate article he makes no bones about postulating "a hypothesis by which the literary process is seen as a continuing movement away from representational meaning or symbol toward abstraction and unintelligibility."[41] While granting that some "interesting abstractionist experiments are undertaken in the 1960s and 1970s" (p. 25), he characterizes extreme Boom experimentalism as "the cult of creative nothingness" (p. 25). In Earle's view, the Post-Boom, by contrast, is governed primarily by the fact that "consciously or subconsciously, writers want to recover [the] world's ethical center" (p. 29). This, he argues, joining hands with the left-wing writers and critics, represents a return to Spanish American fiction's traditional mainstream, which was always more "ethical" (i.e., content centered) than "aesthetic" (i.e., "writerly" and experimental). Earle's article begs a great many questions, chiefly because it fails to confront the question of the dynamic that underlies experimentation in literature: consciousness of a need to find new ways to express a new vision of the human condition. Nonetheless it articulates a widespread criticism of the Boom that helps to explain the urge in the Post-Boom to recover greater immediacy of impact on the nonelite reader.

Those critics who have attempted to describe the Post-Boom as such have produced a number of other very useful items. They include an updated version of a 1978 *Texto Crítico* 1978 article by Juan Armando Epple that is now called "El contexto histórico-generacional de la literatura de Antonio Skármeta."[42] Another is the introduction by Angel Rama to his 1981 anthology of new fiction, *Novísimos narradores hispanoamericanos en marcha*; this has been republished as "Los contestatorios del poder" in his *La novela latinoamericana, 1920–80.*[43] Epple makes an important point, which will be confirmed presently by Duncan, when he reminds us that "no toda la literatura que se escribe hoy, me refiero a lo que produce un conocimiento 'nuevo' del mundo, está siendo escrito por jóvenes, y no todos los jóvenes están escribiendo una literatura nueva" (p. 103). That is to say, alongside the authentic Post-Boom, there is a highly creative prolongation of the Boom itself, whose patterns continue to be exploited both by the established Boom writers and by younger writers who, instead of reacting against it, push its techniques and attitudes to new limits. So far as the truly Post-Boom writers are concerned, Epple suggests that they exhibit three distinguishing characteristics: "la parodia de los géneros literarios y los códigos oficiales del lenguaje"; "la caracterización protagónica del estrato adolescente y juvenil de la sociedad"; and "la incorporación a la textualidad narrativa de la expresividad poética, como forma natural de decir" (p. 107). These give us in fact the three Ps of the Post-Boom: parody, poetry and "pop."

Unquestionably the most important element here is the reference to the role in the Post-Boom of youth culture: television and films, pop music, sport, casual sex, and drugs: a fun-culture that provides the context for accounts of the rites of passage into adult life. What more than anything established this tendency to "instalar en los personajes adolescentes el núcleo básico de la experiencia y la aprensión de lo real"[44] was, of course, the huge success of the first two novels of Manuel Puig, *La traición de Rita Hayworth* (1968) and *Boquitas pintadas* (1969). But Puig did not initiate the trend; the initiator was Gustavo Sainz, who, as his compatriot and fellow-novelist José Agustín has pointed out, was "one of the first authors to write about youth while still being young himself."[45] *Gazapo* (1965) was the key work, followed in 1974 by the enchanting *La Princesa del Palacio de Hierro*. I have argued that an even earlier example of the trend was Skármeta's prize-winning short story "La Cenicienta en San Francisco" (1963), which later introduced his first collection of tales, *El entusiasmo* (1967).[46] All this seems to confirm that while the Boom itself was still developing during the 1960s, the Post-Boom was already in gestation.

Such is the view of Angel Rama, who in a 1985 interview included Skármeta, Puig, and Sainz among "el conjunto de escritores que han aparecido en los 60 [y] . . . que han ido construyendo una nueva literatura."[47] He describes it as "una literatura urbana, muy sostenida en el habla . . . mucho más libre, más desembarazada y, al mismo tiempo, más realista." Calling it "una fuerza que efectivamente muestra un nuevo mundo," Rama mentions in passing, alongside the influence of the mass media, especially the cinema and pop music, an interesting characteristic already hinted at by Skármeta: the renewed preoccupation with Latin American society itself, its contemporary lifestyle and specific problems, rather than emphasizing the general human condition as it just happens to manifest itself in a Latin American setting. This seems to be what Rama is alluding to when he asserts that "gran parte de los narradores . . . trabajan dentro de la tradición del continente": a conscious return to the primacy of "lo americano."

Rama's prologue to *Novísimos narradores hispanoamericanos en marcha* dilutes the impact of the Post-Boom by trying to say too much and by mentioning too many names without putting them into clearly defined categories. Still, it reiterates familiar characteristics, above all the "recuperación del realismo," with a corresponding shift of alle- giances which has brought a renewal of interest in relevant older writ- ers from Roberto Arlt to Mario Benedetti. Rama also lists a parallel "retorno a la historia, en el intento de otorgar sentido a la aventura del hombre americano," urban settings, exile perspective (in some cases), colloquialism, "rechazo de la retórica," youth themes, pop culture, humor, and sexuality.[48] More particularly since this was until recently a neglected aspect of the Post-Boom "la masiva irrupción de escritoras." Two features of Rama's essay deserve further discussion. One concerns the joint impact of exile experience and the return to a strong interest in the destinies of Latin America itself. In one of his late interviews Cortázar had expressed to Saúl Sosnowski a certain disquiet about pre- cisely this aspect of the Post-Boom, that is, its failure to confront ade- quately the questions "¿qué es un latinoamericano, cuál es la identidad de un latinoamericano?" He went on to say: "Yo creo que no se ha con- testado en parte porque nuestra nueva literatura, la literatura de los últi- mos 20 años, es una literatura joven . . . todo está todavía por hacerse y entonces la búsqueda de los problemas de identidad debe ser, me imag- ino, un proceso muy lento."[49]

Rama is clearly conscious of this aspect of the Post-Boom and refers specifically to the "challenge" faced by "aquellos escritores que aspiran a preservar lo que llaman la 'identidad' de los hombres de sus culturas."[50] It is interesting that such an old-established (and perhaps old-fashioned) concept as the search for the foundations of national or racial identity should still have currency among young writers of today in Latin Amer- ica. Rama correctly views it with suspicion and tends to associate it with a rigid and conservative idea of Latin American-ness. We cannot fault his advocacy of the counterconcept of "integración transculturadora" as one of the imperatives of the Post-Boom: the effort, that is, to incorporate Latin American culture into that of the end of the twentieth century, while at the same time preserving its "identidad esencial." The other fea- ture of Rama's essay that strikes the alert reader is the absence of any sys- tematic attempt to face the question of changes in fictional technique. Apart from noting, as other commentators do, the use of colloquial lan- guage and mentioning the impact of the cinema, all that Rama really sug- gests is that there is an absence of distance between the youthful authors and their often youthful characters, an (implicitly uncritical) identifica- tion between author and work. Puig would have to be an exception, since he often uses pop culture—in *Boquitas pintadas*, for example—to com- ment critically on the outlook and lifestyle of his characters.

The novelist who has been most outspoken in his remarks about a change in fictional technique in the Post-Boom period is José Donoso. If we can identify some early signs of an emerging new creative pattern with the novels and short stories already mentioned of Puig, Sainz, and Skármeta in the 1960s (to which we must add, as González Echevarría has shown, those of Sarduy: *Gestos* [1963] and *De donde son los cantantes* [1967]),[51] a major indicator that the shift had taken place was the publication in 1978 of Donoso's *Casa de campo*, for in it Donoso makes fun of the technical innovations characteristic of Boom novels. Specifically, at the beginning of chapter 2 he addresses the reader in his own voice. He does so primarily to insist on the fictionality of the story that is being read and hence to render more difficult reader-identification with the action. But also Donoso is concerned with breaking a lance in favor of "las viejas maquinarias narrativas, hoy en descrédito" (i.e., those of the realist period), which he feels can still be technically effective. The most prominent among these older techniques is, as we see from *Casa de campo* itself, that of authorial omniscience. Skármeta in *Ardiente paciencia* (1985), perhaps significantly, causes his narrator to make the same point in the prologue: "En tanto que otros son maestros del relato lírico en primera persona, de la novela dentro de la novela, del metalenguaje, de la distorsión de tiempos y espacios, yo seguí . . . sobre todo aferrado a lo que un profesor de literatura designó con asco: un narrador omnisciente."

The underlying idea is that of a return to greater simplicity. In an interview with Ronald Christ in 1982, Donoso asked: "Now, in a way, hasn't the time come to turn back a little bit? . . . Of course, one has to arrive at the limit of things to be able to turn back . . . And the whole thing is that we have got to the limit of things."[52] He went on to predict the end of the big, ambitious, "encyclopedic" novels of the Boom (we think of Fuentes's *Terra Nostra*, for example) and to advocate shorter, more plot-centered and in general more accessible fiction. His own *La misteriosa desaparición de la marquesita de Loria* (1980) is an example. But Philip Swanson, in excellent articles and in his book, argues that behind its apparent simplicity of content, a Post-Boom Donoso is subverting realism from within.[53] An interesting feature of this subversion is the use of "a recognizably realistic style which is counteracted by the introduction of fantasy."[54] This is very much what we find in Isabel Allende's first three novels also. It perhaps corresponds to Skármeta's idea of linking the everyday and the lyrical. Swanson has contributed to the discussion the realization that we must always ask, in respect of Post-Boom writers, what ingredient it is that they add to a realistic style or outlook to carry it beyond old-style realism.

In 1986, Donoso's views received support from Vargas Llosa in an interview with Raymond Williams. Asked about the difference between his early (implicitly Boom) novels and his more recent (implicitly Post-Boom) ones, Vargas Llosa replied:

> The main difference I can see . . . was my attitude about form. I was
> so thrilled with form that it was very visible. In *The Green House* form
> was ever-present and quite evident. As was the case with many Latin
> American novels in the sixties, for me form was almost like a theme or
> a character in the novel. Since then things have changed. Now I am
> interested in being less explicit about form itself.

Commenting on the current situation in fiction in Latin America, he
went on to say:

> We Latin American writers discovered the technical and formal possi-
> bilities of the novel in the fifties and sixties. The idea was to experi-
> ment with form, and to show it.

Now, he affirmed, he proposed to hide the structure and technique in
the story, "to be more invisible." But, he concluded, this could not be
generalized: "Many Latin American writers still want to carry out a formal revolution. And this has become in some cases a kind of new tradition—the tradition of experimentation and of being modern."[55] Here we
have in a nutshell the problem facing certain critics of the Post-Boom:
how to handle a movement that both contains a reaction against overt
formal experimentation and at the same time prolongs the Boom tradition of technical innovation. At the same time, Vargas Llosa's acknowl-
edged shift in *La guerra del fin del mundo* (1981) and *Historia de Mayta*
(1984) to greater emphasis on historical and political themes, to say
nothing of his subsequent incursions into the detective-type novel and to
the semipornographic novel (*¿Quién mató a Palomino Molero?* [1986]
and *Elogio de la madrastra* [1988]), illustrate the ability of the Boom
writers to achieve the transition to more popular genres.

Like Donoso and Vargas Llosa, several other Boom writers had
evolved away from extreme complexity. In 1978 Fuentes had produced
*La cabeza de la hidra*, a parodic thriller whose narrator, in chapter 39,
deliberately draws the reader's attention to the fact that the book contains "escasas reflexiones internas." Vargas Llosa had already produced
*La tía Julia y el escribidor* (1977), which includes nine radio serials of
an exaggeratedly popular and melodramatic kind as a background for a
love story that shares some of their characteristics. The case of García
Márquez is, as always, more complex; but not long after Donoso's 1982
interview with Ronald Christ he was to publish the most startling of all
the illustrations of the internal shift taking place in the Boom: *El amor
en los tiempos del cólera* (1985), which from its title on contradicted one
of the basic Boom characteristics. In each of these cases a "low" or
"popular" fictional genre is adapted to serve a different (but always, in
the end, "higher") literary purpose, developing Puig's pioneering use of
"pop" material in his early novels.

Among the critics who have most recently taken up the issue we are considering is Roberto González Echevarría, who addresses it in "Sarduy, the Boom and the Post-Boom" and *La ruta de Severo Sarduy*. In part his views accord with those of Donoso and Vargas Llosa. Where he differs is in his attempt to identify Boom writing with modernism, in the North American and European sense of the term, and therefore Post-Boom writing with postmodernism. He too, stresses the collapse of the "encyclopedic" novel: "lo que la narrativa postmoderna [i.e., of the Post-Boom] hace es abolir la nostalgia de la totalización."[56] In its place González Echevarría, following Lyotard, postulates a return to *narratividad*, a "retorno del relato," a rediscovery of linear storytelling without the fragmentation and the unexpected shifts in time sequence, undermining patterns of cause and effect, that were prominent in Boom novels from *Pedro Páramo* to *Terra Nostra*. But, he insists, this return to plot centeredness is not accompanied by any return to narrative authority on the part of the author/narrator: "Cuando el autor aparece en la obra . . . lo hace como un personaje más de la ficción sin poderes superiores . . . En la última novela hispanoamericana el relato es más importante que el lenguaje o el narrador" (p. 250). Similarly he argues that the Post-Boom no longer contains "un metadiscurso crítico, literario o cultural" (p. 251), a deep theme underlying the surface content, often involving "ironic reflexivity" on the part of the author about the processes of writing themselves. In view of the remarks by Rama and Cortázar, it is interesting that González Echevarría specifically singles out the search for Latin American identity as one of the deep themes that have been eliminated: "la novela del post-Boom abandona la saudade de la identidad" (p. 251). Finally he suggests that *mise en abîme,* internal reduplication and other forms of ambiguity are also less prominent in Post-Boom fiction, which instead presents an appearance of superficiality.

It will not escape the notice of careful readers that González Echevarría's account of the novel of the Post-Boom betrays a certain uneasiness and even ambivalence. For if the Post-Boom novel is presented as more plot centered, more reader orientated, less thematically and technically complex, it is hard not to think that in some way (as Donoso candidly suggested) it is a turning back. Like Swanson, González Echevarría hastenes to deprecate any such suggestion: "este retorno del relato no significa que haya un regreso a la novelística tradicional ni mucho menos" (p. 249). But can we be so sure, if we think, for example, of the novels of Isabel Allende, especially *De amor y de sombra* (1984)? The remarkable success of her work seems to be partly due to the presence of the characteristics—or some of them—that González Echevarría indicates, but the net result is in fact a much more traditional kind of narrative than we have recently been used to. The same seems to be true of the Boom works that align themselves with the Post-Boom: is not García Márquez's *El amor en los tiempos del cólera* a case in point, compared with the "splintered mirror" effect of *Crónica de una muerte anunciada*? Nor should we completely overlook in this connection the renewal of popularity in the Post-Boom period of documentary fiction, much of which is not far removed from a traditional narrative stance.

In contrast to the views of the writers and critics so far mentioned are those of J. Ann Duncan. Her *Voices, Visions and a New Reality: Mexican Fiction since 1970* is the most carefully researched monograph on a single country's Post-Boom fiction to have appeared so far. Her choice of authors is, of course, selective. She admits that she has not included authors like Juan García Ponce and Angelina Muñiz, whose work might perhaps be seen as more in line with what we have been discussing. The importance of Duncan's book, however, lies in the fact that it shows how any attempt to associate fiction in the Post-Boom period exclusively with more "accessible" story-orientated works is quite partial, and, in Mexico, at least, ignores some of the evidence. Duncan reminds us how many examples there are of Mexican contemporary fiction which "generally relate nothing";[57] how, in contrast to the supposed absense of deep theme, much of the work of Carlos Montemayor, José Emilio Pacheco, and Esther Seligson "centers on the metaphysical quest" (p. 7); and how, contrary to the idea that that innovatory narrative techniques are out of favor, many of the younger Mexican novelists are still concerned with exploring "new ways of creating fiction " (p. 10). At the extreme she describes Humberto Guzmán as "antiliterary (in the traditional sense), antipsychological as well as anti-consumer-orientated art [and] opposed to social commitment in literature" (p. 94). Of Antonio Delgado's *Figuraciones en el fuego* (1980) she writes implacably: "it is not *about* anything; it *is* . . . it can be termed a novel only in that it is a more or less continuous piece of prose narrative . . . it does not tell a story, develop characters or deliver a message (p. 165). We are clearly a long way from other views of Post-Boom fiction, but rather close to R. L. Williams's emphasis on continuing radical experimentalism in his *The Postmodern Novel in Latin America*.

On the other hand sundry writers carry the reaction against the Boom to its logical extreme, publishing documentary narratives that, far from questioning reality, privilege it, usually for purposes of protest. This is an important part of of Post-Boom narrative, as Foster, Jara and Vidal, and Sklodowska[58] have all shown. As an early example we might mention Elena Poniatowska's *La noche de Tlatelolco* (1971), which deals with the repression of the student demonstrations in Mexico in October 1968. Between the two extremes of *narrativa testimonial* and persisting experimentalism we find a range of novelists from the Cuban neorealists, such as Manuel Cofiño, to a figure like Luisa Valenzuela, whose *Cola de lagartijo* (1983) reads in many ways like a Boom novel, *inter alia* because of its extremely sophisticated approach to language, while in fact it explores fiction's relationship to the political situation. Since then Valenzuela, in typical Post-Boom fashion, has moved closer to direct political commitment.

What, in conclusion, does all this suggest? It seems to be widely accepted that the shift from observed reality to created reality, from mimesis to myth, from confidence in to questioning of, our ability to understand ourselves or the world around us (as well as of the power of language to express any such presumed understanding), a shift characteristic of the Boom, is no longer the most prominent feature of Spanish American fiction. Gutiérrez Mouat, at the end of an excellent article, argues that the Post-Boom "representa la 'desliteraturización' de la novela" and that this "responde a la masificación del público lector."[59] This is putting it a bit strong. But it seems that there is a definite move back from the "interrogative" novel toward the "declaratory" novel, toward less complicated story lines, reader identification (in contrast to requiring readers to "crack" some Boom novels as if they were puzzles); recognizable, nonsymbolic, local Latin American settings; familiar references to youth culture; and even a measure of social commitment. But this is not an across-the-board phenomenon. Rather we should think in terms of a set of coexisting trends. At one end of the spectrum we have the *novela testimonial*, based on personal observation of people and events and the more or less direct recording of them using reportage techniques. This type of novel flourishes all the way from Mexico to Argentina and Chile. Conspicuous examples are, as mentioned, Poniatowska's *La noche de Tlatelolco* (1971) and Aníbal Quijada Cerda's *Cerco de púas* (1977). The critical questions raised by works of this kind have to do with the degree of fictionalization employed, and similarly (in the case of a work like Vicente Leñero's *Los periodistas* [1978], for example) the formal innovations brought into play. Hence we can situate the *novela testimonial* close to the traditional neorealistic novel still being produced, for example, by Cofiño in Cuba.

At the other extreme we can situate novels that approximate to pure *écriture* and represent attempts to thrust the experimentation and and anti-mimesis of the Boom novels to their limits. Contemporary Mexican fiction, from Elizondo's *El grafólogo* (1972) to works by Antonio Delgado and Humberto Guzmán, seems to be particularly rich in productions of this sort. In between, we can set the novels of the Post-Boom proper, beginning in the mid-1970s after Sainz, Puig, and Sarduy among others had begun in the previous decade to break away from the mainstream of the Boom with its tendency toward the *novela totalizadora*, its questioning of the human condition, its experimentalism and anti-mimesis. The new young writers, including by that time a contingent of women novelists, set a trend toward greater accessibility, which in retrospect seems to have affected the later writing of some of their elders, including García Márquez, Vargas Llosa, and Donoso. This accessibility seems to be based on a renewal of confidence in the writer's ability to observe and report everyday reality and in the referential power of language. The here and now of Latin America figures prominently as a theme—along with fictional treatments of the continent's history designed to comment indirectly on the here and now. There is a return to love as a major theme.

A nagging question remains, however: How is it possible to return to a more realistic mode of fiction after the radical critique to which realism has been subjected with the advent of literary modernism? This question has not been squarely faced, much less clearly articulated, by Post-Boom writers or critics in sympathy with them. A possible answer is that the Boom writer's view of truth, representation, and language, insofar as there was one, was no more than an ideological convention imposed by a given historico-cultural situation. In other words it was part of the cultural logic of dependency on late capitalism, a pseudo-discovery, a power ploy, and a constraining influence on other forms of writing, which are now shaking it off. Such an answer, of course, would imply a rather uncritical acceptance of the "sociogenesis" of literary texts, in terms of which Boom attitudes and textual strategies merely reflect the moment of the movement's hegemony, which coincided with a peak of authoritarian regimes and of cultural imperialism. In turn, the Post-Boom's return to accessibility, greater realism, pop elements, and so on would reflect greater cultural autonomy and the revival of democracy in parts of the continent. If not this one, some other theoretical underpinning of Post-Boom literary ideas will presumably have to be found.

# CHAPTER 2

# *The Transition*

The appropriate way to envisage the Boom seems to be to see the Boom novelists as succeeding, with the help of certain prizes and publishing houses, in imposing a measure of hegemony on the novel in Spanish America. The result was that a new pattern of fictional discourse became accepted. But we know that, whenever such a situation arises, alternative modes of writing are always waiting in the wings for their opportunity and jockeying for position. Literary and artistic movements tend to enjoy a period during which the creative pattern that manifests itself in them is at its peak. But immediately before and after that peak period, there are often other stages of development within which we can usually identify a certain number of authors who from different individual positions represent a *transition to* the new movement and, on the other side, writers who represent a *transition from* it toward the next; why such transitions occur at the time they do is of course a mystery. However, for those who consider the Boom to be associated essentially with the 1960s and the first half of the 1970s, writers like Sábato, Onetti, Rulfo, and Carpentier, who came to prominence in the 1950s or earlier, are apt to be regarded as precursors.

If so, who were the major writers who marked the transition from the Boom to the Post-Boom? I shall discuss four. On the one hand, as was suggested in chapter 1, Puig and Sarduy are often cited as obvious candidates for the role, though for very different reasons. But on the other hand, we must recognize that if, as almost all critics and commentators seem to agree, the main strand in the Post-Boom is a return to a more realistic, representational form of fiction, with clearer emphasis on history and sociopolitical commitment, then writers who go on throughout the Boom practicing something like this kind of writing, Benedetti and Viñas, for example, represent an element of continuity, the importance of which is only now becoming visible. Thus Elsa Dehennin points out: "Benedetti se sitúa en la corriente (*mainstream* dicen los ingleses) del realismo. No cuestiona la mímesis . . . No hay experimentación ni juego discursivo. Impera la seriedad que no excluye la risa negra, una ironía crítica."[1] This is clearly the correct view. It is not invalidated by Eileen Zeitz's rather uncritical attempt to present Benedetti as an innovative and and even experimental writer.[2] Some of Dehennin's assertions derive from a speech by Benedetti in Caracas in 1977[3] (just as the Post-Boom was getting under way), an address that deserves to be considered alonside the articles by Skármeta, Allende, and Giardinelli mentioned in chapter 1.

Like Skármeta, Benedetti sharply criticizes certain (unnamed) Boom writers in whom "aquel horror a la realidad circundante los lleva a escribir como si estuvieran alojados en cámaras herméticas, a prueba de sonidos y revoluciones" (p. 7). Where Boom writers are specifically named (Rulfo, Arguedas, Onetti, García Márquez) Benedetti argues that they represent a privileged class that had access to universal culture and were thus utterly unrepresentative of average people in Latin America. However, while (in 1977) "todavía existen algunos narradores latinoamericanos que virtualmente no escriben para que los lea el lector común" (p. 11), there is, Benedetti affirms, a growing tendency to return to reality. This he, like Giardinelli, associates with the terrible realities of Latin America in the 60s and 70s. When so many people, including intellectuals and writers, were imprisoned, exiled, tortured or murdered, how, he asks, can writing be aseptic and technical? More ideologically commited than Skármeta, Benedetti does not hide his conviction that much writing in the Boom years and much critical response to it belonged, consciously or not, to a "cultura del dominador." In particular, forms of writing that privilege language itself over its referential function and forms of criticism that accept or advocate such a prioritization, in his view, represent cultural imperialism. These ideas, we recall, were already present in Benedetti's "Subdesarrollo y letras de osadía" (1968) later included in *El escritor latinoamericano y la revolución posible* and hence were not new to him.

The role of the Post-Boom, as Benedetti sees it, is to "de-mythify" the aesthetic of the sixties and early seventies, to reject excessive preoccupation with the novel as an "hazaña verbal," and to adhere consciously to a "cultura de la liberación" founded on realism and on faithfulness to the human condition: "la palabra no existe, como quieren algunos ideólogos de la derecha, para ser el protagonista de la nueva narrativa latinoamericana. No, el protagonista sigue y seguirá siendo el hombre; la palabra su instrumento" (p. 11). This is a fundamentally important approach and one that widens the scope of the debate considerably. It reminds us of the crucial fact that we cannot entirely disassociate the attempt to define and interpret the Post-Boom from "cultural politics," especially in view of the left-wing stance of many Post-Boom writers.

Given such an uncompromising standpoint, it is hardly surprising that Benedetti should have found the Boom difficult to handle. In fact, his criticism, notably in *Letras del continente mestizo* (1967, 3rd amplified edition, 1974), reveals a clear unwillingness to face squarely the issues raised by the movement. In *El escritor latinoamericano y la revolución posible* (1974) the Cuban revolution is predictably awarded the credit for unleashing the Boom and with it a new phase of experimentalism in fiction. But this is perceived as carrying with it the risk of writing "para una *élite* más amplia pero igualmente refinada y *snob*, capaz de disfrutar de esas nuevas invenciones y usos de la palabra, pero a partir de una frívola concepción del mundo."[4] It is not made clear whether Benedetti regarded this risk as having become a reality or whether the other risk which he mentions—that "Imperialism" might instrumentalize the success of the Boom writers—was also in the end a fact. Instead of offering any pronouncement on these questions, Benedetti prefers to leave them open and to affirm (rather prescriptively) that if experimentalism in fiction is directed at reserving pleasure in novels for an elite, it will fail. "Pero si la intención es, pese a la dificultad que implica un trabajo experimental, llegar al pueblo, en ese caso el autor (sea o no consciente de ello) sembrará en su experiencia los necesarios indicios para que el lector, o el espectador, o el oyente, tenga por fin acceso a su invención" (p. 98). However, in the last analysis, it is perfectly clear that for Benedetti what matters is not questioning reality but questioning the "system." Like Skármeta, Benedetti exemplifies the conscious radicalization of many intellectuals that took place during the 1970s as a result of the rise of authoritarian regimes. At the beginning of the decade he joined the "26 de Marzo" Movement "y ya en ese instante advertí que . . . podía significar un cambio profundo en mi vida" (p. 17). The Frente Amplio which subsequently came into being in Uruguay performed the same function of *concientización* for him as Unidad Popular in Chile did for Skármeta. This links him to the central current of the Post-Boom.

In retrospect we can see that what is significant for the transition from Boom to Post-Boom in Benedetti's critical writings (supported, of course by his own fictional practice) is:

1.  His critique of the Boom for its tendency toward elitism, excessive experimentation and tendency to turn its back on social responsibility

2.  His confident attachment to realism and to fellow novelists like David Viñas and critics like Juan Marinello, who practiced and advocated realism even during the Boom period

3.  His rejection of the central role of language in fiction

4. His insistence on the importance for the contemporary novel of the here and now of Latin America and his confidence in the power of the common people to change the continent's social and political reality

5. The radicalization of outlook that becomes visible in his work during the 1970s

6. The importance attached to love throughout his work, as distinct from the Boom's emphasis on sex. We may note, for example, the remark by Ramón Budiño in *Gracias por el fuego:*[5] "Dolores es sexo y algo más. Y sólo ese algo más convierte lo sexual en el deleite torturado, condenado y urgente, que viene a ser el amor, ya que hay que nombrarlo de algún modo"

7. His experience of political upheaval in his native country and of involuntary exile

8. His ultimately optimistic outlook in the later novels, despite the setbacks to progress that he has experienced at first hand, his overt political commitment to the Left and the pattern of values, including emphasis on meaningful struggle, that goes along with this

In Benedetti, then, we have an established senior figure who, both as a novelist and as a critic, encouraged the rejection of much that writers and critics of the Boom had taken for granted. In him, as in David Viñas, Post-Boom writers could see a figure who linked aspects of their outlook with the central tradition of the novel in Latin America. Like Benedetti, Viñas published through the entire high Boom period of the sixties and early seventies, without ever really being thought of as part of it, and for the same basic reason: he was willing, within certain limits, to incorporate a degree of experimentalism into his novels (especially *Los hombres de a caballo*, 1968), but this did not carry with it any serious intention of casting doubt on the relationship between language and reality, or of questioning the ability of the writer to exercise authorial authority in the reflection and interpretation of this last. David William Foster in his useful *Alternate Voices in the Contemporary Latin American Narrative* stresses that in "contemporary narrative that bears witness to the conflict of Latin American society, there has been an emphasis on fiction as an especially productive form of documentary." He continues: "Perhaps the most sustained example is the work of David Viñas, who for almost thirty years has been proposing a revisionist history of Argentine society in his novels."[6] The prime importance of the new historical novel in the Post-Boom makes a glance at Viñas even more obligatory.

Where Viñas and Benedetti coincide is in their rejection of the

Boom, in both cases for the same reason: the Boom writers moved away from reality. For Viñas, whose ideas we saw Vidal mechanically echoing in chapter 1, the shift to the Boom represents the climax of a trend toward "genteel," liberal-bourgeois writing whose origins go back to the romanticism of the 1830s. Elitist and individualistic, the Boom writers are characterized by "la separación del escritor de los términos más amplios de su comunidad" and by surrender to the "ideología del colonizado."[7] Borges, above all, discovered that "No hay como el arte fantástico para resolver—a través del ensueño—un utopismo absoluto y una marginalidad empecinada" (p. 95). The ideal of Borges is "de desacreditar la realidad concreta y de construir un producto que se le oponga" (p. 95); just as the ideal of Cortázar is the achievement of a (spurious) universality by turning his back, in Paris, on the "especificidad" of his native country (pp. 126–27).

In an article on the negative influence of Cortázar Viñas amplifies his criticism of the literary outlook of the Boom writers, seeing Cortázar as their supreme representative in Argentina.[8] The article acuses him of influencing Ricardo Piglia, Néstor Sánchez, Manuel Puig, and others in the direction of "torpeza frente al concreto cotidiano" and "abdicación de todo proyector modificador" (p. 738), that is to say, in the direction of merely prolonging objectionable aspects of the Boom. Fajardo, in his interesting doctoral thesis, sums up Viñas's complaint about the influence of the Boom in terms of: "la exaltación del quehacer literario exclusivamente recortado del resto. Es decir, ocupémonos de lo literario sin tener en cuenta las otras dimensiones que hacen el código, al contexto que subsume la tarea específica de lo literario."[9] In this Viñas is at one with the criticisms of the Boom's formalism by Post-Boom writers and their allied critics mentioned thus far. In his thesis, Fajardo makes a valiant effort to counteract the prevailing critical opinion about Viñas represented, for example, by Angela Dellepiane. She writes of him and those like him, in the middle of the Boom period:

> de la lectura de esta novelística no se deriva placer estético alguno, no hay destreza en el manejo de la lengua o un sólido conocimiento de ella. Hay que escribir, eso es todo; hay que hacerlo de alguna manera. Y esta subordinación del *cómo* al *qué* implica excesos que conducen directamente a la trivialidad cuando no a la barbarie. La novela es arte, mas no en estos escritores.[10]

Fajardo contends, "Si desde el punto de vista del compromiso se pudiera decir que la obra de Viñas no ha evolucionado (lo cual no es rigurosamente exacto), desde la perspectiva artística se puede apreciar todo un proceso de maduración . . . Con cada obra, el novelista profundiza en el manejo de las técnicas narrativas" (p. 151). In one sense this is perfectly true. *Los hombres de a caballo* (1968) and even more *Cuerpo a cuerpo* (1979) do employ techniques of fragmentation and "dato escondido" that are familiar from Boom novels proper. But the fact that neither of these novels has been incorporated into the canon of the Boom illustrates precisely what Viñas as a critic was reluctant to accept, that technical innovation is not connected with some alleged desire to arbitrarily cut off literary creation from its social and ideological context, but has to do with the bona fide need to express a different vision of the real. Wilful failure to accord adequate recognition to this obvious point invalidates much of the Post-Boom's criticism of the Boom.

A later essay, "Pareceres y digresiones en torno a la nueva narrativa latinoamericana" (1981), confirms the view that, like Benedetti, Viñas was ill at ease when discussing the Boom. Characteristically, he begins by suggesting that the Boom writers, by their overwhelming success, "impedían oír otras voces" and that the Boom itself was "la única voz, privilegiada e impuesta o manipulada, que el imperialismo cultural y la academia metropolitana querían escuchar de América Latina."[11] He goes on to advance the childishly simplificatory argument that much of the prestige of the Boom writers derived from the Ph.D. industry in the United States ("tesidolatría") and that the writers of the theses in question took for granted the superiority of "autonomous" fiction over the socially orientated kind. The result was a "star system" based on "complacencias" and "complicidades" on the part of the major authors. Predictably he asserts that the Boom was followed by a crash in the early 1970s. However, reversing an earlier judgement in the light of later experience, he now sees Cortázar as the one writer who was able to transcend the limitations of the Boom writers and bridge the gap that separated them from such figures as Rodolfo Walsh, Haroldo Conti, and Paco Urondo, whom Viñas seems to want to endorse as Post-Boom figures by virtue of their reaction against "el discurso del poder" before which the Boom writers as a whole had prostrated themselves.

In brief, Viñas criticized the Boom writers for:

1. "Vedetismo."
2. Cultural dependency and market orientation
3. Indiference to the "especificidad nacional" of their mother countries
4. Lack of a clear ideological center

In the end, however, he faces the central dilemma of the Post-Boom writers: how to write realistic, socially orientated fiction without seeming to perform a U-turn back toward old-fashioned models. A glance at his "Hacia una literatura socialista con fronteras" in *De Sarmiento a Cortázar* (1971), with its grotesque suggestions for liberating Latin

American fiction from cosmopolitanism and individualism, shows that he had no viable direction to commend to the movement which was soon to get under way. Nonetheless we should notice that Gustavo Sainz writes in his autobiography, "David Viñas me ayudó a definirme."[12]

Viñas views clearly have much in common with Benedetti's. In particular, they share the pattern of radicalization that was not characteristic of the Boom writers generally (hence the exceptionality of Cortázar in his later work). Tealdi, commenting on Viñas's middle period, writes: "en *Los hombres de a caballo* y *Cuerpo a cuerpo* lo que salta a un primer término son los enfrentamientos que dejan relegados a un segundo plano, cada vez menos importante, a los cuestionamientos críticos. Se ha ido pasando de una situación acentuada sobre los problemas individuales y subjetivos en crisis con lo social, a otra situación en la cual la primacía de lo social ha ido estrechando los límites de lo subjetivo."[13] This evolution, already visible in Benedetti after he joined the "26 de Marzo" movement, is, as we have mentioned, equally a feature of the work of Skármeta, Valenzuela, and other Post-Boom writers.

In essence, whereas for the Boom's mainstream critics, led initially by Rodríguez Monegal, the novels of the Boom represented a "salto de calidad" by comparison with those of the Regionalist and *criollista* writers who preceeded them, for Benedetti, Viñas, and others, including Marcos and Vidal, the Boom was a dead end. Only to the minor extent that it could sporadically be seen as including the elements of the tradition of social criticism and protest did it escape the charge that what it really illustrated was the intellectual crisis of the bourgeois elite, the last great sell-out to cultural dependency and spurious universalism. Both Benedetti and Viñas seem initially to be fighting a rearguard action against the growing tendency in Spanish American fiction after mid-century to replace observed reality with created reality (mythic, fantastic, magical realist, etc.) and as a corollary to consider that the writer's task was in the first instance to revolutionize literature rather than to harness literature to the chariot of the Revolution. But in retrospect, in the context of the 1990s, Benedetti and Viñas can now be seen as representing the desire to retain continuity with the older corpus of critical and testimonial writing that has commonly been thought of, by the Left especially, as constituting the central tradition of Spanish American letters. As the Boom ran out of steam, this tradition, stimulated by the failure of the Cuban Revolution to spread to the rest of Spanish America during the 1960s while authoritarian regimes flourished and guerrilla wars raged in Central America, reasserted itself vigorously. It bifurcated into two main currents: testimonial writing as such and the new historical novel of the Post-Boom, which went far beyond the shrill revisionism of Viñas's *Los dueños de la tierra* or *Los hombres de a caballo*. In the Boom, history tended to be presented as static, circular, or at best (in Carpentier) as moving in terribly slow upward spirals, which human effort and sacrifice could not greatly accelerate. The Post-Boom writers, by contrast, despite setbacks to progress in the 1960s and 1970s in Spanish America, generally returned to the faith in progress of Benedetti and Viñas. Those who had doubts (such as Abel Posse in *Los perros del paraíso*, 1987) often expressed them via forms of parody which reveal how deep their basic attachment remained.

However, compared with a novel like Skármeta's *La insurrección* (1982), which deals with the Sandenista rebellion against Somoza in Nicaragua, the novels of Benedetti and Viñas remain within the limits of a prudent revisionism. Significantly, perhaps, we read at the end of Viñas's *Dar la cara* (1975): "Más allá, empezaba el campo de batalla." Tealdi, in an important passage of his book, criticizes Viñas for limiting himself to denunciation of the dominant class without identifying himself clearly in his novels with the alternative: "¿Se puede erigir en personajes positivos a los guerilleros, a los obreros combativos, a los estudiantes y maestros?, he asks, and replies: "Si Viñas cree que ello es posible, debiera justificar su exclusión" (p. 141). Tealdi's stress on the limits imposed on Viñas's radicalism by his middle-class background is equally valid for Benedetti. In both writers, denunciation of the present or recent past does not lead to open advocacy of a revolutionary alternative. The working class remains largely absent from their fiction. There is no contact with the youth culture, so prominent in some Post-Boom writers. Though the question of the marginalization of, for example, Jews and homosexuals is alluded to, virtually for the first time, in the work of Viñas, love plays a less significant role in his novels than in Benedetti's. Although their work looks forward to the central element in the Post-Boom, there are certain differences, as one would expect from generation to generation. Tealdi's conclusions deserve quoting in full, since they were elaborated in the early 1980s, in other words, in the early Post-Boom period. They present Viñas as the main forerunner of what Tealdi thought Post-Boom literature should be like, in Argentina and implicitly in the rest of the continent:

> La literatura de Viñas ofrece, de todas maneras, aspectos fundamentales para la elaboración de una literatura argentina identificada con los problemas sociales sin que por ello necesite ser "social," con la realidad concreta que vivimos sin que por ello haya de ser "realista," con nuestros problemas históricos sin que por ello haya de transformarse en historia. No se trata de hacer sociología, política o historia con la literatura, sino de crear ficciones desde una postura previa de identificación con un proyecto social, político o histórico; y entonces la literatura podrá abordar cualquier tema sin temor a convertirse en defensa

o tolerancia de una visión opuesta. No se trata de definirse a través de la literatura mediante un reclamo mágico de símbolos conjuradores que puedan necesitar entonces de la "política" o del "realismo," sino de ser políticos y realistas para que nuestras obras también lo sean. (p. 158)

Tealdi goes on to credit Viñas with having understood how to "plantearse los verdaderos alcances del oficio de escritor" (p. 158). The whole paragraph reads like a Post-Boom manifesto.

Before leaving this topic a brief postscript is in order with reference to Cortázar, whose name has appeared several times in the previous paragraphs. At first sight there is little to connect him with the Post-Boom, so far as the greater part of his published work is concerned. His insistence on the mysteriousness and ambiguity of reality and the challenges to the reader in his fiction place him, as a writer, unequivocally with his peers in the Boom. However, from the late seventies to the time of his death in the mid-eighties, he emerged as the most authoritative voice of the older generation to encourage the incorporation into Spanish American fiction of many of the features which we associate with the Post-Boom. While he was almost always careful to qualify his remarks so as to safeguard the creative liberty of his fellow writers, it is evident that in articles like "La literatura latinoamericana a la luz de la historia contemporánea" (1979), "Realidad y literatura en América Latina" (1981), and above all "El escritor y su quehacer en América Latina" (1982), he was concerned with emphasizing his approval of the shift that was taking place, even to the extent of implicitly criticizing Boom writing as representative of the "culturas sojuzgadas, aculturadas, ridículamente minoritarias y elitistas, culturas para hombres cultos."[14] "Huelga decir," he insists on the same page, "que no estoy abogando por la facilidad, por la simplificación que tantos reclaman todavía en nombre de [la] inserción popular," but at the same time he calls for much closer contact with the reader and with the problems of the here and now in Latin America. The articles he writes around this time constitute a call for greater social and political engagement on the part of writers in their work and a turning away consciously from "falsas culturas estabilizantes." In the first of the articles mentioned above he specifically welcomed the rise of new "testimonial" literature and called for "una intención de análisis, de toma de contacto, que sigue siendo literatura en la mejor aceptación del término, pero que a la vez entra a formar parte de las vivencias históricas y sociales de cada uno de nuestros pueblos."[15] The importance of Cortázar's *toma de posición*, coming as it did from a major Boom writer, just as the Post-Boom was taking shape, should not be overlooked. As we shall see below, Rosario Ferré, a prominent figure in the Post-Boom, wrote a useful critical monograph on Cortázar as a short story writer that characteristically emphasizes those aspects of his tales which can be regarded as prefiguring the shift back toward greater sociopolitical commitment and more directly "referential" language.

What all this ultimately suggests is that we must read and criticize Post-Boom novels in a quite different way from the way in which we read and criticize Boom novels. Whereas we tend to approach the latter from the standpoint of their view of the human condition generally (however much its setting happens to be Spanish American) and of their link with "high" literature, now we may be better advised to approach Post-Boom novels bearing in mind primarily their relevance to the specific condition of Spanish American men and women and their tendency to react against the notion of "high" canonical literature.

Turning now to two other writers who, in a quite different way, may be regarded as transitional between the Boom and the Post-Boom, Puig and Sarduy, we find ourselves faced with one of the major issues facing critics in this area of Spanish American fiction: the possible relationship between the Boom and the Post-Boom, on the one hand, and modernism and postmodernism, on the other. This is because both novelists have been regarded as representatives of postmodernism in one way or another.[16] In attempting to confront this issue, however tentatively (given that we do not know with any degree of certainty what either of the terms postmodernism or Post-Boom means and are thus in danger of discussing one mystery in terms of another), we must beware of surrendering to the desire for a quick-fix solution to this very complex problem. Concepts can be purloined from the vast mass of writings about postmodernism and applied by a familiar process of lateral thinking to the Post-Boom, instead of working inductively from data supplied by direct research; but good criticism is rarely produced by this approach.

More important is to keep before us the fact that postmodernism is a far wider ranging concept than is Post-Boom. It marks what many regard as a shift in the whole contemporary reception of culture. Beginning in the field of architecture, it has become relevant, not merely to all the arts, but to philosophy, history, political and sociological thinking and to interpretations of trends in science. By contrast, Post-Boom is a much narrower and humbler term restricted to fiction in one continent. Moreover, we must not lose sight of the fact that the notion of postmodernism arose and developed in relation to the culture of advanced industrial or post-industrial societies in Europe and North America and thus may not be properly applicable without much modification to the culture of underdevelopment. Finally, it is perhaps worth passing mention that it is possible to read entire books in this field (for example Peter Brooker's excellent *Modernism/Postmodernism*) and seldom meet with applications of the theory to specific texts, least of all to Spanish American texts. These considerations do not invalidate the attempt to link the Post-Boom to postmodernism (or to some interpretation of it), but they indicate the need for extreme caution in formulating any conclusions.

A suitable place to begin is with what Fredric Jameson has called "a crisis of representation," that is, a loss of confidence in "a mirror theory of knowledge and art, whose fundamental evaluative categories are those of adequacy, accuracy and Truth itself."[17] It is not at all difficult to trace this questioning of older assumptions about truth and knowledge of the real to the father figures of the Boom, especially Borges and Asturias. We recall the latter's famous assertion at the beginning of chapter 26 of *El Señor Presidente* (1946) that "Entre la realidad y el sueño la diferencia es puramente mecánica" and the former's frequent reminders to his readers that all our certainties are probably fictions and that, if there are laws governing reality and our existence, we are probably not programmed to understand them. As we saw in chapter 1, we can, and probably should, relate the Boom to the crisis that Jameson postulates and that lies at the heart of modernism. Can we then proceed to relate the Post-Boom to postmodernism and, if we can, does it help?

Let us consider two possible scenarios, bearing in mind all the time that we are dealing with issues that entirely transcend literature and have crucially important philosophical, political, and social dimensions. In the first scenario the Post-Boom considered as bearing some relationship with postmodernism would have to be seen as reacting directly against the Boom at the literary level (the Boom being regarded as having imposed a false hegemony on fiction, especially via a "high-art" sense of form, often used as a refuge from the crisis postulated by Jameson). It would also have to be seen as reacting indirectly against the authoritarian regimes of Pinochet, Videla, and others at the political level (such regimes being regarded as having imposed some form of "privileged" ideology on their respective societies). The reaction, in both cases, would be in the name of pluralism, heterogeneity, challenge to "master-narratives," whether these take the form of all-embracing philosophic or political ideologies or their literary equivalent, "totalizing" encyclopedic novels. It would propose dissensus, multiplicity, subversion of all grand metadiscourses that purport to offer explanations of the human condition, the abandonment of any search for foundations (in this case, e.g., national, ethnic "essences" or unified theories of fiction), and satisfaction with mere context-relevance rather than universality. There would be advocacy of constant change and experimentation; Post-Boom novels would become "events" in search of a form or rationale that could be discoverable only ex post facto on a basis of the performativeness of the work in question. Indeterminacy, invention, variation and risk would prevail. A problem with this scenario would be that it contains no real hope of progress. It merely emphasizes creative play and difference, rejecting any large-scale project or explanatory rationale but providing no stable alternative stance.

The other scenario is quite different. Here the Post-Boom would be seen as rooted in a nostalgic desire for a return to a communicative approach to language on the part of responsible (i.e., "committed") novelists. They would be presented as addressing a public characterized by some degree of consensus about objective reality and the existence of verifiable referents. This would lead (back?) to a new figuratism, based on widely acceptable presuppositions about meaning, truth, justice, and freedom, a reconstruction of normative criteria, albeit of a temporary, consensual kind. Such norms would have to be posited on the basis of the here and now of the present-day culture itself, not deduced from any allegedly universal or eternal truths. This would be possible only by readopting certain assumptions about language, reality, and the intelligibility of things that modernism seemed in its time to have subverted. But this is another, different time.

The first of these scenarios stresses continuous "new moves"; the other emphasizes the need to legitimize the more important "new moves" by appealing to some supposed underlying consensus about their direction and meaning: some minimal, nontranscendental model of intelligibility. Much of what we can see here is fully consistent with the ideas put forward in chapter 1. There the question was posed: Is the Post-Boom a radicalization of some occasionally overlooked aspects of the Boom itself or does it contain an attempt to contradict some of the central presuppositions of the Boom writers? Consideration of the two foregoing scenarios prompts the conclusion that both are in some degree relevant to the Post-Boom but that there is a majority and a minority position. We can postulate, in other words, a double situation in which one side of the Post-Boom, in Derrida's words "affirms play," while the other side "dreams of deciphering a truth which escapes play."[18] In the first case, Sarduy seems rather relevant as the transitional figure, and in connection with this aspect of the movement we may recall Skármeta's reference to the deliberate "intranscendence" of the work of his peers. But over against this we must postulate a more committed majority sector of the Post-Boom. In this sector the shift in fiction can be presented as a creative return to what, following Foucault, we could call "the collective archive," that is, to an older collective project, still unrealized, that the Boom subordinated to its aesthetic project and commonly repressed (except where, to take only the most obvious example, it broke surface in the description of the banana-workers massacre, which suddenly breaks the predominantly comic tone in *Cien años de soledad*). The difference is rooted, as we might expect if we have read our Carpentier properly, in the conception of history and the idea of progress arising from individual and collective endeavor. For Abel Posse in his Rómulo Gallegos Prize novel *Los perros del paraíso* (1987), to take an illustrative example, historical change seems to be either illusory or mere happenstance, unpredictable or uncontrollable. By contrast, for Skármeta in *La insurrección* (1982) it is the outcome of intentional acts on the part of a people leading to real improvement in social conditions. It is perhaps not entirely irrelevant in this connection that Puig's *El beso de la mujer araña* (1976), generally regarded as his most complete and powerful work, is situated in a prison and that of its three major themes one is revolutionary activity and another the relationship between sexual freedom and political freedom. This is not, of course, to argue that we can draw obvious parallels between Puig's early novels and those of Skármeta. It is merely intended to make the point that the presence of Valentín in *El beso* involves what Tittler calls "the sustained treatment accorded to the possibility of a macropolitical solution to human problems."[19] This is something we do not readily associate with Boom writing and accords with the second scenario postulated above. While the existence of this element in the novel already sets Puig somewhat apart from the Boom writers generally, the fact that Valentín to some extent evolves away from his early arrogance and dogmatism toward a greater awareness of the complexity of human reality represents a critique of direct political commitment. To that extent, it distances Puig from a central strand of the Post-Boom: he is essentially transitional.

Nineteen sixty-eight, the year of *La traición de Rita Hayworth*, marked a turning point in the emergence of the Post-Boom. By then the Boom had passed its first peak with *Cien años de soledad* (1967) and its writers had largely established their hegemony as practitioners of the dominant fictional mode. Most of the Boom's characteristics were already recognizable, and in 1970 were to be given an early codification by Vargas Llosa and Rodríguez Monegal in *Books Abroad*.[20] By this time, too, Sarduy was on the scene with two novels to his credit, while Sainz and Skármeta had already published first novels. In retrospect we can see that a challenge to the Boom was taking shape. It is noteworthy, however, that Puig was chronologically the oldest of the challenging group, five years older than Sarduy and eight years older than Sainz and Skármeta. The last two, it will be argued here, belong to the Post-Boom proper. Opinions about Puig, informed and otherwise, differ on this point. Fredric Jameson, Linda Hutcheon, and Lucille Kerr, for instance, all seem to think that he is characteristically postmodernist.[21] Tittler sees him as a "secondary" figure of the Boom, while Bacarisse associates him fully with the Post-Boom.[22] But this has not been discussed at any length.

Puig's significance with respect to the Post-Boom derives from several aspects of his work, but there can be no doubt that the principal one, which is crucial to the new movement, as we saw in chapter 1, was his deliberate rebellion against the concept of "high" literature and his functional incorporation of "pop" and "low" culture elements into the Spanish American novel. This involved not only incorporating references to (for example) sport and mass-entertainment, but also using "low" culture genres as models and adapting "low" culture techniques to the writing process. He was not the first to go in this general direction. Borges had written about Billy the Kid in *Historia universal de la infamia* as early as 1935 and had used the detective story format in "La muerte y la brújula" (1942). In addition there are the Bustos Domenq and Parodi stories, written in collaboration with Bioy Casares. Cortázar had written about boxing in "Torito" (1956) and had Charlie Parker and bebop in mind when he wrote *El persiguidor* (1959). As we saw earlier, youth culture was a prominent feature of the "Onda" in Mexico in the sixties, a movement that was led by Sainz and Agustín. But it was not until *El beso de la mujer araña* emerged as a cult classic after its publication in 1976, and was subsequently consecrated by Babenco's film in 1985, that it was possible to see with hindsight the importance of what had really only begun to achieve full momentum with *La traición de Rita Hayworth* in the late sixties. By the time the film version became popular, Vargas Llosa had published *La tía Julia y el escribidor* (1977); Fuentes, *La cabeza de la hidra* (1978); Donoso, *La misteriosa desaparición de la marquesita de Loria* (1980); and García Márquez, *El amor en los tiempos del cólera* (1985), to name only the most obvious examples of the way the Boom went pop after Puig had eclipsed the Mexicans in leading the way.

What began to happen in Spanish American fiction after 1968 was what Jameson, referring to "metropolitan" literature, calls "the effacement of the older (essentially High-Modernist) frontier between high culture and so-called mass or commercial culture and the emergence of new kinds of texts infused with the forms, categories and contents of that Culture Industry so passionately denounced by the ideologues of the modern."[23] The tendency, as Linda Hutcheon observes, involved "reappraising existing representations that are effective precisely because they are loaded with pre-existing meaning and putting them into new and ironic contexts."[24] This sentence could serve as a definition of what it is that Puig brought to the Spanish American novel in his early work. Jean Franco writes:

La cultura de masas, especialmente el cine y los cuentos policíacas
habían ejercido anteriormente una fascinación sobre Borges, para
quien el problema de la repetición es central. García Márquez, Roa
Bastos, Vargas Llosa, Cabrera Infante y Fuentes escribieron guiones
cinematográficos y además es evidente el impacto de la cultura de
masas en su narrativa. La novela de Fuentes *Cambio de Piel* está dedi-
cada a Shirley McClaine e ilustrada con fotografías de estrellas de cine;
las novelas de Manuel Puig emplean el lenguaje de la literatura popular y las imágenes del cine; Cabrera Infante y Luis Rafael Sánchez se
apoderan de las canciones populares, Vargas Llosa de la radionovela y
Cortázar de la tira cómica.[25]

While this passage shows a tendency to flatten out the differences
among the uses of popular culture made by the various authors mentioned—and they differ very significantly—it indicates an important
aspect of the transition from Boom to Post-Boom, a transition whose
clearest examples can be found in Puig's work. Franco herself admits as
much at the end of her essay: "Al comparar las novelas mencionadas de
Fuentes y Vargas Llosa con las de Manuel Puig se percibe un manejo
mucho más sofisticado en el último" (p. 129). Nonetheless, it deserves
to be reiterated that, so far as the mainstream of their work is concerned,
the Boom writers, conscious of what they regarded as the excessive
localism and technical inadequacies of the earlier Regionalist novelists,
moved most of the time in the direction of "high" literature with emphasis on experimentalism and writerliness.

In contrast, writers like Benedetti and Viñas resisted this trend in
most of their fiction, and critics rejected it as élitist and as breaking with
the entire tradition of the Spanish American novel. As we read on the
one hand *El escritor latinoamericano y la revolución posible* or *De
Sarmiento a Cortázar* and on the other hand the replies of the Boom
writers (for example, in Oscar Collazos's *Literatura en la revolución y
revolución en la literatura*), we have the sensation of voices talking past
each other. There was virtually no common ground. What was necessary, as Tittler points out, was the emergence of a novelist who was
capable of being "at odds" with the "serious high culture" which was
the result of the Boom's *salto de calidad*, without moving either in the
direction of neorealism or, worse still, in the direction of mass culture
itself.[26] He argues persuasively that Puig was able to occupy "an innovative middle ground" (p. 8). Essentially, Puig himself asserted, he was
reaching out towards a wider public than the Boom writers had envisaged.[27] But as he later told Gazarian Gautier: "I am not interested in the
least in a purely realistic approach. I want to recreate reality to understand it, to illuminate it, but always in terms of an aesthetic elabora-
tion."[28] Here we can see what Tittler was referring to: Puig wanted to

find a more accessible, reader-friendly approach in fiction, without giving up the Boom's insistence on literariness or moving toward the views
of Benedetti and Viñas.

To the extent that he clearly exemplifies what Leslie Fiedler was the
first to identify in 1965 as the tendency of postmodernism to seek materials and models from popular subliterary genres, and to the extent that
the Jencksian concept of postmodernist "double-coding" (one part
modern, one part more traditional) is equally applicable to his novels,
Puig could be regarded as postmodernist. At the same time, the problem
with seeing him as a fully Post-Boom writer is connected with his tendency to separate the "pop" elements in his work from the serious, or
"high" literature ones rather than synthesizing them. Characteristic is
the way the film plots in *El beso* are related by Molina to Valentín in
the context of the imprisonment of both and their different evolutions
during the ordeal. Similarly, as late as *Pubis angelical*, there is a sharp
distinction drawn between Ana's daydreams about herself as Ana/actriz
and what Tittler calls the "markedly mimetic or realistic" modality of
the novel (p. 66). The use of the more vapid or "pop" elements in Puig's
novels is always functional, but they are kept apart; we are always conscious of the difference between them and the drabness and even danger
of real life. In Puig, that is, they tend to be part of an "other life" of the
characters, whereas in the Post-Boom proper they are part of the characters' real experience and presented as life enhancing rather than
escapist.

We must, of course, distinguish between Puig's use of pop elements
within the novels and his use of low literary models, such as the crime
novel in *La traición* or the novelette in *Boquitas pintadas*. This use is
highly innovative and historically significant since it long predates the
adoption of similar models by Vargas Llosa, Fuentes, Donoso, and García Márquez. But it is the intention that matters. What Puig is doing,
especially in his early work, is to instrumentalize pop material in order
to get back to a social vision that the Boom had tended to subordinate.
He is using the products of the entertainment industry to challenge its
impact from within. To understand this we need to recall that (to take
the most obvious example) pop music has undergone a very visible evolution since the late fifties. Prior to that time it was generally nostalgic,
sentimental, and, sociologically speaking, largely in the business of reinforcing social and sexual conventions. It was only in the sixties that pop
music began to espouse oppositional stances toward established values
and to be related to youthful rebelliousness. Moreover it was not until
the recent arrival of the rock video that pop music became genuinely
postmodernist, in the sense of tending to exclude story or message in
favor of utterly nonrealistic fantasy or (to use the jargon) the free play

of the signifier. To see again why Puig is a transitional figure, we must notice that in his early work (in *Boquitas pintadas* especially, which is set in pre–World War II Argentina) he uses references to the oldest of the three phases just mentioned, represented in Argentina by prewar tangos and boleros. Moreover he uses them, not as markers of a youth culture, but explicitly for purposes of social criticism. In his often quoted interview with M. Osorio in 1977, he was unequivocal about his objective: "Yo quise . . . contar una historia de cálculos fríos en términos de una novela apasionada." In defending his use of a popular novelette model he said: "Me gusta entretener, me gusta divertir al contar algo. No creo que esté reñido con el *decir algo*, con hacer un discurso complejo y comprometido."[29] Puig employs this popular model and incorporates references to music, films, and radio soap opera to emphasize the banality and hypocrisy of the characters' lives. This is very different from the use by Skármeta, for example, of references to pop music, films, and sport to establish his young protagonists as representatives of their sixties generation, that is, as fans of Ella Fitzgerald, the Beatles, John Coltrane, Chet Baker, George Raft, Gregory Peck, Mike Todd, Robert Mitchum, and so on. Moreover in Skármeta's short story "Basketball," for example, the young narrator deliberately uses pop music and film references to express his ironic self-vision, and when he refers to his generation's equivalent of Puig's Alfredo La Pera and Gardel—Mantovani—it is to make fun of his own emotions and desires. Puig, that is, uses an earlier and a different kind of pop culture in *La traición* and *Boquitas pintadas* from the one used by the later, fully Post-Boom writer, and he uses it for a quite different purpose, the effect of which is paradoxically to emphasize his serious intention.

Failure to recognize adequately what this means about his attitude toward reality and hence his place in contemporary Spanish American fiction is the basic weakness of Kerr's *Suspended Fictions*, a book which one can read from end to end without realizing that Puig is a key figure in the shift from Boom to Post-Boom. There is an unresolved tension in it between the author's desire to present Puig as a fully fledged postmodernist, on the one hand, and her recognition that he is a subversive "political" writer, on the other. Although she specifically accepts that "it would be possible to show how the radical transvaluations of discourses and genres, for example, are tied to the political structure of parody itself,"[30] she never develops what she calls on the same page the "radical thrust" of Puig's work—which is precisely what links him with the Post-Boom. In her anxiety to present his flight from omniscient narration to multiple discourse and to the creation of novels that are "doubly dialogized hybrids" (p. 15), she completely loses sight of the very aspect that differentiates the complexities we encounter in his novels from the at times similar complexities achieved by the Boom's emphasis on formal experimentation and emphasis on the narrative act.

By contrast, Enrique Giordano more convincingly highlights the second feature of Puig's work that points forward to what will become a major strand in Post-Boom fiction, when he writes, "la obra de Puig marca una instancia fundamental en el proceso de la novelística hispanoamericana: el paso de una escritura irrealista a otra forma de concebir el texto, lo cual implica una transgresión a los modos anteriores de composición y una vuelta hacia lo referencial, a una forma de realismo más depurado."[31] It is this referentiality that Puig constantly insists on in relation to his early work and that critics of every stripe have accepted as significant in his writing. Especially in his first two works, he continues the linguistic and narratorial experimentalism we associate with the Boom. Indeed, as Kerr's analyses indicate, he takes it in novel directions. But rather than exploring the universal human condition as it just happened to manifest itself in a Spanish American setting, an approach that set the Boom writers off from the earlier Regionalists, he emphasizes the condition of Spanish American man (and woman) much more specifically than had usually been the case in the earlier movement. There is room for argument about whether we all tend to live the banal lives of characters in a B movie, which, if true, would confer universality on Puig's novels and perhaps explain their popularity outside Latin America. But it seems clear that his original intention in the Coronel Vallejos novels was to explore critically the lifestyle of the provincial Argentina he had grown up in, seen as dominated by the exercise of power, on the one hand, and by modes of escape from it, on the other. Thus, *Boquitas pintadas* is presented as a *folletín*, and Puig on one occasion asserts, "Del folletín quise tomar la estructura atenta al interés anecdótico, la emotividad, la aparente simplicidad en el trazo de los personajes,"[32] emphasizing features of love interest and plot centeredness which were destined to become basic to much Post-Boom fiction. But Bella Josef points out that, in contrast to that of the *folletín*, "el tono narrativo es el de implacable objetividad, de precisión documentaria," (p. 112) and, in full accord with Giordano: "El proceso narrativo será de base referencial, a través de los índices de verosimilitud: cartas, anuncios, album de fotos, documentación oficial, periódicos y revistas y la precisión de horarios" (p. 113).

That is to say: if Puig's early novels "break the mold" of Boom fiction, it is partly in order to bring the novel back to its traditional role in Spanish America, that of social commentary and criticism. This, with its emphasis on what Giordano calls "irrealismo" (fantasy, myth, emphasis on the mystery or unintelligibility of reality), the Boom had pushed into second place. Puig's work marks its return to favor. The "objectivity" of Puig, which Josef stresses, is not a return to old-style, pre-Boom realism. Indeed her whole approach, like that of Kerr, foregrounds his formal, and linguistic innovations. But she indicates, as her choice of vocabulary (*objetividad, documentaria, referencial*) makes clear, something fundamental about the shift Giordano postulates: the return to greater referentiality indicates a return to a concept of reality as inherently intelligible. As indicated in chapter 1 and in my comments on the ideas of Benedetti and Viñas, the problem posed by the Boom for a significant group of writers and critics, chiefly on the Left, was that, by questioning our ability to know and interpret the reality of our experiences, the Boom writers undermined in principle any realistic attempt to deal with social problems. The process began to be apparent when Asturias attempted to unite social protest in *El Señor Presidente* with a mythical subtext and innovations of technique which were not entirely compatible with his intention. This produced in the novel the ambiguity first properly recognized by Guillermo Yepes Boscán and later discussed by Nelson Osorio.[33] It was a process which thereafter became dominant in the sixties and early seventies. But in the early work of Puig we see its breakdown. The reason is, as Puig remarked to Reina Roffé, "No pude aceptar la realidad que me tocó."[34]

The incorporation of pop material and the return to referentiality and social criticism both tend to distance Puig from the Boom writers. Unlike Skármeta and others, however, he has not specifically criticized the older generation of novelists. Still, his comment on the writers of the French "nouveau roman" reveals his priorities, which are those of the central strand of the Post-Boom. Of the French writers, he asserts, "cometían lo que creo que es un error básico, posponer el contenido a la forma," whereas, in his view, "lo importante es la necesidad de investigar algo por una necesidad de cambiarlo, la forma viene sola."[35] Along with this goes his rejection of the "gusto por lo cerebral" (609), which he felt typified the culture of Argentina (and by extension much of Latin America) during the rise of the Boom writers. By contrast he emphasizes the need for reader friendliness, which was to become so prominent in the Post-Boom: "trato de no pedir esfuerzos especiales de la atención por parte del lector" (593).

Central to this intention is Puig's use of language; in two senses, both of which portend language use during the Post-Boom. One, of course, colloquiality. From *La traición* onward, as Puig himself and numerous critics (especially Kerr, Josef, and Echevarren) have noted, his desire to avoid the third person, and its assumption of authorial authority and omniscience, has resulted in the foregrounding of individual "hablas sociales." These ideolects both differentiate and personalize the characters, as well as, in certain cases, present them in a gently humorous light. Characteristic of his interest in colloquiality is the fact that the style of *Sangre de amor correspondido* was influenced by tapes Puig made of conversations with a building worker whom he met by chance in Brasil.[36] The emphasis laid on colloquiality as part of his generation's practice by Skármeta, mentioned in chapter one, cannot be separated from Puig's pioneering explorations of oral discourse. But secondly, as Sarduy points out, Puig's language represents the necessary corollary to his return to more direct representation of reality: "lo que en él [el lenguaje] se subraya es su carácter de vehículo, de medio de transmisión y soporte de ideas recibidas," in contrast to the much more literary codes predominantly used by the Boom writers, whose confidence in the relationship between signifier and signified was much less great.

Finally we must mention two other relevant features of Puig's work, especially prominent in his earlier writings, though still visible in *Sangre de amor correspondido* (1982): the heavy emphasis on emotionality and a love interest and the incorporation of working-class characters. Milagros Ezquerro, discussing the pop art characteristics Puig incorporated into his work, notes that, "Lo más importante es el sentimentalismo, o sea la preeminencia de la sensibilidad y de los sentimientos, particularmente—claro está—del amor en toda su gama."[37] The Boom was antiromantic in the extreme. The Post-Boom, by contrast, tends to revindicate the role of love in everyday life. Once again it is Puig who marks the transition, though, given his emphasis on forms of oppression and response through illusion, he rarely presents love in the positive light we notice, for example, in Skármeta's *Ardiente paciencia* or Allende's *De amor y de sombra*.

If, by and large, the majority of Puig's characters are in the very broadest sense middle class, the appearance of Raba and her seducer Pancho, the policeman, in prominent roles in *Boquitas pintadas* is of historical significance for the Spanish American novel in our time. They are treated quite differently from the young workers in Skármeta's *Soñé que la nieve ardía*, or from Allende's Eva Luna, who is the daughter of a servant. All the same, far more than Mauricio Babilonia, the mechanic's apprentice in *Cien años de soledad*, who is sometimes mentioned as representing the emergence of the working class into high Boom fiction, they mark the convincing arrival of the modern proletariat in the Spanish American novel.

Bearing in mind the model suggested in chapter 1, much of the above points toward a confirmation of Giordano's postulate that Puig's early work constitutes a watershed. Puig himself has stated categorically, "Yo no me propuse una renovación de nada"[38] and we can take him at his word. But when he told Corbatta, "Sólo intentaba reproducir algo real," in his early work,[39] he was voicing a central tenet of the Post-

Boom and must be regarded as the writer who best illustrates the turning point we are concerned with here.

The fiction of Severo Sarduy illustrates the shift in a quite different way. Whereas Puig's earliest novels break away from the Boom in what is already clearly distinguishable as a Post-Boom direction, Sarduy first carries the idea of the novel as language, already endorsed by Fuentes in his *La nueva novela hispanoamericana* (1969) and elsewhere, to its furthest extreme, "revolutionizing" Spanish American fiction in this way, according to René Prieto,[40] before returning unexpectedly to a more traditionally realistic mode in *Cocuyo* (1990). There is, in other words, first a violent shift in the opposite direction, followed only much later by a qualified acceptance of the mainstream Post-Boom trend. In retrospect, however, we can see that Sarduy's earlier practice of fiction only serves to throw into higher relief his subsequent partial alignment with the new movement and to confirm not only its most basic characteristic but also its impact on writers who initially were of quite another persuasion. Sarduy, then, is not a precoursor of the Post-Boom in the sense that Puig is; rather, he is the youngest of the group of writers, including García Márquez, Fuentes, Donoso and Vargas Llosa, whose work illustrates an awareness of the transition that was under way.

This has only recently become apparent. Giordano, writing in the mid-eighties, saw Sarduy's work as having nothing in common with the shift in Spanish American fiction, whose origins, he argues, are most visible in the early work of Puig:

> A partir del modernismo y las orientaciones de vanguardia suprarrealistas," he writes, "la narrativa hispanoamericana—a la par del drama y la lírica—ha tendido al discurso autosignificante e intransitivo: al lenguaje autónomo (lenguaje considerado en cuanto lenguaje) . . . a la mismidad de la narración, al discurso centrado en sí mismo, cuya máxima expresión estaría en Lezama Lima y Sarduy. En Puig, en cambio, observamos un vuelco definitivo hacia una forma de 'alteridad' que implicaría una vuelta al discurso referencial.[41]

González Echevarría, only slightly later, could see the change coming, to the extent of arguing that since *Maitreya* (1978) Sarduy had begun to return to plot and in *Colibrí* (1984) had shown more interest in Latin America itself and the theme of the jungle. What is implied is that, since the late 1970s, Sarduy has become increasingly aware of what González Echevarría calls the "exhaustion of theory" and has been moving in a new Post-Boom direction.[42] This fits well with Suzanne Jill Levine's assertion in the preface to her translation of *Cobra* (1972) that that novel "represents in many ways the culmination of the New Latin American Novel."[43] If these critics are correct, a discernible shift in Sarduy's work took place during the mid-seventies, which are generally accepted as the years of transition from Boom to Post-Boom.

To the question, Of what is *Cobra* a "culmination"? Sarduy himself gave a short answer in a 1991 interview when he declared, "En *De donde son los cantantes* se trata en todo caso de una idea que es muy del barroco, es decir el hecho de que una literatura es autónoma, que está organizada como un código particular y no tiene nada que ver con la supuesta realidad que puede mimetizar, que puede reproducir o no."[44] More than twenty years earlier he had expressed the same idea in *Escrito sobre un cuerpo* (1969), dismissing as a mere prejudice the notion that visual signifiers, that is, words on a page, could somehow express content, ideas, messages, or an imaginary realm. Modern literary criticism, he argued, has destroyed this myth of meaning and focused attention exclusively on the writerly nature of the text, from which significance is a necessarily absent feature. There is no referent outside the book itself, he writes approvingly of Maurice Roche's *Compact* (1966).

This was not a new idea in 1969, even in Spanish America. In the 1920s Macedonio Fernández was already arguing that the various literary genres "nada deben copiar de una Realidad Presente y todo debe incesantemente jugar."[45] The concepts of the total autonomy of the work of art and of the free play of the signifier derive from the crisis of old-style that which we see as giving rise to modernism in Western literature. The Boom writers in Spanish America were deeply conscious of this crisis and to that extent are associated with modernism. But they were far from breaking entirely with referentiality. As González Echevarría writes in his preface to the English version of Sarduy's *Maitreya*: "Characters in their novels have the appearance, mannerisms of speech and behavior sanctioned by society and novelistic tradition."[46] By contrast, the historical significance of Sarduy's early novels lies precisely in the fact that he, like Elizondo in Mexico, was memorably practicing in them, during the peak decade of the Boom, a form of writing that deliberately sabotaged the literary dream of a world where words can create a construct that can be in some sense compared with, and validated by, its similarity to or correspondence with a world "out there." Sarduy's work stands in contrast to the return to reality and referentiality commonly seen in Post-Boom writing; for Sarduy, Montero writes, "'reality' is a metaphysical category in a system which his textual practice contests."[47] In that sense, as the most "theory-informed" writer of the sixties and seventies, Sarduy reveals the impact of that form of postmodernism that emphasizes the free play of signifiers, *jouissance*, an aesthetics of the body, and the direct expression of sensations and images without any necessary links to any "really" real beyond the text.

This, some critics have seen as possibly the dominant mode in metropolitan cultures, but it is resisted for ideological reasons in the Third World as it is, for the most part, in black and feminist writing. An example of this resistance, directed at the two authors mentioned above, can be noted in these comments made in 1978 by José Agustín, a Mexican novelist:

> I find only one serious flaw in Sarduy and Elizondo, both of whom have created a strong following in Latin America and also in Europe. They love their literary theories so much that they consider them as the only valid ones, the ultimate truth of all artistic laws . . . Joyce's *Ulysses* and Proust's *A la recherche du temps perdu* initiated a literary movement leading inward . . . But now, almost at the end of the century, the pendulum has reached the subjective extreme, and any dogmatic attempt to keep it there disrupts this natural development, which now needs to turn back to external reality to rediscover, with our perception enriched from these inner journeys, just how much we have been missing in this external reality. Thus, when Sarduy and Elizondo maintain that the only true way to write is theirs, they obstruct this multiplicity, the multifaced richness of styles and world-views presently growing in Latin America.[48]

Without losing sight of the technical achievements of the Boom writers or of the dangers inherent in what Sarduy called the "myth" of old-style realism and the assumption that language "es un puro práctico-inerte,"[49] we recognize in this passage another clear indication that the mainstream element in the Post-Boom is a tendency back to referentiality.[43]

What is significant, from the standpoint of the present attempt to characterize the Post-Boom, is Sarduy's return, after establishing himself as the leading exponent of nonmimetic fiction, to a more traditional form of linear structure with coherent character presentation and in the case of *Cocuyo* even an omniscient narrator. In one sense, therefore, *Cocuyo* might be seen as another example of submission to a new "dominant," an example similar to but even more significant than that presented in other novels by the older writers. However, I must enter a caveat. Sarduy remains, even in this novel, a transitional writer. This is partly because, after the struggle in *Colibrí* perceptively postulated by Méndez Rodenas,[50] he began to align himself with some aspects of the Post-Boom only in 1990. However, it is also partly for a quite different reason. In his interview with Ada Teja in 1991, Sarduy rather unexpectedly asserted that his writing corresponded at the personal level to a kind of "logoterapia" designed to cure him of an inner anguish by writing it out of himself.[51] Montero notes that this is relevant as early as Sarduy's second novel: "The tales that compose *De donde son los cantantes* began with desire and end with death."[52] Even so, he qualifies his remark later by adding: "As in a New Orleans funeral, however, what matters most in Sarduy is not the drive towards death but the dancing jig punctuating it" (p. 68). *Cocuyo*, with its more explicit treatment of man's existential "orfandad" and anguish, must cause us to modify that judgement in turn. The issue is, however, that such a pessimistic vision of the human condition tends to be far more typical of the Boom than of the Post-Boom. Thus, just as Sarduy was changing his mind about the baroque and discovering in it, not "una proliferación incontrolable de signos," as he had previously thought, but rather "un enderezamiento, una reestructuración,"[53] and restoring visible structure to his novelistic practice, he was meanwhile expressing a worldview that we associate in Spanish America with the fifties and sixties. Nevertheless Sarduy's development as a novelist is crucial to our argument. The shift in his work from the Kristevan notion of the text as productivity, foregrounding the evidence of its own writing, back to something much more like the traditional representational novel is one more piece of evidence with respect to the process I am attempting to describe. The tendency in Levine, Prieto, and Montero to see in the early Sarduy an author who "explodes," "subverts," or "revolutionizes" the older practice of fiction in Spanish America is overdramatic. He merely extends a tendency already present in the work of other novelists. But the more extreme that extension can be seen to be, up to and including *Cobra*, the more significant is the change illustrated by *Colibrí* and more fully manifest in *Cocuyo*.

An interesting parallel to the case of Sarduy is offered by that of Salvador Elizondo, of whom Cadena (forgetting Sarduy) has written that, up to the point at which he wrote *Elsinore* (1988) he was "El exponente por excelencia, en lengua española, del *nouveau roman*."[54] Exactly like Sarduy, Elizondo began by totally rejecting observed reality. "No hay realidad en ninguno de mis escritos," he proclaimed, referring to his earlier work. "Ella no cuenta, no existe, no interesa; hablo de la realidad *real*, anecdótica."[55] Cadena comments, "Su interés no radica en el mensaje comunicado; de hecho, el mensaje es lo de menos: algo tiene que servir como soporte a las palabras . . . lo único que existe en la narrativa de Salvador Elizondo [up to *Elsinore*] es el lenguaje" (p. 41). But, as Sarduy with *Cocuyo*, Elizondo with *Elsinore* came to recognize that his earlier fiction had reached a limit. "He llegado a la conclusión," he confessed in the interview just mentioned (p. 38), "un poco deplorable para mí, de que ya no hay campo para los experimentos." In and after *Elsinore*, he asserted, he intended to write more "normal" fiction. This remarkable shift in the work of both the two leading exponents of antirealist prose fiction in Spanish America cannot be without significance in relation to the wider shift from Boom to Post-Boom.

A pendant to the above is developed by Kenton Stone in his *Utopia Undone: The Fall of Uruguay in the Novels of Carlos Martínez Moreno.*[56] He shows convincingly how this undervalued Uruguayan writer of the Boom period evolved. He moved from the production of highly complex novels, which illustrate many of the characteristics of the Boom listed in chapter 1, to a transitional phase. This phase was marked by his *Tierra en la boca* (1974, a date that emphasizes afresh the importance of the mid-1970s as the period of shift from Boom to Post-Boom). Finally in 1981 he wrote the denunciatory, testimonial novel of torture and oppression, *El color que el infierno me escondiera*. As Stone points out, even Martínez Moreno's attitude toward language changes at this point and "distinguishes this novel from those of his boom period in the 1960s. Martínez Moreno appears to have completed the transition noted in the 1974 novel *Tierra en la boca* from the style of his boom novels to a postboom aesthetic" (p. 177). He continues: "In Martínez Moreno's postboom view . . . the writer's role in society is to rescue society from the hell it creates for itself. While not claiming the power to transform society, literature can heal by bringing humanity into painful contact with even the most atrocious but true aspects of human nature. This is an interesting case of an author's coming about full circle in his attitude towards the relationship between literature and society in narrative" (p. 178). We should probably not have to look far for other examples. Commenting specifically on *El color*, Stone suggests that it illustrates "a return to a more straightforward social realism, though one informed by the experiments of the boom all the same" (p. 179).

It seems to follow that we can tentatively postulate two especially significant trends within the Post-Boom. The majority trend, which it seems relevant to point out is the one that was adopted by the older writers who became alive to the change coming over fiction, is the one I attempted to characterize in chapter 1. Its basic characteristic is the one restated above by Agustín: a renewal of interest in referentiality. Along with this go reader friendliness, plot centeredness, the return to the here and now of Spanish America, and the other traits so far argued to be relevant. But partly stemming from Sarduy and Elizondo and the notions that the former put forward in *Escrito sobre un cuerpo* in 1969—"la instancia absoluta del significante" and "la literatura en tanto que arte no comunicativo" (*Escrito*, p. 51)—and reinforced by the theoretical investigations that have led from formalism to poststructuralism, and postmodernism, there is also a second trend. Manifested in the "Escritura" movement in Mexico, for example, it carries the reaction against old-style realism, already prominent in the Boom, to the extreme of what Santí has called "the nihilism of a total fiction."[57] Perhaps, then, a suitable tactic for dealing with Post-Boom authors is to try to situate them along a line representing a continuum that runs from extreme documentality/testimoniality to patterns of writing in which referentiality is subordinated, though, as we have just seen in Sarduy, rarely eliminated entirely. Finally it seems plausible to argue that of the two trends mentioned, the second seems more in line with current definitions of postmodernism. This is more or less the view of Raymond L. Williams in *The Postmodern Novel in Latin America* (1995).

PART 2

# Some Post-Boom Novelists

# CHAPTER 3

# *Isabel Allende*

Without question the major literary event in Spanish America during the early eighties was the publication in 1982 of Isabel Allende's runaway success *La Casa de los Espíritus*. Its extreme accessibility to the general reader, its prominent love interest, and its intriguing combination of the marvelous with social involvement seemed to announce it as the novel which would be to the Post-Boom what *Cien años de soledad* was to the Boom. Since then the dust has settled somewhat and Allende's position as the leading Post-Boom novelist has come to seem less obvious. But the historical importance of *La Casa de los Espíritus* remains unchallenged. In what does it basically consist? In chapter 2, I quoted a statement by José Agustín that was in line with several others arguing in favor of returning to a form of realism while remaining mindful of the crisis of referentiality that had been a factor in the rise of the Boom. In what now seems a rather cruder sense than was to be the case with *Eva Luna*, *La Casa de los Espíritus* can be seen as illustrating this alleged imperative of Spanish American fiction.

On the whole, the various forms of realism tend to rely on two major supports. One is a more-or-less linear chronological arrangement of episodes. The other is a general postulate of the intelligibility of experience perceived in terms of causes and effects. Both of these supports were frequently questioned by Boom writers, who commonly broke with conventional chronology—a noteworthy figure being Carpentier in *Guerra del tiempo* and in a different sense *Los pasos perdidos*—and undermined our confidence in simple causality. Borges explored the idea of circular time but also, in "La lotería en Babilonia" (*Ficciones*), suggested that our lives might be governed by "un infinito juego de azares." Cortázar rejected what he called "false realism" based on old-fashioned presumptions about cause and effect.[1] Méndez Rodenas, with her usual lucidity, points out that one of the salient features of Sarduy's first novel,

---

The chapters in this part are not intended to offer systematic general studies of the work of the novelists under review. Rather the aim is to discuss it in the context of the scenario developed in part 1. That is, to attempt to discuss these writers specifically in relation to the Post-Boom, in the hope that this will provide some illustration of what the term might mean.

*Gestos* (1963), is that the arrangement of events in chapter 4 "tiene como propósito el destruir el concepto de causa/efecto que fundamenta una idea progresiva de la historia," a process that Guerrero sees as peaking in the second part of *Cobra*.[2] At first sight Allende appears to react against both these tendencies. To Gloria Gutiérrez she said, "En general uso el tiempo cronológico. No hago experimentos con el texto, procuro contar con sencillez"[3] (a classic Post-Boom affirmation). Equally, although she is usually careful to qualify her remarks in a way which reveals her awareness of boom influence (as when to Moody she referred to "el mundo *aparentemente* ordenado, donde vivimos y cuyas leyes *creemos* conocer" [emphasis added]),[4] she seems to have little doubt about the principle of causality in general, though this may be open to some question in view of her penchant for using details that seem magical.

One of the unresolved critical questions with respect to *La casa de los Espíritus* concerns precisely its blend of "magical" or "fantastic elements" with a story line reflecting the twentieth-century social and political history of Chile. Critics usually refer to this blend, and a whole book has been written about "narrative magic" in Allende's work.[5] However, the issues regarding this blend have not been clearly defined. There are three. First, Is the fantasy intended to reflect something mysterious and ambiguous about reality itself everywhere? Or, second, Is the fantasy intended to reflect something specific (or more specific) to Latin American reality? Third and most important, What is its function in relation to the more conventional presentation of reality, especially after the pivotal ninth chapter in *La Casa de los Espíritus*? Allende herself wavers. Sometimes she associates the fantastic elements in her work with what she calls "el lado oculto de la realidad";[6] at other times she associates them with Latin America as "a land where anything can happen" and explicitly follows the notion of "lo real maravilloso americano" of Alejo Carpentier.[7] She has linked them in the case of her first novel with the passions and obsessions of the Trueba family, but she also related them to her childhood imaginings and to the influence of her clairvoyant grandmother. It is clear from her interview with Gloria Gutiérrez, mentioned above, that an important part of her literary personality has to do with her unwillingness to draw any hard and fast line between reality and fantasy. But this presents critics with a problem, for the importance of fantasy in literature lies usually in what it tells us about reality. We automatically wish to be able to impute a symbolic or metaphorical dimension to the fantastic elements in *La Casa de los Espíritus*, to be able to interpret meaningfully the references to the spirit world even if they do not always seem very serious. This desire is all the more acute because of the way this novel straddles the Boom and the

Post-Boom, looking back to García Márquez, Cortázar, and ultimately Borges, on the one hand, and forward to the more conscious commitment of *De amor y de sombra*, on the other.

Hart makes a convincing case for concluding that *La Casa de los Espíritus* is written, in a sense, to debunk some aspects of García Márquez's presentation of reality in *Cien años de soledad*. The essence of her argument is that, in contrast to García Márquez's practice in his best-known work, Allende's first novel is characterized by "the way the real is used to undercut the magical."[8] If this were the whole truth of the matter, *La Casa de los Espíritus* would be a more important marker in the shift from Boom to Post-Boom than it actually is. The problem lies in the fact that not all the "magic" is connected with prescience (the issue on which Hart bases her case) and thus not as much of it is "undercut," to use one of her favorite verbs, as she tries to make out. Allende affirmed categorically to Gazarian Gautier her view that "The world has no explanation" and that it is "ruled by invisible forces," a view that she reiterated to Gloria Gutiérrez.[9] In the latter case she added that the "elementos invisibles que afectan nuestras vidas" may belong to a spiritual realm from which explanations and sources of hope can be drawn. Agosín has developed this idea, arguing that the mysterious forces to which Clara apparently has access in *La Casa de los Espíritus* are basically benevolent.[10] As against this, on the other hand, we must notice that the chief invisible force governing life postulated by Allende in her first novel is determinism. At the climax Alba reflects:

> Sospecho que todo lo ocurrido no es fortuito, sino que corresponde a un destino dibujado antes de mi nacimiento . . . una cadena de hechos que debían cumplirse . . . un rompecabezas en que cada pieza tiene una ubicación precisa . . . no alcanzamos a ver la relación entre los acontecimientos, no podemos medir la consecuencia de los actos, creemos en la ficción del tiempo, en el presente, el pasado y el futuro, pero puede ser también que todo ocurre simultáneamente.[11]

Here we have an echo not merely of the futile circularity of events that seems to underlie *Cien años de soledad* but also of the suspicion circulated by Borges that the world may operate according to laws we are not programmed to understand. Hart (p. 45) recognizes momentarily that this notion of determinism is crucial to the whole novel, which deals after all with a long span of recent Chilean history, but she fails to develop her insight. The notion is, however, more crucial than she perceives; for only to the extent that Allende suppresses it, and the sense of powerlessness to affect events which goes with it, does she move away from the Boom's underlying pessimism and emphasis on the unintelligibility of time and causality toward the positive view of her literary activity that she has expressed in "Por qué y para quién escribo" and in many interviews. However, such initial doubt and disquiet about the human condition, and about the way things are, is not uncommon in the early Post-Boom, being part of the legacy of modernism. We shall see it again in Skármeta, for instance.

Where the suppression of the notions of determinism and the unintelligibility of reality are at their most visible is in the treatment of history in *La Casa de los Espíritus*. In the sense that the novel chronicles the decadence of an oligarchic class, symbolized by Trueba, the novel looks back toward a well-worn Spanish American and even distinctively Chilean theme, recognizable in Donoso's *Coronación* (1956) and earlier in Barrios's *Gran Señor y rajadiablos* (1948). But it is forward looking in the sense that it is linked with one of the central genres of the Post-Boom: the new historical novel as practiced by Posse, Paternain, Benítez Rojo, and others, inevitably including some of the Boom writers such as Fuentes, Vargas Llosa, Roa Bastos, and García Márquez. It is possible to argue that this genre interestingly reflects in reverse the postulate that, while probably the majority of mainstream Post-Boom writers practice a return to modified mimesis, to a certain optimism, and to a certain confidence in their ability to understand how things are, a minority develop the opposite line. Following the early Sarduy and Elizondo, they reveal continuing scepticism about the author's power to interpret reality or to express any interpretation meaningfully. A number of the new historical novels, that is, illustrate what Hutcheon calls "historiographic metafiction," whose chief characteristic is that it tends to "problematize the entire question of historical knowledge."[12] For all her references to our inability to relate events to each other or to explain the world, something that can be seen to affect *La Casa de los Espíritus*—for example, when Clara is situated in a world where "el pasado y el futuro eran parte de la misma cosa y la realidad del presente era un caleidoscopio de espejos desordenados donde todo podía ocurrir" (p. 78)—Allende belongs to the former group. In her first novel, that is, she confidently discusses the historical process in Chile, much as Viñas has done with respect to Argentina. She makes no serious attempt to deconstruct historical reality, but rather, as Coddou asserts, ultimately places her imagination "al servicio de un desentrañamiento de lo real" from a clearly evident ideological standpoint.[13] Hart agrees, the whole thrust of her book being to argue that in Allende "the magical aspect is ultimately subordinated to the real."[14] The real in this case is the conviction that history does illustrate real progress, albeit not in a simple linear fashion. Aligning herself once more with Carpentier, Allende has affirmed unequivocally: "creo que avanzamos en una espiral ascendente, a veces parece que andáramos en círculos sin movernos del mismo nivel, pero no es así. Progresamos, crecemos, aprendemos."[15]

While, then, we perceive a certain ambivalence in Allende about the complete intelligibility of reality, an ambivalence that expresses itself in the fantasy elements in her earlier work, we can recognize that even in her first novel she tends ultimately to write *as if* reality could be generally understood in terms of chronological chains of causes and effects and *as if* the ability to detect historical progress formed part of that understanding. This already marks her as a Post-Boom writer. In her subsequent fiction these presumptions about the real intensify, though Coddou's assertion that "El suyo es un caso de *superreferencialidad*, que lleva hasta la exasperación el diálogo con el referente, afirmando de tal modo las relaciones lenguaje-literatura-mundo" seems to overstate the case.[16] The whole problem of Post-Boom writers in Allende's category is precisely to avoid this extreme and to walk an uneasy path between the Barthes—*Tel Quel*—Sarduyian notion that the text can have no exterior referent and the old-fashioned idea that the relationship between signifier and signified is completely unproblematic.

Numerous other elements of *La Casa de los Espíritus*, apart from the author's attitude toward reality and historical progress, mark the novel as belonging to the Post-Boom. One of the most important is the return to "strong" characterization. This is not to suggest that such characterization was absent from Boom fiction. We find it prominently, for instance, throughout the work of Vargas Llosa. But several critics— including Barrenechea with reference to Elizondo and Guerrero with reference to Sarduy, two novelists who represent the extreme—have suggested that the Boom writers' tendency toward scepticism about our ability to understand ourselves and our behavior produced a blurring of outline in character presentation.[17] It is symbolized at an early stage by the characters in Bioy Casares's *La invención de Morel* (1940), in which they are reduced to mere images, and at a late stage of the Boom by Vargas Llosa's Mayta in *Historia de Mayta* (1984), in which the "real" Mayta is completely elusive. The longing of Humberto Peñaloza, for instance, in Donoso's *El obsceno pájaro de la noche* (1970) for "una máscara definitiva," a recognizable self however unreal, is representative of a trend in the Boom away from the notion of fixed identity. Skármeta, as we saw in chapter 1, has suggested that the paradigm in many cases became Zavalita of Vargas Llosa's *Conversación en La Catedral* (1969), producing figures characterized by scepticism, cowardice, and hyperintellectualism. This last may be the key concept. Many Boom characters are or become deeply aware of the human condition as potentially tragic, so that their status as "weak" characters often derives from inner existential doubt and conflict. This is less prominent in Post-Boom fictional characters, whose struggle is not so much internal as external, against conditions, not against themselves.

Virginia Invernizzi, in an unpublished doctoral thesis on Allende, makes a convincing case following the work of Frank Rahill, Robert Heilman, and John Cawelti on melodrama, for classifying Allende's first three novels as social melodramas, characterized by plot centeredness with highly dramatic incidents, strong emotionalism, and above all an extreme polarization between good and evil that expresses confidence in a value orientated reality.[18] Since the struggle of the major characters tends to be directed against forces outside themselves, there is little stress on inner division and complexity. What is particularly prominent in Allende is, of course, that the "strong" characters who thus emerge are predominently women. To understand the importance of this—as an almost totally Post-Boom phenomenon—one must examine, as Sharon Magnarelli has done in *The Lost Rib*, female characterization in the Spanish American novel from the 1860s to the 1970s. Magnarelli concludes that right up to the 1970s female figures in Spanish American fiction were missing or perceived in terms of the prostitute/madonna dichotomy or seen as threatening presences. That is, their presentation was conditioned by male insecurity and the will "to invalidate and/or obliterate covert or latent female power."[19]

Perhaps more than anything else, what makes *La Casa de los Espíritus* a genuinely "inaugural" novel is its strong presentation of women and of the way they have been able to empower themselves over the period of time covered by the novel. In 1984 Allende said to Marjorie Agosín:

> I chose extraordinary women who could symbolize my vision of what is meant by *feminine*, characters who could illustrate the destinies of women in Latin America . . . All the women in my book are feminists in their fashion; that is, they ask to be free and complete human beings, to be able to fulfil themselves, not to be dependent on men. Each one battles according to her own character.[20]

The two female characters most closely connected with Allende herself and with her subsequent heroines are Clara and Alba. It is important to notice that both *write* as a reaction to an oppressive patriarcal society. Clara periodically retreats into silence, especially after being struck by her husband; but in that silence, she writes. Alba writes after she has a vision of Clara while she is in prison for political subversion. That is, Clara retreats inward while Alba rebels outwardly, but in the end it is by writing that they hope to bring about change. Subsequently Irene in *De amor y de sombra* rebels outwardly more successfully than Alba does, and it is through a form of verbal communication (the tapes she makes, documenting the crimes of the regime) that she is successful in influencing reality by embarassing the dictator. Finally Eva Luna both involves herself in guerrilla activity (though half-heartedly) and writes extremely successfully at a less overtly committed level than does Alba, but, in the end, no less referentially to the society around her. In each of Allende's first three novels, that is, we see that the key activities are love, social activism, and writing, and that these seem to go closely together. At the same time writing and the self-definition of the women who perform it are equally inseparable. In turn, as we see in Eva Luna's reflections on her initiation into love by Halabí, it is primarily the discovery of love that stimulates a woman's total sense of her own femininity. Halabí, too, is instrumental in seeing to it that Eva learns to read and write. Thus, whichever way we look, the triad of love, activism, and writing dominates Allende's first three novels.

We may also notice in passing that it is writing that appears to break the negative influence of determinism in *La Casa de los Espíritus*. It does so in two ways. First, Clara writes the notebooks that Alba will use fifty years later. In other words, writing can turn determinism quite specifically into a positive force. Second, as we observe, the notebooks are useful to Alba in the sense that they help her to perceive an underlying *order* in events. Recall Swanson's perceptive comment on Donoso's *El obsceno pájaro de la noche*: certain events in it make it a novel that "marks the transition from an ordered vision of the universe to an awareness of its truly chaotic and therefore terrifying nature."[21] By contrast, Allende told Gazarian Gautier that "Through [the novel] we can give a fictional order to chaos" and in 1991 amplified the remark, saying that "The first lie of fiction is that you are going to put in some order the chaos of life," but "All that is a lie because life is not that way. Everything happens simultaneously in a chaotic way."[22] Nothing is more thoroughly Post-Boom than this sense of a return to an ordered universe, however fictional the imputed order may be.

The emergence of strong female characters in Allende's novels is a historically important shift not only in itself but also in the effect it has on the presentation of the male characters. Esteban Trueba borrows from the stereotype established in Chile by Barrios's Valverde in *Gran Señor y rajadiablos* the characteristics of powerful individualism, strength of character, and ambition, combined with lack of self-control, macho sexuality, violence, selfishness, and irrationality. These qualities mask a genuine dependency and weakness at the level of the emotions and a certain infantilism at the level of thought. Impulsive, domineering, self-indulgent, but by and large good hearted (if wrong headed), Trueba, like Valverde, stands for the old oligarchic class blindly resisting socioeconomic and political change. The difference lies in the fact that he is now seen from a critical feminine standpoint. Reemphasizing it is the presentation of two other male characters, Pedro Segundo García "leal y silencioso" (p. 148) and Jaime "generoso, cándido y tenía una gran capacidad de ternura" (p. 167). They are the forerunners of Francisco Leal in *De amor y de sombra*. Characterized by loyalty, sensitivity, and supportiveness, these slightly idealized male characters in Allende's early novels are in their way as important historically as the strong females. While Lagos-Pope perhaps exaggerates when she refers to Francisco as "a new type of male hero,"[23] there is no doubt that we can perceive here an evolution in the fictional presentation of masculinity. Love and understanding from the other sex rank high in the list of human aspirations. Hitherto love, both romantic and sexual, has figured prominently in the Spanish American novel. But supportive understanding, especially of women by men, has rarely been incorporated into fictional relationships. It is unquestionably one of Allende's major contributions. The danger is that the simplified whore/madonna dichotomy noted by Magnarelli in older fiction may be paralleled in the works of the new women writers by a simplified macho/antimacho dichotomy.

Two characters remain to be mentioned: Tránsito Soto and Esteban García. It is their presence and activities in the novel that most of all situate it in the category of social melodrama, that is to say, a combination of melodrama, with its polarization of good and evil, and a social setting dominated by a specific historical event (in this case the *pinochetazo*). The dramatization of the moral order, which is fundamental to melodrama, requires the conflict of good and evil to be expressed by unambiguous characters. Trueba is not in this class, because it is not Allende's main purpose to attack the old Chilean oligarchy. Hence he is treated ambivalently with a certain affection on the part of the narrator and allowed to try to justify himself in his own first-person contributions to the story. But Esteban García is an old-fashioned villain whose role in the novel, it has to be said candidly, makes nonsense of Allende's repeated assertions that she aims to avoid reducing her novels to the level of political pamphlets. Like Skármeta's Sergeant Cifuentes in *La insurrección*, Esteban García is a cardboard figure of unrelieved evil. His presence contradicts Marcos's uncritical attempt to present Post-Boom novelists as consistently re-elaborating popular elements in their works in such a way as to create in each case "un texto intensamente referencial, pero no monosémico ni mucho menos simplista."[24] Tránsito Soto is a less flat character, but her role as the prostitute/good fairy, solving Trueba's problems four times in succession, though symbolic of women's self-empowerment, is simply a remake of the "Diamond Lil"–type whore-with-a-heart-of-gold, a stock figure of popular fiction, not excluding *Gone with the Wind*. In contrast to Puig's more subtle use of folletinesque figures (for example those of the radio soap opera that Mabel and Nené listen to in *Boquitas pin-*

*tadas*) to comment on the banality and frustration of his own person-
ages, the presentation of Esteban García and Tránsito are part of *La
Casa de los Espíritus* itself, on a par with the other characters. They
illustrate the danger inherent in the Post-Boom's return to social commitment in preference to literary distance.

Panjabi writes: "All the Trueba women in the novel—Clara, Blanca
and Alba—are fiercely independent, and participate indirectly in the
transition from the feudal to a socialist to a military rule by either aid-
ing the campesinos, or hiding arms and revolutionaries in the hacienda;
yet they always return to the shelter of this patriarcal institution because
of their social and economic dependence upon it."[25] The fact that this is
not the case with Irene in *De amor y de sombra* (1984) indicates the next
stage in Allende's presentation of the social role of women. Irene, that
is, develops the role of Alba in the earlier novel to the point at which the
process of her growing political awareness after the Pinochet military
coup is the novel's basic theme. This use of a pattern of ongoing *concientización* is standard in protest fiction, as we see, for example, in Carpentier's *La Consagración de la Primavera* and in Skármeta's *Soñé que
la nieve ardía*, when Vera and Arturo respectively evolve away from
their earlier apolitical stances. By inducing us to follow this evolution,
the novelist hopes to stimulate a similar process in us as readers, or at
least to explain how such a process occurs. What is important for the
present purpose is that it is the opposite of the process of growing disil-
lusionment, scepticism, and sense of failure that typifies so many modern fictional heroes.

Irene begins with an inner problem of lack of direction in her life, a
problem that Francisco will solve at the emotional level and political
commitment will solve at the ideological level. The novel's key episode,
which links Irene's evolution to the theme of oppression, is the murder
of Evangelina Ranquileo by Lieutenant Ramírez. Thirty pages after
learning of it, she admits, "hasta ahora he vivido soñando y temo des-
pertar."[26] As from the beginning of the third part of the novel it is she
who assumes the initiative in placing responsibility for the crime on the
regime and, as in the case of Carpentier's and Skármeta's characters, is
rewarded with authentic fulfilment with Francisco, as distinct from the
inauthentic relationship she had had with her fiancé Morante, or the
even more inauthentic affair her mother carries on with her young lover
Michel. We should notice that, like Viñas in *Dar la cara* Allende does
not follow through with a plot development involving active armed
rebellion against the regime, for which she has been ritually castigated
by Gabriela Mora and Monique Lemaitre.[27]

Francisco Leal, as I have already implied, is a novel Spanish American fictional hero because of his combination of gentleness and strength.

We know nothing of him except what is attractive: his attachment to his parents, his attempt to protect Irene when the shooting begins at the Riquelme's farm, his understanding of Mario's homosexuality, and his defence of Mario in the face of Morante's contempt. Kind, intelligent, humorous, supportive, virile without machismo, and sexy but at the same time tender and self-sacrificing, he is about as convincing as Carpentier's Rosario in *Los pasos perdidos*. Like her, his main characteristic is that he never gives his mate any trouble. He is never moody or difficult, never refuses attention, never wants time on his own or makes any of the standard male demands that fuel the war of the sexes.

A problem with *De amor y de sombra* that characterizes it even more than *La Casa de los Espíritus* as social melodrama is the lack of a convincing conterforce to Irene and Francisco other than the next of Allende's villains, Lieutenant Ramírez. Lagos Pope convincingly emphasizes "the absence of a strong male figure to represent the traditional man who embodies unmistakably the military regime."[28] It is not the business of the critic to discuss the might have been; but it is difficult to avoid the conclusion that Allende here lost the same opportunity that Gallegos did in *Doña Bárbara*, How much more convincing *Doña Bárbara* would have been if Santos had been allowed to fall in love, even briefly, with Bárbara and thus acquire an element of inner conflict. Similarly, what interesting possibilities would have opened up had Irene been faced with a convincing representative of the *golpistas* and each had felt attracted to the other. The missing novel here is not about Irene and Francisco, but about an Irene who is conscious that the Left and the working class in Chile are not without responsibility for some aspects of the state of affairs preceding the coup and is emotionally drawn to a Morante who is conscious of the criminality of the Right and the armed forces but regards them as inevitable in the circumstances.

Instead, in order to get the novel's message across, the representatives of the oppressed classes and the progressive side must be idealized, while those of the dominant social group, whether passive like Irene's mother Beatriz, or active like Ramírez, must be vilified. A major shortcoming of ideological fiction of this kind (a shortcoming that threatens a whole area of Post-Boom writing, as it did the old "anti-imperialist" novel in Spanish America before the Boom) is that it tends to trivialize the standpoints of both sides in the social struggle—each of which contains within itself areas of conflict. There are, of course, counterarguments. One is that any simplification of the issues is offset by the raising of the reader's threshold of awareness. Another is that some degree of simplification and melodrama is inevitable if the work is to transmit its message to a genuinely popular audience. A third is that there is a need to restate in unambiguous terms the existence of a broadly consensual moral order governing social behavior and to reinforce adhesion to it. The Boom writers tended to challenge readers with works figuring forth disturbing metaphors of the human condition. By contrast the Post-Boom writers tend to present an ultimately more reassuring picture of the way things are. Allende in her first four novels is unquestionably in the forefront of this trend. She has repeatedly emphasized the fact that she is an incorrigible optimist, that despair is a sell-out to reactionaries, and that the aim of her work is to contribute to a "destino más feliz" for Latin Americans and to influence her readers "so that people will love each other more."[29] Perhaps most significantly of all, she told Virginia Invernizzi: "In my books bad people are punished in one way or another. I know it is not so in real life most of the time, but that's how I would like it to be."[30] The idea surfaces again in Eva Luna's approach to fiction.

Writing *De amor y de sombra* from the standpoint of the way Allende would like things to be has two consequences. The first is the tendency of the novel to develop the technique of sharp contrast between good and evil already adumbrated in *La Casa de los Espíritus* via the presentation of Tránsito Soto and Esteban García. As Beatriz Hernández-Gómez has pointed out, from the title on "Isabel Allende en esta novela . . . ha desarrollado toda una serie de elementos (situaciones y estructuras) que se oponen."[31] These include the "barrio alto" of the city, where the Alcántara's mansion is situated, as against the rural farm of the Ranquileos and thus the upper bourgeoisie against the working class; the supporters of the coup and the regime as against the opposers; the strong women as against the weaker or absent men; and most of all, of course, love, goodness, and justice as against evil and violence. The themes of Irene's evolution and the murderous cruelty of the regime, that is, dictate the choice of episodes and the division of the characters into attractive ones and their sometimes repulsive counterparts. Allende avoids Skármeta's well-founded charge that the novel in Latin America has ignored the working class; but the lesson of *De amor y de sombra* for Post-Boom writing is that ignoring the working class is not the only problem. The real difficulty is to deal with it without idealizing it.

The second consequence of Allende's reluctance to distance herself from her material is the emphasis on emotion rather than on action. The appropriate responses to military oppression may indeed include a strengthening of love and human solidarity between and among individuals, but Gabriela Mora's article reminds us that they are hardly enough. *De amor y de sombra* is without question one of the archetypally neoromantic novels of the Post-Boom, reversing a major tendency of the Boom in which love never plays a serious role, since the Boom writers tended to subordinate it to their legitimate desire to break the taboo on dealing openly with sexuality. The importance of love in human affairs is a matter of simple observation, and one can only welcome its reinstatement in the Post-Boom novel. But it is not the most obvious response to the sort of situation that obtained in Chile under Pinochet. Susan de Carvalho, in a percipient article, may have the answer to this criticism when she writes: "In all the female characters in her novels—Alba (*Casa*), Irene (*De amor y de sombra*), Eva Luna— Isabel Allende links political commentary with romantic love. In all three novels the protagonists initially involve themselves in the revolution only to help or protect their lovers, but soon their participation and level of commitment become very real."[32] Allende, that is, presents love, not as a social force in itself, but as part of the dynamic underlying open denunciation of injustice and potential insurrection against it.

*Eva Luna* (1987) combines two kinds of oppositional discourse: one connected with feminism and the other with social protest. The work belongs to the class of feminist novels that Ellen Friedman describes as incorporating a quest for selfhood. In them, women protagonists use "strangeness," outsider status, and "nomadism" to elude patriarcal convention. Rejecting past models without nostalgia, the protagonists of such novels look forward to a new female/social condition that has not yet taken shape.[33] The point of departure is important. *Eva Luna* is an illustrative Post-Boom novel, not only because of its feminism and its overt social commentary, but also because, unlike Clara and Irene who are white and rich, Eva is dark skinned and the child of a servant and an Indian gardener. An interesting article could be written on the almost symbolic contrast between her and the equally dark-skinned and proletarian male in Puig's *Sangre de amor correspondido* (1982). The latter is lost in a paralyzing machistic daydream of sport and sex, while Eva finds herself through love, activism, and creativity.

Eva reveals the Post-Boom tendency, also noted by critics of Skármeta and visible in Sainz as well, for the writer to be much closer emotionally to his or her principal characters than was usual in the Boom. Allende said in 1989:

> Eva Luna . . . habla por mí. Ella dice todo lo que yo tenía ganas de decir sobre la vida, el hombre, la revolución, la literatura, la relación de las mujeres . . . todo eso ella lo dice por mí. Ella se acepta a sí misma, se quiere, está orgullosa de sí misma . . . es esencialmente mujer. Su espíritu, su intelecto, su cuerpo, todo está amalgamado, todo le funciona coordinadamente. No es ni cerebral ni puramente emotiva, ni puramente espiritual. Todo en ella es armonioso, equilibrado.[34]

Two years later, she added in another interview:

> My first book—*The House of the Spirits*—was born, was triggered I'd say, by nostalgia, by the desire to recover the world that I had lost after

I had to leave my country and live in exile. My second book—*Of Love and Shadows*—was triggered by anger, anger and sadness at the abuses of the dictatorship. *Eva Luna* had a wonderful, positive feeling. That was the discovery that I finally liked being a woman; for forty years I wanted to be a man; I thought that it was much better to be a man. When I was in my forties, I discovered that I had done all the things that men do and many more, that I had succeeded in my life. I was okay. And that's what the story is about: its about storytelling and about being a woman.[35]

As a consequence it is once more about optimism. *La Casa de los Espíritus* is about the approach of severe social conflict; *De amor y de sombra* is about the conflict itself; *Eva Luna* is in many ways about the resolution of conflict. In this case, Wolfgang Karrer is able to posit something quite the opposite of the stark dualities of *De amor y de sombra*: "The central fantasy in *Eva Luna* is to fuse distinctions, to unite opposites. Images of mixture and fusion proliferate throughout the novel."[36] One might even add that these amount to images of reconciliation, especially, as the above quotation specifies, of reconciliation with the feminine condition.

This means that *Eva Luna* is now less a social melodrama than a feminist romance, as we can see by comparing it with, for instance, Luisa Valenzuela's early novel *Hay que sonreír* (1966) and especially with the title story of her *Cambio de armas* (1982) or with Elena Poniatowska's *Hasta no verte, Jesús mío* (1969) and *Querido Diego, te abraza Quiela* (1978)—to say nothing of the stories of Domitila Chungara (*Si me permiten hablar,* 1977) or Rigoberta Menchú (*Me llamo Rigoberta Menchú,* 1985), in which the real feminine condition in Spanish America is made brutally apparent. What both social melodrama and romance have in common is the underlying metaphor of a moral order that both exists and is capable of resisting threats from the chaos and disharmony of life. From Allende's point of view, the reassertion of a moral order is partly expressed in terms of the empowerment of formerly powerless or marginal minorities, empowerment now attained essentially by working within the system. Three figures in *Eva Luna* symbolize this process: Eva herself, Melecio/Mimí, and Rolf Carlé. By contrast, Humberto Naranjo, alias El Comandante Rogelio, represents the element of active rebellion missing from the foreground of the two earlier novels. The key quotation occurs near the end of the novel when Mimí attempts to dissuade Eva from participating in a guerrilla action alongside Naranjo, her former benefactor:

Aquí a nadie le importa nada de nada, tus guerrilleros no tienen ni la menor oportunidad de triunfar. Piensa como empezamos, Eva! Yo tuve la mala suerte de nacer mujer en un cuerpo de hombre, me han perseguido por marica, me han violado, torturado, puesto en prisión y mira dónde estoy ahora por mi propio mérito. ¿Y tú? Lo único que has hecho es trabajar y trabajar.[37]

What this overlooks is that neither Mimí nor Eva succeeds simply by hard work. Mimí is a brilliant actress and Eva becomes a successful writer, just as Rolf overcame his immigrant status by developing his interest in photography to the point of becoming a globe-trotting film reporter. Each has a special talent. In addition, each is given a number of lucky breaks. This is particularly true of Eva, who, as Pilar Rotella cogently observes, is constantly lucky: "At crucial junctures in her life, when disaster threatens and hunger—the ultimate picaresque motif— seems imminent, a rescuer appears (usually a man) to help Eva to reach a more or less safe harbor and preempt any need, on Eva's part, to act in an improper or unethical manner."[38] In fact, precisely what distances *Eva Luna* from the picaresque proper is that she is never forced to compromise her principles.

Clearly there is no longer anything here to threaten the status quo. As for Naranjo/Rogelio's guerrilla activities, Eva has no need of prompting from Mimí to dismiss them. She does so, not on the grounds that they cannot succeed in bringing about revolutionary changes, but on the far more convincing grounds that, even if they did, women as a sex would not share in any transfer of power. As Miguel Alfonso states categorically: "En definitiva, la revolución no le interesa . . . porque su anhelo no es cambiar la sociedad."[39] In other words, in comparison with her two earlier novels, and especially *De amor y de sombra*, Allende has moved from a more radical response to the power structure of society in Latin America (though always avoiding any hint of revolutionary commitment) to a more liberal response that tends to privilege individual initiative. It cannot be without significance that *Eva Luna* is set in (semi-) democratic Venezuela and that Allende's next novel does not deal with Spanish America at all. The evolution here is similar to that of Skármeta, who moves from the radical stance visible in *La insurrección,* set in revolutionary Nicaragua, to *Match Ball,* set entirely in Europe. We also notice that Valenzuela has moved from the political allegory of *Cola de lagartija* and the commitment of *Cambio de armas,* both set in Spanish America, to the more ambiguous message of *Novela negra con argentinos,* set in new York. Something similar can be argued about Giardinelli by comparing *La revolución en bicicleta* (1980) with *Santo Oficio de la memoria* (1991). All four writers illustrate the tendency of the Post-Boom to become less radical with time, but Allende comes closest to reconciliation with the system. While *Eva Luna* contains an obvious metaphor of human liberation, those in whose name Allende now speaks are no longer the Ranquileos and Flores of *De amor y de sombra*. By the same token, Colonel Rodríguez, the representative of the military, is no Lieutenant Ramírez but a rather more acceptable defender of the oligarchy. The fact is that with *Eva Luna* Allende reaches an ideological impasse. The writer who told Gazarian Gautier: "I write so that people will love each other more"[40] could not maintain an adversarial stance once the impact of the coup in Chile became attenuated by time. Defence of groups such as women, homosexuals, and presently Chicanos takes over from the defence of the undifferentiated rural and urban masses. Thus while we may agree with de Carvalho that "Consistent with the trends of the post-boom generation, Allende clearly postulates as a constant in her literary production the overwhelming need to communicate the truth" (p. 65), we must notice that the "truth" in question changes quite noticably with *Eva Luna*,

The other major aspect of the novel that is relevant to the Post-Boom is its status as a "self-aware" piece of fiction, that is, as a novel that (in this case) gradually reveals its own fictional nature. Karrer's blyth assertion that "*Eva Luna* belongs to the metafiction of Postmodernism" (p. 155) overstates the case considerably. But the way in which, as almost every critic has noticed, Eva's autobiographical narrative merges with her *telenovela* script is more than just a gimmick. It is a strategy for attempting to resolve what we have seen is the Post-Boom's worst dilemma: the difficulty of expressing the real while at the same time retaining an awareness that all expressions of reality are fictions. Coddou, Alas-Brun, Rehbein, and de Carvalho[41] have all examined this crucial aspect of *Eva Luna*, chiefly noting the importance of Eva's shift to writing as the culmination of her growing self-awarenees and "control" of reality via her imagination. But what none of them indicates clearly enough is that the moment Eva merges her life story with a television script, the "artificio del texto" is transfered both to her as a representative figure and to the exterior "real" reality that is supposed to be the referent of the novel. We are back, in other words, to the Borgesian notion that all reality is a construct that may bear little relation, or at best an unverifiable relation, to any possible reality that may exist outside the text. Here we see how the Boom's problematization of reality left the Post-Boom with an awkward legacy. What credit can we attach to Allende's insistence that her work explores people's hidden motives and the "deeper" features of reality, if all is imaginary? Similarly, if any "order" is a "lying" (imaginary) construct that we impose on the chaos of reality, how can we make the leap from this to some form of social action? If *Eva Luna* were to be classified as a postmodernist novel, it would follow that it would run counter to de Carvalho's above-mentioned postulate that the Post-Boom exhibits an "overwhelming need to communicate the truth." Can writers have it both ways?

The stories of *Cuentos de Eva Luna* (1990) have yet to be closely analyzed, but in general seem marginal to Allende's mainstream development as a writer of fiction and as a representative of the Post-Boom. An exception is "Un camino hacia el norte," designed to draw attention to the use of children's body parts fraudulently obtained from the poorest Latin American parents by organ banks in the United States. Here we see Allende living up to her often repeated claim to speak for those in Latin America whose voices are not heard and thereby reestablishing the link between literature and overt protest, something that was not a prominent feature of the Boom. Other stories, such as "Tosca," confirm Allende as the leading figure in Post-Boom neoromanticism. Where this leadership is most accentuated, however, is in *El Plan Infinito* (1991). Based on the life of her second husband and set in California, it has elements in common with *Eva Luna*, at least to the extent that the central character, Gregory Reeves, at one point in the novel "pensaba que le tocó nacer entre los de abajo y hasta ese momento su vida había sido sólo trabajo y escasez"[42] Like Eva, however, he is completely untypical of the masses and partly through the assistance (once more) of a succession of helpers, including Cyrus, who helps to get him to the University of California, the old lawyer who later takes him into his prestigious firm, and Ming, who becomes his analyst, he joins the ranks of the upper bourgeoisie, but not to remain there.

*El Plan Infinito* is still a romance, but since Greg is his own worst enemy, it is not a melodrama. There is no specific evil counterforce built into the novel except North American society itself. Greg's life story indicates that its influence can be resisted and its injusticies attenuated. The novel has three interlocking themes. The first theme is racial harmony: Greg is white, the son of a an American father and a Russian immigrant mother, but is brought up in a latino barrio of Los Angeles amid Chicanos, represented by the Morales family. The second theme, inherited from Rodó's *Ariel* (1900), is that of the gross materialism and the false values of North America, to which Greg temporarily sells out. They are represented by his boss in the legal firm and a range of other characters including the parents of his friend Timothy Duane and Greg's wife, Samantha. The chief victim of United States society, apart from Greg himself, is his daughter, Margaret, who becomes a junkie and a prostitute at an early age. The third theme is Greg's increasingly despairing quest for the kind of true love that will enable him to overcome the lust for wealth and immediate gratification to which he had succumbed while hospitalized after serving (with distinction) in Vietnam.

The basic problem with regard to *El Plan Infinito* can be summed up in the remark attributed to Vargas Llosa that optimistic writers are liars. Generally speaking, as I attempted to suggest in the conclusion of my *Nueva narrativa hispanoamericana*, the outlook of the Boom was deeply pessimistic. It reflected a crisis of values, certainties, and existential confidence "en que se ha dislocado una imagen del mundo" as Ernesto Sábato accurately expressed it.[43] The Post-Boom tends to modified optimism. Allende has gradually moved to the extreme pole of this recovery of confidence, just as Skármeta did in *La insurrección*, a novel whose theme of successful rebellion later events in Nicaragua have tended to contradict. Giardinelli, quoted in chapter 1, wisely dissented.

Mention of Skármeta, however, is quite relevant. In *No pasó nada*, he too provided an optimistic parable of harmony between northern Europeans and Latins, but the harmony is achieved only after violence. More especially Skármeta examined in *Match Ball*, as we shall see, a figure who was even more successful as a society doctor than Greg was as a company lawyer, but who, like him, was deeply dissatisfied by material success. Papst also follows love, albeit of a highly erotic and *Lolita*-esque kind, but it proves to be illusory and leads to murderous violence. However, Greg, Allende's first male central character, is an important Post-Boom figure because his development, which takes over from the other themes in the latter part of *El Plan Infinito*, illustrates at great length the reaction against the traditional macho hero already visible in Francisco Leal in *De amor y de sombra*. The difference is that Francisco is mature, tender, and supportive from the beginning, whereas Greg is in his fifties before he realizes that sexuality as such is not the answer. His realization is more important than it seems, for throughout the Boom sexuality tended to be seen as a valid weapon against the *otredad* of the other partner and as a way out of *incomunicación* and even out of existential insecurity.[44] Greg, however, in relation to his high-bourgeois period, confesses that "en esa etapa de mi vida la sexualidad equivalía a la violencia de la guerra" (p. 242). Having given way to it was only one of the "suma de tropiezos" (p. 172) that he has to accumulate before a "lento y doloroso viaje hacia el interior de sí mismo" (p. 321) reveals to him that, for reasons partly connected with his childhood, "nunca pude establecer una relación sana porque no sabía rendirme ni aceptar la entrega completa de una compañera de verdad, nada sospechaba de la comunión en el amor" (p. 327).

No study of the Post-Boom fictional hero, therefore, could avoid reference to Greg Reeves. But equally it is important to bear in mind that his redemption at the end is part of a much wider pattern of harmony that the text postulates. It operates a several levels. Thus Greg evolves positively not only at the emotional level but also at the spiritual one, leaving behind his childhood sense of "la angustia de estar vivo" (p.

133) and accepting that his father had been right to preach "el equilibrio perfecto del universo" (p. 35). "De acuerdo con el Plan Infinito de mi padre," he concludes, "nada sucede por azar" (p. 273). Even more than in *Eva Luna* it appears that if our lives are governed by deterministic forces, these forces operate benevolently. At the social level the harmony is symbolized by Greg's unshakable attachment to Carmen Morales, the "strong" woman of the novel. Like the Ranquileos and the Flores of *De amor y de sombra*, the Morales present a cozily idealized picture of humble latino folk who, Reeves informs a fellow gringo: "Tienen más habilidad y sentido de honor que tú y yo. Has vivido en este barrio toda tu vida y no sabes una palabra de español, en cambio cualquiera de ellos aprende inglés en pocas semanas. Tampoco son flojos, trabajan más que cualquier blanco por la mitad del pago" (p. 122). The Morales's son is not allowed to become a macho layabout in the barrio and their daughter Carmen somewhat improbably becomes an internationally known jewelry and fashion designer: "Carmen morena y esencial. Carmen valiente y sabia, con quinientos años de tradición indígena y castellana en la sangre y un sólido sentido común anglo-sajón" (p. 318). By contrast, Greg's wife, Samantha, a woman in the line of Beatriz Beltrán in *De amor y de sombra*, is completely sacrificed, being presented as idle, greedy, an unloving wife and mother, and utterly cut off from reality. She is the caricature of a Californian upper class woman as seen by a Latin. We may be forgiven for finding the whole picture somewhat slanted, though the ways in which it is slanted are of interest to students of the Post-Boom.

There are two worrying aspects of Allende's literary personality, given her prominence in the movement. The first is that, in the novels briefly discussed here, her formulation of social problems has come to be increasingly in terms of of an emotional idealism that shows little real understanding of the forces in play. The process intensifies during the writing of these four novels, and by the 1990s it is at variance with her claim to speak for the silenced majority of her fellow Latin Americans. The second is that from the outset we are conscious of a series of unresolved contradictions in her work. The key to the Post-Boom is the attitude of its writers to reality, at both the philosophical and the social level. As we have seen, Allende's attitude has been from the first ambivalent. She sees it, on the one hand, as undifferentiated chaos, on which art feigns to impose an order; an order, in other words that is essentially a *construct* rather than something actually perceived. On the other hand, she she sees her writing as somehow explaining the meaning of events and the human motivation that often underlies them, as if they were part of an intrinsically intelligible prior framework. At the same time she has on occasion professed not to be able to distinguish clearly the real from the fantastic and to believe in mysterious but not necessarily malevolent forces that intervene in human affairs. Are such fantastic elements part of the literary construct, or of some sort of "real" reality, and if the latter, how far do they compromise its intelligibility? Finally, Allende sometimes seems to believe (and her frequent use in her novels of flash-forward comments relating to the future may offer confirmation of it) that reality is subject to some degree of determinism. At the same time human effort appears to be able to collaborate with deterministic processes in furtherance of progress, which is said to occur as a slow upward spiral. It is not clear how these different notions fit together.

At the social level, despite her belief that any sort of "order" perceivable in reality is no more than an imaginary construct, Allende has continued to assert the writer's responsability to protest against misery, violence, inequality, and injustice. But in Eva Luna, Carmen Morales, and Greg Reeves we see quite unrepresentative individuals who thrive in unjust societies by using their own enterprise and talents. Although Allende once admitted that revolution might be the only answer in Latin America,[45] in her work emphasis is gradually increased on love, hope, and individual human solidarity with no real indication of a need for collective action. By the same token, her feminism, though it fits in quite well with the pattern postulated by Friedman on the basis of North American women's fiction, is not very well integrated with her sense of social injustice, as Mora's aggressive article stresses. To critics like Coddou and Muñoz who would dearly like to bring to bear on Allende's novels a critical perspective nourished by modern literary theory and by notions of postmodernism, the magical/fantastic element in her work is difficult to reconcile with her social commitment, while the existence of this last, of the prominent love interest, melodrama, and the linear non-experimental technique of her novels seem unsophisticated. Their discomfort is as obvious as that of Marcos and Mora, to whom her ideology seems confused and suspiciously bourgeois.

What can we conclude? Whatever her future status in the canon turns out to be, Allende has earned the distinction of having written the most popular and famous novel of the early Post-Boom. With *La Casa de los Espíritus* the phalanx of new women novelists, whose emergence is perhaps the most significant single feature of the Post-Boom, found its best-known representative, and feminist writing a strong and authoritative voice. From *La Casa de los Espíritus* we can date the triumphant appearance of Post-Boom neo-romanticism and optimism in contrast to the anti-romanticism and pessimism of the Boom. In addition, her work, with its feature of melodrama and romance, illustrates the continuing incorporation of "popular" elements in to "higher" forms of fiction.

The "specificity" of Post-Boom themes to Latin America itself in contrast to the Boom's reaching out toward greater universality and cosmopolitanism, and the Post-Boom's radical outlook on contemporary issues, are prominent in her work before *El Plan Infinito*, as is the Post-Boom's incorporation of marginalized and working-class figures into fiction. Above all we can point to the reader-friendliness and the confident treatment of reality as characteristically Post-Boom.

At the same time the defensive tone adopted by Patricia Hart and others writing about Allende's work puts us on our guard. When Allende said to Rodden "Maybe [my books] are sentimental very often, and maybe they are kitsch very often. And I'm not afraid of that . . . I never think of my books as art . . . I write them with feelings, not with much thinking," she is surely making—though perhaps disingenuously—some rather damaging admissions.[46] Her line of defence is twofold. On the one hand, in "Por qué y para quién escribo," she argues that her sentimentalism is a form of defiance of the masculine tendency to impose fake canons of rationality and good taste on art (p. 159). On the other hand, in the same article, she argues persuasively that if literature is to have a social role, it must borrow from the mass media and even try to infiltrate the media in order to undermine their function of endorsing a "colonialist" culture and an unjust social system. Most authorial declarations of this kind, whether in print or in interviews, are apt to be self-serving, and we can perhaps take these and others by Allende with a grain of salt. But they underline important aspects of her work that are clearly related to a central issue of Post-Boom writing: the need to escape from what was seen by younger writers as the constricting intellectualism of the Boom.

# CHAPTER 4

# *Antonio Skármeta*

Antonio Skármeta (b. 1940) is both the source of some of the most insightful comments on the Post-Boom and one of its best-known writers.[1] As we saw earlier, he is one of the few younger figures who react consciously against their elders in the Boom and even criticize their outlook openly. But like Allende in her earliest work, he shows in his early stories a certain affinity with the pessimism and existential malaise that we associate with the older movement. A case in point is his early, prize-winning story "La Cenicienta en San Francisco" (?1963), the best of those in his first short story collection *El entusiasmo* (1967).[2] That volume already suggests the beginnings of a shift away from the Boom, whose collective outlook was not, in general, enthusiastic about the human condition. But the shift itself is still some years away. For the moment, the autobiographical protagonist of "La Cenicienta," Antonio, reflects, albeit in a restrained and slightly self-ironic way, Skármeta's youthful "sentimientos de soledad y angustia"[3] that also seem to be shared by Abby, his casual sexual partner. Here, for the first time, Skármeta offsets his characters' awareness of the "enigma" of reality, the unintelligibility and aimlessness of life (symbolized by the two young wanderers who briefly make love and then part) with their joint discovery of affection, warm sexuality, and mutual understanding. In the Boom there are few such moments in which the act of love produces a moment of reconciliation with life and seems to overcome man's existential orphanhood and the "otherness" of other people. Similarly in "El joven con el cuento," in the same collection, the young writer's sense of the mystery and the probable "sin sentido" of existence is replaced by emphasis on human warmth and solidarity as he comes into contact with a migrant worker and his son. In all the young men in *El entusiasmo* some form of intellectual preoccupation seems to be present, but the stories reveal a certain confidence on the author's part that, in the young especially, there is a kind of instinctive vitality that allows them to reach an accommodation with life and even to enjoy its happier possibilities.

Another feature of Skármeta's early work that we can relate to the outlook of the Boom is his use of fantasy as "un intento de responder al enigma que el mundo nos propone."⁴ A characteristic story here is "El ciclista del San Cristóbal" (1968), which belongs to the collection *Desnudo en el tejado* with which Skármeta won the Casa de las Américas Prize in 1969. In it a young participant in a bicycle race undergoes a series of experiences that seem to empower him mysteriously against the darker forces of life, specifically those threatening his mother, who is seriously ill. There is a link between his winning the race and the recovery of his mother that has nothing to do with the ordinary operations of cause and effect. Conventional reality is subverted, as it often is in the work of Julio Cortázar, on whom Skármeta wrote his master's thesis at Columbia University (New York). Yet the result of the subversion, in this case, is reassuring, not disquieting. Elsewhere, moving ever closer to the Post-Boom, whose emphasis on youth culture is illustrated by the lifestyles of the young protagonists of his early stories, Skármeta uses a performance by Ella Fitzgerald in "En las arenas" and sport in "Basketball" (both in *Desnudo en el tejado*) as preludes to love making and the surge of vitality that accompanies it, bringing life into happier focus. Dorfman correctly emphasizes "la experiencia transformadora que cada personaje siente."⁵ The sense of life's negativity is temporarily overcome.

The key to the evolution of Skármeta's literary personality at the time of his third short story collection, *Tiro libre* (1973), is the installation in Chile of the Allende government, which he supported. It stimulated an outburst of creativity by a number of "committed" young writers and artists. In the case of Skármeta it provoked a marked shift of outlook. The awareness of solitude and disquiet sporadically discernible in *El entusiasmo* and *Desnudo en el tejado* gives way to more concrete social preoccupation and eventually, after his first novel, the all-but-complete disappearance of imaginative fantasy from his writing. The most important comment by Skármeta on his change of stance at this time was made in 1986:

> Antes que se produjera la Unidad Política [i.e., Unidad Popular] en Chile, mi literatura era individualista y egocéntrica. El auge del Socialismo, por el contrario, conllevó la necesidad de hacer una apreciación realista de la situación política del país, y en el terreno personal me impulso hacia lo "otro," no sólo para amarlo, sino para abarcarlo en tanto que 'cuerpo social.'⁶

In an earlier interview he had described his early stories as "una literatura de un adolescente fascinado por el espectáculo del mundo e indeciso con respecto a su papel en él."⁷ But already his life was on the verge of a violent transformation. The rise of the Allende administration radicalized his outlook. As a result, his earlier lyrical and exhuberant individualism gave way to the sense of exaltation based on collective social endeavor that dominates *Soñé que la nieve ardía* (1975) and *La insurrección* (1982). The Allende years altered his vison of himself as a writer and affected both his choice of themes and his techniques.

The change first becomes clearly visible in "En la área chica," a section of *Tiro libre*. The section contains four stories in which the affirmation of life that is generally present in Skármeta's earlier stories is replaced by a serious political overtone. "Primera preparatoria" is one of his favorites. It illustrates better than any other how he was able to incorporate the theme of political awareness into his work without exhibiting stridency or taking an unduly partisan stance, blending it into a family situation so as to create a doubly effective result. At first sight the story is about the divisive effect of political polarization inside a small family. At this level the tale has great meaning for anyone able to identify with rifts of this kind in family solidarity. They are not the least of the wounds left by political strife. But as the story develops we see that its technique is based on the manipulation of the reader by the narrator, who is gradually revealed to be jealous and envious of his brother. Ideological differences blend with sibling rivalry to produce a story that combines two levels of pathos and human insight. This is the Post-Boom at its best. "Primera preparatoria" is at once inextricably linked to its specific time and place, but, like some of Valenzuela's short stories, it transcends its setting and presents a universally recognizable dilemma.

However, "El cigarrillo," from the same section of *Tiro libre*, illustrates the open political commitment toward which Skármeta gravitated in the early 1970s and which links him and his fellow Post-Boom writers, through Benedetti and Viñas, to the tradition of "civic" involvement that left-wing critics in particular still regard as the central strand in Spanish American literature. "El cigarrillo" is about a young working-class thug hired by the Right to help break up a left-wing demonstration under Allende. On one side of the young man Skármeta situates a wealthy, middle-aged woman, representing the oligarchic class, who encourages his mindless violence and uses him briefly as a boy-toy. On the other side stand the boy's mother and a group of his fellow workers, whose class solidarity and aspirations he has selfishly betrayed. The story hits hard and fulfils its function of raising our threshold of awareness by using the same kind of melodramatic juxtaposition we found in the early Isabel Allende. The familiar arguments against committed writing come into play afresh. For some, perhaps most, Spanish American readers, this is literature performing a totally valid social function, testifying to a hideous reality and expressing a collectively felt indignation at the human degradation it produces. For those readers to whom the reality is less familiar, the writer's stance is apt to seem simplificatory and lacking in the ambiguity that seems to confer on "Primera preparatoria" a deeper level of human insight. Be that as it may, both stories exemplify parallel aspects of Post-Boom fiction. Since *Tiro libre*, Skármeta has written only a handful of short stories, the best of which is "La composición" (?1978), which, like "Primera preparatoria," is an archetypal Post-Boom tale, combining as it does sport, as a metaphor of life under Pinochet, with an angry criticism of the regime's ignoble attempt to instrumentalize the school system in order to trick children into betraying their parents. The sensitive presentation of the nine-year-old narrator and the functional use of soccer (and in the parents' case, chess) to symbolize the moves and stratagems by which the people can score off their oppressors, makes this one of Skármeta's most strikingly successful stories.

A version of the last story in *Tiro libre*, "Profesionales," is incorporated as a sort of contrapuntal, contrasting subplot in Skármeta's first novel *Soñé que la nieve ardía* (1975), begun in Chile and finished in exile in Argentina. The story concerns two grotesques, a diminutive entertainer and his gigantic stooge. We gradually recognize in the latter a kind of guardian angel of his midget partner leading him out of misery and insecurity to a secure emotional refuge. Behind the fantasy and humor, that is, there is—typically of Skármeta and much of Post-Boom writing—a warm and comforting metaphor. This is perhaps why the story is woven into *Soñé*, to offset, at least partially, the bitter presentation of the collapse of the Allende government and the crushing of the idealism which accompanied it.

Apart from its intrinsic merit, *Soñé* is historically important as one of the first novels to mark the shift from Boom to Post-Boom. This is a novel which not only deals directly with what Skármeta considered the Boom had neglected, the here and now of Latin American social and political conditions, but also presents them through the experiences of a group of politically active, urban, working-class young people, a category scarcely ever present in Boom fiction. It is necessary only to compare *Soñé* with Donoso's *Casa de Campo*, published three years later and containing a rather contrived literary metaphor of the Allende experiment, to see how radically the Spanish American novel was changing. The elements in the novel based on "Profesionales" represent Skármeta's farewell to fantasy and the breaking of his last link with the Boom. Later he was to state: "No me interesa la fantasía por la fantasía, y en este sentido encuentro que mucha parte de la literatura latinoamericana es bastante aburrida. Me parece que nuestra realidad está totalmente inexplorada, que todavía en América latina no hay literatura realista . . . las posibilidades de lo real, de lo cotidiano, recién comienzan a ser exploradas."[8] In this declaration we hear once more the authentic voice of the Post-Boom. The emphasis has to be, Skármeta asserts, on Latin Americans, not as representatives of the Western human condition generally, but as set in their own historical situation.

The tendency of Skármeta's major characters to undergo some "transforming experience" (mentioned by Dorfman), which often coincides with or culminates in the sexual act, is the key to a large portion of Skármeta's work. In this case, the subject of the transformation is Arturo, a young soccer player from the provinces, who arrives in Santiago seeking fame and fortune as a professional. As with Irene in Allende's *De amor y de sombra*, what matters is Arturo's gradual development of sociopolitical consciousness as he comes into contact with the young workers in the rooming house where he lives during the last phase of the Allende government. There are two basic symbols in the novel. One is commercialized, professional soccer, in which team spirit has been eroded by the star system and the commodity value of individual outstanding players. Skármeta uses Arturo's desire to triumph through this system as a classic sign of his greedy, self-centered, bourgeois individualism. Arturo refuses to teach his skills to his semiprofessional fellow players, because to do so would reduce his own market value. Predictably, however, it is his excessively individualistic style of play and his absorption with his own image as a top player that produces his downfall. His bid for stardom fails for the very reasons that impelled him to make it. This use of soccer as a symbolic metaphor is both highly original and typical of the functional incorporation of popular culture into certain areas of Post-Boom fiction, not just to provide familiarizing references, but to make some kind of social statement.

The other important symbol in the novel is Arturo's virginity. In all Skármeta's work sexuality tends to acquire symbolic overtones. These may be existential, as in "La Cenicienta en San Francisco" or "Basketball" and through to *Match Ball*, where sexual activity is associated with self-liberation and joyful acceptance of the human condition, or basically political, as here and in *La insurrección*. In *Soñé*, Arturo's virginity, which he loses only late in the novel, combined with his desire for merely physical relationships with women, symbolizes his lack of political maturity and class solidarity. It has associations of lack of virility, ingenuousness, and unwillingness to open oneself emotionally to others, to accept a genuinely reciprocal relationship. These associations Skármeta wishes to transfer, in the reader's mind, to all those who accept the bourgeois ideals of competitiveness and individualism.

The standard against which Arturo is intended to be measured is provided by Osorio, the leader of the group of young workers in Arturo's rooming house. In the worker-occupied factory he helps to run, Osorio emerges as a competent personnel manager calling to order a backsliding fellow-operative. Outside the factory it is he who presents Arturo with a more mature view of sexual relationships and a model of active social commitment. The crux of the novel comes when Arturo fails to come to the aid of Osorio (who is attacked by right-wing thugs) and is subsequently expelled from the world of soccer for selfish indiscipline. At this point he turns to his proletarian friends for consolation and a kind of absolution. He finds it in making love to one of them, Susana, whose embrace symbolizes the warmth of worker solidarity. But at the end of the novel he is still not completely won over.

Silva Cáceres stresses the significance of Susana, not only in Skármeta's early fiction, but also in current Spanish American fiction generally.[9] We saw in chapter 3 that feminism is an important feature of some Post-Boom writing, as part of a tendency in the movement to incorporate viewpoints that earlier had been denied a voice. But feminism does not make its appearance only with Allende. It is already implicit in Valenzuela's *Hay que sonreír* as early as 1966 and is explicit in both *Soñé* and *La insurrección*. Susana breaks the mold of conventional female characters in Spanish American fiction, portending some of the new "strong" heroines of the Post-Boom. This is another feature which makes *Soñé* one of the inaugural novels of the movement.

Given that *Soñé* is Skármeta's first novel, a glance at its technique is obligatory. Apart from the introduction as a subplot of elements based on the earlier short story ("Profesionales," mentioned above) whose humor and fantasy provide relief from the seriousness of the central theme, the chief features are the novel's deliberate return to linearity and reader-friendly construction. By this time, Skármeta was advocating, in true Post-Boom fashion, a mode of fiction which "renuncia a algunos efectos y técnicas en función de lograr la comunicabilidad de contenidos sociales." This stands in deliberate contrast to what he saw as the Boom's tendency to "escrib[ir] abrumadoramente bajo la forma de una meditación o cuestionamiento de la misma obra que se está escribiendo."[10] We have already suggested that what is regularly questioned in the Boom is not so much the act of writing itself (though this is certainly prominent) as the intelligibility of the reality to which fiction is traditionally related. Hitherto, Skármeta had toyed in some of his short stories with a "fantastic" or imaginative vision of reality in which simple cause and effect does not always seem to operate. The story of "El Señor Pequeño" and his stooge in *Soñé* belongs in part to this phase of Skármeta's work and for that reason jars to a certain extent with the unambiguous realism of the story of Arturo.

What characterizes the latter is the carefully symmetrical arrangement of the narrative that—in contrast to the "splintered mirror" effect, not unusual in Boom narration—already expresses a quite different and more confident approach to reality. Nothing in *Soñé* suggests any doubt in the author's mind with respect to Arturo's evolution or the events that produce it in the specific social context of the Allende administration. The novel, which has twenty-two chapters of widely different lengths, is centered around chapters 11, 12, and 13, with chapter 11 functioning as the pivot of the whole narrative. It is here that Osorio assumes the narrative voice (after an interior monologue in chapter 6) and is set up as the role model for Arturo. In chapter 12, the latter touches the lowest point in his moral parabola, while in chapter 13 almost all the main characters are brought on stage (there is even a personal appearance by the author), and all the threads of the narrative are woven together. On each side of this central narrative-sequence there are sets of chapters (6, 7 and 8, balanced later by 17, 18, and 19) that emphasize, respectively, Arturo's negative characteristics, and his growing sense of solidarity with the others, and the final loss of his virginity.[11] *Soñé* illustrates other Post-Boom characteristics, particularly the various registers of spoken language, ranging from the colloquialism of the youngsters to the pretentiousness of the football commentators and the emphasis on *cotidianeidad*, the everyday life of ordinary people. If as a novel it does not quite come off, it is because of the schematization of Arturo's evolution and a certain idealization of the young folk in the rooming house. But it has delightful freshness of humor and human appeal different from anything else one can easily think of in Boom fiction.

Skármeta's next novel *No pasó nada* (1980) belongs to the important Post-Boom category of novels of exile, in this case the exile of a Chilean family in Germany as perceived by one of the children, Lucho, who is in his early teens. Thus the strain of living in another country as political refugees is seen not from an adult standpoint of nostalgia, resentment, or frustrated heroism but from a more innocent, nonideological position that underlines the pathos and precariousness of the family situation. Skármeta has taken an anecdote he had used in an early short story, "Relaciones públicas" (in *El entusiasmo*), and developed it into a novella in which a fight with a German youth followed by a reconciliation becomes symbolic of the need to overcome ethnic differences. The theme, as we saw, surfaced again in Allende's *El Plan Infinito* and, like the general Post-Boom tendency to defend and give expression to minority and marginalized viewpoints, is part of a desire on the part of various Post-Boom writers to emphasize harmony and fusion—solidarity—rather than conflict, solitude, or "otherness." The novel of exile's problem, which Skármeta here resolves brilliantly, is to link the theme to some wider area of human experience without diminishing its impact. The outer frame of this novella, which presents the exiled family and brings out the difficulties surrounding its insertion into a new, racially and culturally different community, encloses and focuses the story of Lucho's relations with two different girlfriends. This in turn becomes the story of a kind of rite of passage from childhood into full adolescence, of which the fight is the climax.

As with most genuine Post-Boom novels, part of the interest of *No pasó nada* derives from the difference between it and the kind of fiction we associate with the Boom, in both subject matter and technique. In appearance nothing could be further from the complexities and occasional portentousness of the Boom than this innocent-seeming account of a banal incident in a distant country. But this should not make us underestimate the novella. The novel emphasis on family life as seen by younger members of the family, an emphasis present in "Primera preparatoria" and "La composición," emerges afresh here to lend the story great charm and appeal. The use of familiar youth-culture elements, soccer (once more) and pop music, to bring Lucho alive and lend credibility to his situation contrast with the Boom's intellectualism. Here there is no pressure on the reader to collaborate with the writing process, no requirement to make sense of a fragmented or nonchronological account of reality. But this does not mean that subtlety of technique is absent.

The apparent artlessness of Lucho's narration, underlined by his asides to the readers ("en confianza, les contaré que . . ."),[12] is designed to induce us to lower our guard and to take his presentation of events on trust. Because of his age and inexperience, he is automatically assumed to tell it like it is. Once this reader reception is established, Skármeta can and does manipulate it to to keep the theme of exile in the foreground. The use of past and present tense verbs, sometimes in the same sentence, establishes a happier, pre-exile "then" in contrast to the oppressive "now," to which corresponds a "there" (Chile) in contrast to a "here" (Berlin), something the reader is never allowed to forget. At the same time, references to Lucho's schoolmates, the Kumides, exiled from Greece, remind us that exile is not only a Latin American phenomenon. The incident with Hans, which leads to the fight between Lucho and Michael, Hans's brother, occurs the day before a demonstration organized by the Chilean community in exile on the first anniversary of the Pinochet coup.

Inevitably, the introduction of the theme of Lucho's relationship with his two successive girlfriends provides a new focus of interest, one that threatens to overshadow the theme of exile. The contrastive presentation of Sophie and Edith, the former some years older and much more liberated and independent than Lucho, the latter simply a classmate, is intended to express two separate options confronting the young narrator. His shift of emotional allegiance from one to the other is, in its way, as important as the subsequent fight. Grinor Rojo is right to see *No pasó nada* as a pocket-sized *Bildungsroman* in which the evolution of Lucho is crucial.[13] The sensitive presentation of an adolescent crisis is what lends the novella universality. But it remains inseparable from the family situation. On the one hand Lucho is painfully aware that the incident with Hans, provoked by Sophie, could, if Hans's injury is serious, lead to deportation for him and his family. On the other hand the opportunity for Lucho to begin an affair with Edith is provided by the demonstration against Pinochet. In reality Sophie and Edith represent different sets of values: the former is an older temptress, contact with whom brings violence and danger, while the latter is specifically connected through her father to solidarity with the Chilean exiles.

The fight between Lucho and Michael is full of symbolic overtones. As in the short story on which the novella is based, it is stage-managed to bring out certain characteristics of conciliation, forbearance, and courage that Skármeta associates deliberately with Lucho's Chileanness. There is the implicit lesson that, by demonstrating such moral qualities, Chileans in exile can retain their self-respect after the defeat of democracy in their country and that these are qualities that in the long run will overturn the military regime and reconcile the nation, as well as attract international solidarity. The theme of exile culminates in the fight, as Lucho reveals not just his own fortitude but implicitly that of his fellow countrymen. At the personal level the fight, which is presented in hallucinatory terms as a kind of nightmare, symbolizes Lucho's passage from the protection of childhood to the reality of young manhood. He is, in a sense, reborn. We notice the key phrase "yo salía del cuerpo de mi mami y todo era un incendio" (p. 67).

But reborn to what? The fight takes place on a piece of waste ground, amid filth and squalor. As the two youths leave afterward, they are leaving behind the hostility of life and riding on Michael's motorbike toward countervailing values of friendship, solidarity, and in Lucho's case real emotional fulfilment with Edith. He ends the novel on good terms with both her and Michael, who becomes a supporter of the German Pro-Chilean Committee. The happy ending, carrying with it the suggestion of the triumph of positive values over temporary adversity, stands (as do, e.g., the endings of *Eva Luna* and *El Plan Infinito*) in marked contrast to the characteristically unhappy or ambiguous endings of key Boom novels, from Cortazar's *El persiguidor* through Onetti's *El astillero* to García Márquez's *Crónica de una muerte anunciada*, Donoso's *Un lugar sin límites*, and Vargas Llosa's *La Casa Verde*. The metaphor of reality has changed.

With *La insurrección* (1982) we reach an extreme of the Post-Boom's radicalism and sometimes imprudent preoccupation with the here and now of Spanish America. It deals with an uprising in the city of León in Nicaragua at the end of the Somoza regime and with the final Sandinista triumph. Once more, as a novel, it is about as different from those we associate with the Boom as one can find. Specifically, an excellent article could be written contrasting it with Vargas Llosa's *Historia de Mayta* (1984), which totally contradicts both its endorsement of revolutionary activity and its confident presentation of character and motivation. At the same time it takes up the challenge of the end of Viñas's *Dar la cara* (mentioned in chapter 2), where the armed struggle is still to begin. The revolution that fails at the end of *Soñé que la nieve ardía* (to the extent that the Allende government could be regarded as revolutionary) or at the end of *La casa de los Espíritus* here—for the time being—overcomes, with the common people in the vanguard of the action.

A commonplace of left-wing writing is the desire to use a collective protagonist instead of a single central character—Brausen, Adán Buenosaires, Artemio Cruz, Mayta, Bolívar—or instead of a compact group of major characters as in Cortázar's *Rayuela* or Carpentier's *El siglo de las luces*. But the intention of getting away from bourgeois individualism is difficult to fulfil, except where, as here, a group of people can be shown to be animated by the same ideal and drawing others toward it. In this case the collective protagonist is made up of the inhabitants of a small neighborhood in León who eventually drive out the local Somocista garrison. Once again the novel is partially built around a series of transforming experiences, notably those of Agustín Menor, a young Somocista army recruit whose family forms the nucleus of the novel's collective protagonist. For most of the novel Agustín is both the protegé and victim of the Somocista military commander of the garrison, Captain Flores. Agustín stands for one of the options open to victims of oppression: unwilling submission. His pay is his family's only income; he hopes to be sent on a course to the U.S.A., and, at the cost of performing humiliating duties at Flores's house, he escapes the rigors of boot camp. However, his father (a development of Arturo's grandfather in *Soñé que la nieve ardía*), despite the family's indigence, condemns his son's submission and unhesitatingly helps Ignacio, an urban guerrilla who blows up a jeep-load of Somocista officers, to escape. Agustín eventually deserts, but he is recaptured and punished. Only at the end of the novel is he able to desert again, participate in the fighting, and die for the cause.

The other major option, open rebellion, is initially represented by Leonel, the boyfriend of Agustín's sister, Victoria, the local beauty queen. Leonel is away fighting with the main body of the Sandinistas. We know him through his letters to Victoria, letters that are full of of love and poetry. He is the idealized revolutionary, whose reunion with Victoria provides the novel's happy ending. Between Leonel and Agustín Skármeta sets Salinas, the local mailman, who evolves from refusing to risk any action that might bring down on him the wrath of the regime to becoming one of the architects of the rebellion. Important to his change of heart is Victoria, who both uses her sex appeal to encourage her numerous admirers to oppose the regime and leads a confrontation with Captain Flores. Her presence, and that of other women, among the leaders of the insurrection, makes this, in places, an overtly feminist novel. In fact, Skármeta has asserted that feminism "está presente en mi literatura, sobre todo a partir de *Soñé que la nieve ardía*, que es una novela radicalmente feminista."[14] The price she pays is to be arrested and raped by Flores's drunken and dull-witted drill sergeant, Cifuentes.

Cifuentes and Flores stand for the two faces of military repression in Latin America: brutality and stupidity in the case of Cifuentes and a strange blend of loyalty to the regime, crude right-wing ideology, and contempt for the masses in the case of Flores. Because of his ambiguity, Flores is the most interesting figure in the novel. Knowing that he is living on borrowed time and that his violent acts of repression are ineffectual or worse, Flores nonetheless persists in his role until he is gunned down at the end. What makes him different from Allende's stereotypical Lieutenant Ramírez in *De amor y de sombra* is his readiness to open fire on innocent people on behalf of a cause that he knows in his heart is already lost. In a less ideological novel he would have been a near-tragic figure.

The emphasis, then, is on the heroism of the common people, led by a woman, Myriam. They move from passive hostility to sporadic protest and, when this is barbarously repressed, to open rebellion. The critical action in the uprising comes when the inhabitants of the neighborhood bore holes in the walls of their houses and pass through a hose-pipe which is used to spray the local barracks with gasoline and set it ablaze. The hose, entering the intimacy of the people's homes through a series of orifices, could be seen in overtly sexual terms. In order to avenge Cifuentes's rape of Victoria, and all the other oppressive acts that it implies, the citizens permit a kind of symbolic rape of their houses.

Where the novel scores, as Dorfman has suggested, is not so much in the exaltation of the people's victory, on which subsequent events have by now cast some doubt, but rather in the brilliant treatment of the process of radicalization of the neighborhood that occupies most of the novel.[15] In reality, *La insurrección* contains a technique of postponement of the actual uprising, in order to emphasize the stages through which the outlook of the neighborhood evolves. At the beginning, Skármeta is concerned to present the various forces in play: the local people, the

Somocista forces, the Church, individual activists (represented by Ignacio), and the regime's spies and collaborators. Chapter 5 introduces Leonel and the love interest and chapter 7, Victoria. Thereafter, three parallel strands of narrative are dextrously interwoven. One centers on Agustín and the pressures on him to desert, his desertion, and the consequences. Another deals with Ignacio's bombing of the army jeep, his escape to join the guerillas at the front, and an important visit that he makes to Salinas back in León. Finally there is the strand devoted to Victoria and Leonel, including her arrest and rape and the announcement of Leonel's impending return. By arranging the action in this way, Skármeta develops the decisions and actions of different components of the collective protagonist without unduly privileging a single central figure.

Between chapters 14 and 17 the focus shifts constantly. After resting briefly on Agustín, after his attempted desertion, it passes to the protest march organized by the women accompanied by the local priest, then to Leonel, and finally to Salinas and his companion Plutarco as they acquire the gasoline for the attack on the barracks. But this is not a case of fragmentation of reality, such as we find in some Boom novels, any more than the obtrusive shifts of narrative viewpoint that we find in chapter 21 are the equivalent of the "splintered mirror" technique. Instead of deconstructing reality in order to express metaphorically its problematic nature, its irreducibility to straight lines of cause and effect, it reflects Skármeta's vision of social change as a construct made possible by the creative interaction of a variety of human forces (the neighborhood women, the individual activists, the organized guerrillas, the youngsters who defy Flores, the Parish Priest, and so on). As in the Boom, the apparently fragmentary presentation of some of the events is intended to encourage reader participation, since we must to some degree supply the links among the different fragments and foci. But the result is wholly different from that which is intended in earlier novels like *Rayuela*, *Pedro Páramo*, *La muerte de Artemio Cruz*, *La Casa Verde*, *Crónica de una muerte anunciada*, or *El obsceno pájaro de la noche*. Whereas they deliberately challenge our notion of reality, the technique of *La insurrección* in the end produces the typical Post-Boom reassuring metaphor of things falling into their proper place. As Verlichak comments, "*La insurrección* es una novela de muchas perspectivas, de muchos fragmentos, y estos fragmentos van formando de pronto un todo."[16]

The march of the women to the barracks in chapter 15 is the pivotal episode in the plot. It offers Flores a last chance to accept moderate demands backed by public opinion, and at the same time it underlines the solidarity of the neighborhood. It is followed by a peaceful and unarmed protest in chapter 21 by a group of local youngsters on whom Flores opens fire. In addition, Victoria is raped by the drink-sodden Cifuentes, a local boy is brutally murdered by Flores's troops, and the parish priest is tortured. We hear from Leonel of other barbarities in the war zone. Only when all these elements are in place does Skármeta initiate the collectivity's active resistence. The long-postponed insurrection begins in chapter 22 after Agustín Menor deserts for the second time, symbolically returning to the community and completing its solidarity. Although the whole novel builds up to the point at which the barracks is attacked and set on fire, we never actually see this happen. The emphasis remains on the readiness of everyone to help, to see holes bored into the walls of their homes and their furniture and fittings destroyed. It is Salinas who turns on the flow of gasoline. By this time even Doña Rosa, an Englishwoman, has identified herself with the Nicaraguans and their revolt, while Ignacio and Leonel return from the front (accompanied by Osorio whom we met in *Soñé que la nieve ardía*). The presence of an English and a Chilean participant in the uprising, like the presence of the Turkish exiles in *No pasó nada*, emphasizes the need for a wider understanding of, and solidarity with, the struggle against social injustice and oppression.

The ending is, of course, the apotheosis of the collective protagonist, with the triumph and sacrifice felt collectively. But the last chapter has a special importance. Predictably, it focuses on the reunion of Victoria and Leonel. As in Allende, love overcomes. The triumph of true, loving, tender sexuality as the lovers go to bed together symbolizes, like the love making of Mario and Beatriz in *Ardiente paciencia*, which coincides with President Allende's assumption of power, the notion that Carpentier indirectly incorporates into *La Consagración de la Primavera*: a fully satisfying and complete love-relationship is possible only in a society that has thrown off both political oppression and bourgeois models of propriety and sexual morality. In fact the fall of the Somoza regime is deliberately associated by Skármeta with a step forward in the sexual revolution. Don Antonio, Victoria's father, though a progressive in politics, is a conservative in sexual outlook. But, in the face of his daughter's determination to sleep with Leonel under his roof, with no regard for convention, he makes no overt protest. The embrace of the lovers symbolizes freedom in a wider sense than mere political freedom. *Per contra*, as we see in Valenzuela's equally symbolic "Cambio de armas," political oppression and sexual oppresion go hand in hand and must be equally resisted.

In Skármeta's next novel, *Ardiente paciencia* (1985), the hero, Mario Jiménez, a young mailman, discovers love and poetry with the assistance of Chile's Nobel Prize–winning poet, Pablo Neruda. His marriage and his apprenticeship as a poet, however, are brutally interrupted by his arrest following the Pinochet coup in 1973. The time frame of the novel is thus clearly symbolic. It begins in June 1969. Mario's first contacts with Neruda and his courtship of the local beauty, Beatriz, take place during the period just before the election which put Salvador Allende in power. The election night coincides with the first sexual encounter between Mario and Beatriz. The period of their marriage broadly corresponds to that of the Allende government, with a high point of happiness attained when Neruda is awarded the Nobel Prize. Thereafter the illness and death of the poet, along with the crisis and fall of the Allende government, are followed by Mario's arrest and probable death. However, despite the unhappy ending, the novel's title, taken from the speech Neruda delivered when accepting the Nobel Prize, suggests that in the end justice and human dignity will prevail.

The novel functions at three different levels. The first is the personal, human level of the love story between Mario and Beatriz. The second is the aesthetic level of Mario's self-discovery as a budding poet, encouraged by his contacts with Neruda. The third is the political level, the rise and fall of the Allende administration, which conditions the movement of the plot. The element linking the three levels is the idea of liberation. In his brief appearance as himself in chapter 13 of *Soñé que la nieve ardía*, Skármeta explains to Susana that he regards poetry writing and all creative activity as forms of self-liberation. His cult of epiphanic sexuality throughout his work makes it clear that he associates sexual activity with another form of personal freedom-seeking. Finally the Allende years are presented as years of liberation of Chile from its bourgeois and conservative political past.

Mario to some extent symbolizes the provincial Chilean proletariat experiencing creative, sexual, and political liberation under Allende only to have it snatched away by Pinochet. Mario is genuinely working-class, the son of an illiterate fisherman, and has no aspirations to be anything else. Unlike Leonel and Victoria in *La insurrección*, who are university students, or the politically active young workers in *Soñé*, he is, with certain reservations, the true "representante de la gente sencilla de Chile" Skármeta would like us to take him for.[17] Nonetheless there is something slightly magical, and thus probably symbolic, about his sudden absorption with poetry (and poetry as language, not as theme, at that!). Those of us who have tried to teach poetry to proletarian students (or anyone else) may be allowed a smile. But Skármeta was keenly aware of the outburst of creative activity on the part of the previously culturally deprived sectors of the people under Allende and indeed eventually returned to Chile from exile in part with the intention of helping to restart the process of tapping the reservoir of talent in the working class. We must view Mario in this context.

The first half or more of *Ardiente paciencia* is light hearted and full of fun. As in *La insurrección*, the different strands of narrative—poetic, emotional, and political—are effectively juxtaposed and fitted together to illustrate democratic egalitarianism (Mario befriended by Neruda), the creative potential of the workers (Mario's discovery of poetry), and self-fulfilment through love under a libertarian government (the marriage of Mario and Beatriz). This stage of the plot comes close to being an allegorical fairy tale, with Neruda as the good fairy and Pinochet lurking in the background as the demon king. Humor, both verbal and situational, abounds, amusing the reader but also presenting the characters in a highly attractive light. There are hilarious descriptions of Mario's involvement of Neruda in his love affair and of the efforts of Doña Rosa, the mailman's future mother-in-law, to thwart the marriage. The interview between Neruda and Doña Rosa in chapter 9 and the celebration of the former's Nobel Prize in chapter 15 produce more high points of comedy.

All the secondary characters, except the hypocritical right-wing politician Labbé, are drolly and affectionately presented. Surrounding the young lovers with an atmosphere of cordiality and jollity, they create a sense of collective sociability and harmony that we are intended to associate with the Allende administration. Humorous writing was one of the new areas colonized by Boom writers like García Márquez, Cabrera Infante, Cortázar, and especially Vargas Llosa, who, after at first rejecting it as frivolous, embraced it triumphantly in *Pantaleón y las visitadoras*. By contrast, it is largely absent from the work of Viñas and Benedetti, banished by their "civic" consciousness and social commitment. Humor flourishes afresh in the Post-Boom, as we perceive from Sainz's delicious *La Princesa del Palacio de Hierro* and del Paso's *Palinuro de México*, as well as in Bryce Echenique, to the extent that the last is related to the movement. Both in the new, ludic, historical novels of Posse and Paternain (as Sklodowska and Menton have indicated) and in others like those of Hiriart, it tends toward parody.[18] But usually it tends to be associated with the somewhat greater optimism of the Post-Boom, compared with the Boom, even when, as here, tragedy is about to strike.

There is an abrupt change of tone after the beginning of chapter 16, when humor, along with poetry and the joys of love and sexuality are overtaken by the events of September 1973, which saw the fall and death of Allende. Up to that time, eroticism plays its usual life-enhancing role, as in the rest of Skármeta's work, culminating, as we shall see in *Match Ball*.[19] The scene of Mario and Beatriz's first love-making, on the evening of Allende's victory, is one of the high points of Post-Boom fiction, as is their participation in the collective orgy celebrating Neruda's Nobel Prize in chapter 15. Their successive orgasms on that occasion are evoked with all the exhuberance characteristic of Skármeta's style at that stage of his career.

By this time Mario's evolution is practically complete. From being a work-shy layabout with his head full of Hollywood films and pop music, he has become socially productive and stably integrated into society as a kitchen hand, husband, and future father. In addition he is intent on producing poetry. All this is designed to offer a positive picture of life under Allende, despite food-shortages and sabotage by the Right of the government's efforts. But as the representative of the Right, the oleaginous Labbé, reappears to take part in a transport strike to embarass the government, and after Neruda announces from Paris what turns out to be his last illness, things unravel rapidly. With the poet's return to Chile to die, the novel plunges downward. The right-wing military coup follows quickly, and Mario is arrested (and, we assume, *desaparecido*) shortly after Neruda's death. Neruda, indeed, presides benignly over the whole novel, infusing it with humor and poetry and conferring happiness and fulfilment on Mario and Beatriz. With his death, the young man's creativity is thwarted, love is destroyed by his arrest, and political liberty and progress are brutally ended.

The arrangement of events in *Ardiente paciencia* is thus in itself a commentary. The first ten chapters constitute an upward movement: with Allende's rise all seems to get better and better. Chapters 11 and 12 provide a pause in the center of the narrative before the downward phase begins in chapter 13 and accelerates in chapter 16. The underlying metaphor is unmistakable and typically Post-Boom in its presentation of a tidy, ideologically explicable reality, less dramatic than that of *La insurrección*, but essentially similar. Conflict is social rather than individual (Mario and Doña Rosa, for instance, never have a showdown), and the simple, ordinary people who figure in the novel, though poor, enjoy life and reveal none of the social ills we associate with proletarian life.

*Ardiente paciencia*, then, is an archetypical Post-Boom novel: plot centered, reader friendly, with a rapid, linear story line and unsophisticated characters, it illustrates Skármeta's opposition to the obtrusive technical devices and tone of pessimism we frequently notice in Boom fiction. In a passage in the prologue, Skármeta makes fun of himself for his apparently old-fashioned ideas about writing:

> En tanto otros son maestros del relato lírico en primera persona, de la novela dentro de la novela, del metalenguaje, de la distorsión de tiempos y espacios, yo seguí adscrito a metaforones trajinados en el periodismo, lugares comunes cosechados de los criollistas, adjetivos chillantes malentendidos en Borges, y sobre todo afferrado a lo que un profesor de literatura designó con asco un narrador omnisciente.[20]

Though this quotation should obviously not be taken too literally, the fact is that *Ardiente paciencia* is written from the standpoint of omniscience, with all its implications of an intelligible world, and does reject distorsions of time and space, even to the extent of avoiding flashbacks. Its setting amid the daily life of "la gente sencilla," and its emphasis on love and the family could hardly be in greater contrast to the mainstream novels of the previous generation.

We should notice that Skármeta's ideological intention tends to remain throughout implicit rather than explicit as is so often seen in writers like Viñas, Benedetti, or, for instance, Manuel Cofiño in Cuba. What produces the change in Mario is his self-discovery as a poet. As Skármeta reminds us in his *Insula* interview, his young protagonist is arrested because of his attachment to Neruda, not to socialism.[21] When don Cosme harangues his fellow workers, Mario reacts with boredom; any change that there is in his political stance is not translated into action, beyond giving public readings of Neruda. *Ardiente paciencia* is plainly a novel a novel with a political dimension; but we must not overlook the facts that Mario's mentor is a poet, and any change the young man undergoes is seen in terms of his creativity and his achievement of emotional/sexual fulfilment, not primarily in terms of *concientización*.

The key to *Match Ball* (1989) is the reaction by the central character, Raymond Papst, a satisfactorily married and successful physician in Berlin, to the poem "The Sea" by Milosz. At fifty-two, Papst has become infatuated with a fifteen-year-old tennis starlet, Sophie Mass, who gives him the poem early in their relationship as an ambiguous sign of encouragement to go on with it. The poem is, in fact, a memorable statement about age and the achievement of insight into the superficiality of sexual passion. But Papst interprets it in the context of his reluctance to accept the ageing process and his frustration with his comfortable but unfulfilling bourgeois lifestyle. "Mi existencia," he complains, "se había convertido en un procurar más poder, más dinero, más escalas que trepar, más ruido y menos nueces."[22] Hence he reads the poem as an incitement to plunge back into a "real" existence, dominated by unrestrained emotion and desire. He does so and is rewarded with the loss of all he has achieved in his career and marriage, as well as profound humiliation and eventual imprisonment. Nonetheless, at the end of the novel he is unrepentant. This is the Post-Boom's reevaluation of love with a vengeance, and it similarly marks the peak of Skármeta's characteristic emphasis on sexuality as the prelude to an epiphanic sense of the wholeness and joyfulness of life.

Like Sábato's *El túnel*, which is mentioned in the text, *Match Ball* is written retrospectively, in the first person, from prison. The contrast between the two novels reemphasizes the difference between Boom and

Post-Boom attitudes toward love. For Sábato, in *El túnel* as in *Sobre héroes y tumbas*, love offers the deceitful hope of overcoming the otherness of others and of finding a way out of the anguish of the human condition.[23] It is love in a metaphysical maze. For Skármeta, on the other hand, it offers the illusion of recaptured youth and life lived to the full once more. The inner theme of *Match Ball* is the universal fear of growing old and being finally forced to acknowledge that passion and sexuality have had their day. Papst, like Skármeta, was young in the swinging sixties when spontaneity, nonconformity, and youthful values left an indelible mark on the minds of all they affected. Papst's heroic, idiotic gesture of throwing away all that he has gained to follow Sophie is the last hurrah of a man of the hippie era in a society taken over by yuppies.

Into his routine and deadened existence, as he sees it, Sophie brings a challenge to dare all for love. As he tells us about what then follows, much of Papst's attractiveness derives from his ability to distance himself occasionally from his plight, recognizing his folly without minimizing it and without adopting a tone of regret he does not feel. As a consequence, he holds on to enough droll self-awareness to retain some degree of respect from the reader despite his behavior. Papst is far more conscious of the risks and rewards involved in identifying erotic love with authentic living than are the young protagonists of some of Skármeta's earlier short stories. Their epiphanies are linked to the present and to a future still there to be enjoyed. His is linked to something they cannot as yet know, the yearning to recover the impossible past, to overcome, not otherness, but time. This is what raises his failings above those of a mere lustful obsession. His misfortune is that, although he never totally loses sight of the reality of his situation, he is unable to heed the warnings he receives from his wife, from Sophie's mother, and from his medical partner, Mollenhauer. Although he is conscious at intervals of behaving against his own interests and better judgement, he does not try to resolve his conflicting impulses. Everything he says about himself, whether reported from the past of the actual events or added from the perspective of his prison cell, underlies his all too human ambiguity, torn as he is between reluctant awareness and overwhelming illusion. His misfortune is not that he is unable to regulate his actions in accordance with his sporadic flashes of self-insight but that he does not really want to. Once he has undergone the experience of apparent rejuvenation and life-enhancement that falling in love with Sophie brings him, there is no going back. Papst is, in one sense, an archetypal figure of the male middle-age crisis. What makes him pathetic is the way he sees the road back to youth and escape from routine in terms of a physical relationship with an adolescent girl. In the last resort Papst is immature, not because he refuses to accept the inevitability of the aging process—we all try to fight it—but because, unlike Milosz, he cannot see that there is an alternative wiser than the one he embraces.

Sophie is, so far, unique among Skármeta's characters. She is quite unlike Abby (in "La Cenicienta"), Victoria Menor, or Beatriz González. There is little that is guileless, warm, or spontaneously attractive about her. Her beauty and desirability are accompanied by an "irónica mirada . . . más experta que la de una adolescente" (p. 22). Her behavior, from the first, is enigmatic and unpredictable; as Papst soon declares: "las contradicciones de su conducta me mareaban" (p. 40). Unlike Nabokov's Lolita, she insists on taking the initiative rather than accepting Papst's fantasy about her. But her motivation remains baffling. She refuses to discuss her emotions or actions and there is little in the way of psychological commentary in the novel to give the reader a lead. We are left to decide whether she is just a thoughtlessly capricious and manipulative spoilt child, or whether there is some unresolved tension in her personality which makes her need both what she can get from Papst and what she can get from his younger rival, Braganza. Papst refers at one point to a "toque de ausencia," common to both him and Sophie. It might mean that neither is able to accept the constraints of their respective careers and lifestyles and that both are searching for an escape. But it remains unclear why she tantalizes both Papst and Braganza. A psychoanalytic approach and a feminist approach could each be relevant here. Since Sophie lacks a father, perhaps she seeks a substitute in Papst. But why then does she victimize him? Is it some kind of vicarious revenge? Equally, her conduct can be seen seen as a form of rebellion against a paternalistic and phallocratic society, symbolized by Papst's middle-aged eroticism. But why then does she seem grateful to him and try to spring him from prison (using Braganza's money)?

Her attempt to restrict both Papst and Braganza to oral sex seems relevant. Like Arturo in *Soñé que la nieve ardía*, Sophie seems unwilling to give herself completely. After Papst asserts himself and sleeps with her, for the only time in the novel, there is an abrupt shift in her attitude, as if she were trying to regain the initiative. But perhaps the truth is that her first full sexual encounter (if it is her first) produces a personal liberation and a flash of self-discovery. This would explain the remark she makes to Papst, "Tú me ayudaste a mí, yo te tengo que ayudar a tí" (p. 159), before she tries to arrange his escape from jail after he has wounded Braganza in a fit of jealousy. But she remains puzzlingly imperturbable amid the dramatic events and conflicting male emotions that she triggers in the latter part of *Match Ball*.

Braganza is as much Sophie's victim as Papst is. The latter strikes us as slightly parodic because he finds in love the path to authentic existence at the wrong age, with the wrong partner. But he is saved from total ridiculousness by his moments of self-insight. Braganza is even more parodic of the love ideal as we saw it in some of Skármeta's "epiphanic" short stories or at the end of *La insurrección*, for example. He combines callowness with melodrama at the beginning of the novel, and vulgarity with indignity later. Sophie tantalizes and humiliates him as much as, if not more than, she does Papst. Despite being aware of the attention dedicated by the press to Papst's affair with Sophie, Braganza tamely follows her to London and is shot by Papst for his pains. The last we hear of him is that he has sunk to the level of lending Sophie the money to pay for Papst's abortive jailbreak. Unlike *Lolita*, *Match Ball* is not a deliberately antiromantic parody, but in it the more romantic elements in Skármeta's earlier fiction enter a phase of crisis.

The novel divides structurally into two unequal sections, with a pivotal episode in chapter 23 when Papst finally gets Sophie into bed. The creation of a dream of self-fulfilment in his mind is followed by his futile attempt to cling to it when events have revealed its utter unreality. In chapters 10 and 11, which hold the key to his deeper motivation, he reached out to universality as he showed himself unable to resist the mirage of reliving the excitement and wonder of youth. From the erotic climax in chapter 23 to the shooting of Braganza in chapter 27, action predominates. But what it shows this time is that the epiphanic moment of love carries no symbolic implication of triumph over the negative forces of life. The novel ends with an anticlimax that conveys a sense of irony with regard to our hopes of what life might offer. The contrast with the end of Allende's *El Plan Infinito* cannot be overlooked.

A final feature of *Match Ball* is that its style is much less exhuberant than that of Skármeta's earlier work. In several interviews in the 1980s Skármeta showed himself to be well aware of the shift. "Yo tenía por vocación un lenguage irrealista, experimental, de muchas imágenes a veces caóticas," he confessed to Pagni in 1985.[24] But exile (and also probably the ageing process itself, so heavily emphasized in *Match Ball*) changed his approach to language. Now, he asserted to Xaubet, "Opto por una selección rigorosa y creo ahora que la calidad de la vida pasa por la consecución de una imágen feliz, contra mis tesis anterior de que la vida pasa cuando muchas imágenes—felices e infelices—chocan entre sí."[25]

To conclude, in his early work Skármeta invented in Chile (in parallel to Sainz and Agustín in Mexico) a new kind of fictional hero. His young men, with their interest in casual sex, pop culture, sport, and fun, are quite unlike anything we find in Boom novels. The traumatic shocks of the fall of the Allende governement and of exile produced a shift in Skármeta's interest in social comment and political commitment in *Soñé que la nieve ardía*, *La insurrección*, and *Ardiente paciencia* together with some late short stories, as well as a memorably original contribution to exile fiction in *No pasó nada*. From *Tiro libre* to *Ardiente paciencia*, Skármeta was among the most clearly visible and articulate representatives of the Post-Boom. *Match Ball* is more difficult to categorize as a mainstream Post-Boom novel. Whether it marks a divergence from some central aspects of the movement remains to be seen.

# CHAPTER 5

# *Luisa Valenzuela*

The problem of periodization of the Boom is highlighted by the fact that the first novel by Luisa Valenzuela (b. 1938), *Hay que sonreír*, was published in 1966, in the middle of what is regarded as the Boom decade, a year before Skármeta's first collection of short stories, *El entusiasmo*, and three years before Poniatowska's *Hasta no verte, Jesús mío*. Just as many of the Boom writers were active before the 1960s, so some of the Post-Boom writers were already in print before the mid-1970s, when the movement is conventionally thought to have started. *Hay que sonreír*, however, contains few of the characteristics we associate with Boom fiction[1] beyond its urban setting, its pessimism, and a slightly ambiguous link with the Boom's emphasis on sex rather than love. It does not question or problematize reality to any significant degree, nor does it really innovate in terms of narrative technique: the only novelty Valenzuela introduces, the reporting of the heroine's thoughts intercalated into the text without warning, is applied inconsistently and soon abandoned. But *Hay que sonreír* prefigures some of the themes and presuppositions that Valenzuela's later work will develop.

It is the story of a naive, good-hearted, provincial girl of twenty-one (Valenzuela's age when she began it) who graduates from being a casual prostitute in Buenos Aires to working for a stage magician who eventually murders her. As a metaphor of reality it is wholly negative and unrelieved either by humor or fantasy, with none of the playfulness of much of the author's later work. It harks back to Arlt's use of sordid settings and presentation of often cruel sexual relationships as well as to the interest of Argentine writers from Gálvez to Sábato in the theme of solitude. But, as we shall see, a major feature of Valenzuela's literary personality is her adoption of the idea that the writer, like the psychologist, should try to raise the threshold of awareness of repressed aspects of human behavior, in the hope that they will thus be exorcised. *Hay que sonreír* shares with Puig's *Boquitas pintadas* (1969) the notion that "sexual oppression is the school for all other oppressions,"[2] an assertion that Valenzuela would later endorse memorably in her short story "Cambio de armas." For the moment, however, she really did not know how to handle it and, in an interview with Magnarelli, described the first draft of her novel as "inflated," "exaggerated" and "archeprototypi-cal."[3] Nevertheless, she went ahead and published it. The result is an unambiguous protest of the behavior of men, from a woman's point of view. But it is not really feminist because of Valenzuela's curiously detached attitude to the heroine, Clara, who is presented as collaborat-ing to some degree with her own degradation. For this reason it is diffi-cult to accept fully Martínez's idea that "En la joven se percibe un potencial subversivo" and that she possesses "una paradójica actitud de invulnerabilidad y autonomía."[4] What Martínez is thinking of are, in fact, no more than unattainable dreams or illusions in Clara's mind. Nor can we concur in Magnarelli's interpretation of the novel as being largely about "contemporary woman's plight in the face of social expec-tations that she will be passive, silent and industrious" and so on because, as this critic herself indicates on the same page, Clara never seems particularly pathetic or tragic.[5] This is not a case of Valenzuela's being "subtle";[6] the problem of the novel is that it is too unsubtle. The male characters, without exception, are selfish, humorless, ill-tempered, sexually demanding exploiters, in contrast to Puig's Massa, who may be unromantic but is a caring husband and father. Clara meets only vari-ants of Puig's Juan Carlos, without his sex appeal.

Still, two aspects of the novel merit attention. One is that Clara's dream of love is never sentimentalized or belittled. Not unlike Allende's Greg Reeves in El Plan Infinito (1991), she is searching for sincere affec-tion. Her reflexions and assumptions in this regard are utterly untypical of the novel of the sixties but come into their own with the Post-Boom. The other is Hay que sonreír's unabashed referentiality; nowhere is the notion of reporting reality challenged. At this stage Valenzuela reveals total confidence in her power to observe and interpret the world around her. This was to be modified later, as we shall see. But enough remains for her to be able to assert fifteen years later: "I think the one thing we [writers] must do is speak about what is going on":[7] another classic Post-Boom affirmation.

By 1966, successive attempts by Frondizi, Guido, and Illía to con-tain Peronismo had failed, and in June a military coup put General Onganía in power until the return of Perón in 1973. He died in 1974, and two years later the military under Videla once more seized power and kept it until 1983. The result, for Valenzuela (as for Allende and Skármeta after the military coup in Chile in 1973), was radicalization. We should note that the rise of Pinochet and Videla coincided with the emergence of the Post-Boom. Valenzuela's relationship to this new movement is more problematic than is Allende's or Skármeta's. For example, in her "Little Manifesto" she writes: "Literature is the site of the crosswaters—the murky and the clear waters—where nothing is exactly in its place because there is no precise place . . . But it is precisely at these crosswaters where it becomes necessary to have a lucid ideology as a base from which problems may be focussed on." However, she insists that, for her, there is always a "conflictive duality" between being a literary animal and a political one. There can be no clear-cut distinction, she argues, between "crude social realism" and "diffuse metaphysical surrealism": there has to be "a mixture of both." The writer must be a witness (a basic Post-Boom position), but one who occupies no "comfortable, solid ground of absolute security." Rather, it is a matter of questioning, of disturbing the reader, of pointing out what it would be more comfortable to forget, both in "our external and our internal realities."[8]

If we think of the Post-Boom as a movement in which fiction tends to reestablish a closer connection with the here and now of Spanish America, Valenzuela's stress on the inner reality of the individual, on the theme of the quest and the paradoxical "search for the reason of the quest,"[9] and on the role of language in fiction seem to look back toward the complexities of the Boom. She admires Borges (a family friend), Cortázar, and other Boom writers and is on record as stating that she and other Argentine writers cannot escape their legacy.[10] Her affirmation in the same essay that "what we call reality usually goes beyond tangible and explicable limitations," together with similar remarks to Gazarian Gautier and her stress on magic and myth, similarly links her to the older movement.[11] Perhaps most of all her belief in the need to "question language" and explore "the possibility of multiple significations for the signifier,"[12] along with her emphasis on linguistic play, masks, ambiguity, and "analysis of the metaphorical and metonymical structure of language," reveal strong links with Boom outlook.[13] When, on the other hand, she insists that *Como en la guerra* is a highly politicized book and that "We are innately political; we need to fight for a cause, an ideal, a hope," when she affirms that "language is always political" and that "the political topic per se as a subject of my writing is there all the time," when she asserts "If we forget to be rebels we are no longer writing" and declares that "What writers in Latin America ultimately do is a kind of *literatura de denuncia*," we hear a familiar Post-Boom ring in her words.[14]

The process that led her in this latter direction did not produce relevant results for our study until 1975 with *Aquí pasan cosas raras*, described by Magnarelli as "surely one of Valenzuela's most overtly political works."[15] In the meantime she published a collection of short stories, *Los heréticos* (1967), and *El gato eficaz* (1972). The former contains her first published story, "Ciudad ajena," written in 1955 when she was seventeen, in imitation of "a certain fashionable author of that time,"[16] possibly Borges. It is predictably mysterious and contains a contemptuous reference to "los que viven del mal lado de las cosas y sólo conocen las realidades más palpables."[17] In deference to the prevailing trend away from direct referentiality, it challenges our notion of everyday reality. The other tales in *Los heréticos*, however, do not develop this feature significantly but, rather, deal with themes involving satire of religion and male sexuality, witchcraft, and mental alienation, using various techniques that seem to reflect the young writer's effort to find her own direction. At this stage, it is not toward the mainstream of the Post-Boom. There is no interest in youth or pop culture, no real social commitment, and little humor. Only in "Una familia para Clotilde" do we note a wryly ironic depiction of male behavior from a feminine viewpoint somewhat in advance of what we saw in *Hay que sonreír*. Probably the most important story in *Los heréticos* is "Proceso a la Virgen." Conventional religion does not figure significantly in Valenzuela's work except on rare occasions (beginning here) on which she satirizes people's often distorted vision of it. Of this story, she said to Mull and de Angulo: "La idea es que todos están esperando algo de la religión que no puede pasar, que la religión está distorsionada, que la gente persiste en eregir dioses falsos."[18] Martínez suggests that the denunciation of religion in "Proceso a la Virgen," "Nihil obstat," "El pecado de la manzana," and elsewhere in the volume prefigures her subsequent attacks on dictatorship as another form of absolutism.[19]

*El gato eficaz* was written in the late sixties, when Valenzuela had a fellowship at the University of Iowa's International Creative Writing Program, along with Néstor Sánchez, Fernando del Paso, and Gustavo Sainz, among others. Of it she has said: "Until that moment, my narrative was very linear. I was repeating myself. It was a time of change in Latin American literature, and I wanted to get into the trend and change my voice at the same time."[20] Clearly, what she was referring to here was the Boom, with its stress on narrative experimentalism. The key to *El gato eficaz* is a remark Valenzuela makes in her essay "Dangerous Words": "what I write isn't as interesting as how I write it."[21] She asserted that this idea was shared by Joyce and Felisberto Hernández. Both the remark itself and the reference to the two writers point in the opposite direction from that of mainstream Post-Boom writing.

Ana Fores decribes *El gato eficaz*, which has no consistently recognizable theme or plot and uses a deliberately teasing narrative voice, as "filled with a terrorizing surrealism." She continues: "She wants to say that life is chaotic; through that same language which she explores, she forms, purposely, a labyrinth of confusion."[22] Such an innovative text, which is intentionally ludic in its presentation of behavior and whose "language is playful and meaningful in its creation of a signified which is non-referential,"[23] fits some descriptions of postmodernism. But to the extent that it does so, it reveals that postmodernism, at least of this sort, is hard to relate to much of the Post-Boom. According to Cordones-Cook, in *El gato eficaz* "se intenta sustituir abruptamente la estabilidad de la percepción de una realidad ordenada y lógica por un campo móvil donde desaparecen [sic] la oposición entre lo verdadero y lo falso, entre la razón y la locura. Se plantea un universo sin normas."[24] It is not obvious how such a conception can be reconciled with the advocacy of "committed" writing in some of the remarks mentioned above. But this is a problem shared by other Post-Boom writers, who tend to be uneasily aware of the difficulty created by the Boom writers' tendency to doubt our ability to observe and express reality. It is one of the central dilemmas of the movement. An important point with regard to this text is made by Martínez in *El silencio*, when she cogently points out that "la liberación de Eros," which first comes to real prominence in *El gato eficaz*, is symbolic, and "señala el acceso a las fuerzas eminentemente creadoras de la vida."[25] By contrast, Valenzuela herself has described the work as "filled with the idea of death" and as "a book about death."[26] The verdict of criticism on this difficult text is still open.

The zigzag process by which Valenzuela subsequently moves back closer toward referentiality is never complete. As late as *Novela negra con argentinos* (1990) she is still prudently referring to "la llamada realidad." But *Aquí pasan cosas raras* (1975) marks a turning point. In the prologue to *Open Door* (1988), a collection of some of her stories in translation, she tells how she returned to Buenos Aires in 1975 to find it in the grip of violence and state terrorism, its people afflicted with "general paranoia." She continues: "*Strange Things Happen Here* was born, and with it a new political awareness. And action."[27] In her essay "A Legacy of Poets and Cannibals," she tells us, "To write those stories I would go to cafés every day and pick up phrases or moods that would trigger them, and I used humor, the absurd, the grotesque, to break through the barrier of censorship,"[28] adding to Gazarian Gautier that change of identity, masks, and disguise were specially important in the tales and stating that "the book became a metaphor for everything that was going on [in Argentina] at the time."[29] Magnarelli asserts: "the collection focuses on the oppression of human beings by other human beings and our apparently limitless capacity for double thinking, double speaking and virtual blindness, as once again Valenzuela suggests that the political is defined by its misuse of a discourse which supports and justifies governmental oppression."[30] Two features of the text make *Aquí pasan cosas raras* interesting as a work published just as the Post-Boom is supposed to have begun. The first is that oppression is often revealed indirectly or by means of satire (presumably in part to confuse the censor); the second is the fact that, unlike Allende and Skármeta, Valenzuela does not tend to exempt the oppressed themselves from surrendering, with part of their minds, to the tyranny. At this point the ambiguity she associates with her use of language spills over into one of her central themes.

Let us glance at some examples. The title story is ironic in tone with a double-take ending. Like Skármeta's "La llamada," it explores the theme of living in a police state. What adds the irony is that the main characters, instead of being right-thinking people with whom we can identify easily, are a couple of penniless young men living on their wits. In the outer frame of the story they steal a briefcase, a package, and a jacket. But this is the Buenos Aires of 1975; instead of feeling anticipation, they feel tension. Either the briefcase or the package could explode at any moment. They throw the latter away. A second internal episode concerns an unemployed man whom they befriend in contrasting scenes of human solidarity. When they take leave of him and abandon the briefcase and the jacket, we seem to see that anti-climax is the point: in a terrorized society, not even sneak thieves can operate without finding themselves in a nightmare situation. But then the thieves hear what might have been an explosion. We are reminded that their hitherto slightly comic sense of an inversion of normality, which has prevented them from enjoying the results of their theft, is all too real.

Another example is "Camino al Ministerio." It is an extended satirical metaphor. The candidate for a ministerial appointment has to learn a masochistic technique of groveling self-abasement in order to fit himself for the hoped-for position. But, in a device borrowed from many of Borges's stories, this one tips over unexpectedly in the middle. The candidate's neighbors, instead of despising him, have been supporting him in his training program in the hope of future ministerial favors. The people, that is, share responsibility for the degradation of Argentine political life. But now, swayed afresh by greed, fear and ignorance, they suddenly reinterpret his self-humiliation in terms of a quest for saintliness and again try to jump on his bandwagon. But in the meantime the candidate has starved to death. Even so, the self-deceiving populace decide that the smell of his decaying corpse is the odor of sanctity. A similar shift is perceivable in "El don de las palabras," which begins in the first person with the "Leader" (Perón) speaking but ends with an omniscient narrator sarcastically describing the masses, permanently packed into symbolic trenches from which they listen enraptured. The "Leader" despises the people, whom he intoxicates with fustian rhetoric and who are only too ready to listen instead of thinking, and to accept annointment with pigeon droppings or possibly his urine. But the really hardhitting part of the tale develops the parallel, already present in *Los heréticos*, between religious and political gullibility. Valenzuela was to return to this issue in *Cola de lagartija*. By making the central figures in "Aquí pasan cosas raras" sneak thieves and by shifting the emphasis in "Camino del Ministerio" and "El don de las palabras" from politicos to the credulous masses, Valenzuela injects an element of intellectualization and irony into her social criticism. As a result she perhaps loses some of the direct impact of a story like Skármeta's "La composición." The reader must decide whether there is a corresponding gain in universality.

Como en la guerra (1977), while slightly less baffling in some respects than *El gato eficaz*, is specifically presented as a "*rompecabezas*," a puzzle for the reader to figure out.[31] Attempts on the part of critics to assist with the process have not been conspicuously successful and seem to suggest that the novel fails to communicate its message adequately.[32] The English translation is preceded by a "Page Zero," which was omitted from the Argentine edition.[33] It tells us that the central character AZ is being tortured to obtain information about "ella," with whom he has recently been conducting sessions of psychoanalysis. It then appears that, at the time of these sessions, "ella" was working as a waitress and part-time whore in a sleazy nightclub in Barcelona, though earlier she had belonged to an unsuccessful guerrilla group in Buenos Aires. The meaningfulness of this is never explained; "Page Zero" itself shifts confusingly from dialogue in the torture chamber to interior monologue by AZ, with intercalated comments of a highly abstract, metaphysical kind. We perhaps should assume that the novel that follows takes place in AZ's mind in response to the questioning.

It is divided into four parts: "El descubrimiento," "La pérdida," "El viaje," and "El encuentro." The first describes a series of visits to "ella" by AZ, then working as a professor of semiotics, in various disguises (which do not fool her), ostensibly to psychoanalyze her, though their relationship partly parodies and partly goes beyond psychoanalisis, notably when they become lovers. This section of the novel begins with a cry of "angustia por la raza humana" (p. 11) when "ella" is born. At this point she is presented as either male or female, that is, as an archetype of humanity. Thereafter the signals we receive about her are both chaotic and contradictory, so that any interpretation is apt to be grounded simply on a selection of the textual evidence. What seem significant are the implications that she was an urban guerrilla, that she was in love with Navoni (who reappears in *Cambio de armas* and *Cola de lagartija*), that she is in exile, that she appears to be collaborating with AZ in a quest, that she associates her former activism in Argentina in "esos tiempos cuando hubo ideales" (p. 81) with a hated twin sister, that she is trying to "encontrarse a sí misma" (p. 81) and to recover a sense of "pureza" (p. 80), instead of what AZ calls "los malolientes internos que cada uno acuna dentro de uno" (p. 85). The end of "El descubrimiento" suggests that if AZ had been able to grasp her real relationship with the guerrilla organization, he would have understood much more and his interrogation under torture would have had some meaning. But at the same time "ella," obsessed by "la irracionalidad que implica la condición humana," considers that to postulate a "cause" for subsequent "effects," to impose a rational, predictable structure on events, is unbearable (p. 93). For his part, AZ sees her, at least on one page, as having given up the guardianship of one set of values and ideals (*alturas*), presumably those of the armed struggle, and as having taken over another set, which remain unspecified but are associated with the Andes. Similarly he concludes that her personality, which he is investigating, is a mirror image of his own, so that her quest is in fact his own (p. 74). Martínez's identification of her simply with the positive forces underlying the concept of "la madre" (*El silencio* p. 105) and her earlier suggestion that AZ at the end of the novel "se entrega a la madre inminente" (p. 95) seem simplistic, as does Martínez's whole *madre/padre* dichotomy as she applies it to the work of Venezuela.

The description of the novel on the cover of the first edition, which may have been written or authorized by Valenzuela, describes it as an "aventura verbal" in which the theme is the search by the protagonist for his own identity via "un yo diferente pero especular y que quizá refleje la identidad deseada." If this is the key, there seems to be the implication that AZ has been associated with revolutionary activities which have failed and perhaps been betrayed. His quest appears to be for a new pattern of beliefs, a new source of love and fulfilment, which will reconcile him with himself and silence the howl of existential despair with which the novel begins. From a passage in the novel's second section, it seems clear that he suffers from a sense of disintegration of the self and that his consciousness of "ella's" absence and need for her indicate a need to reintegrate his personality (p. 106). The process of meeting that need appears to begin in the second section of the novel, with its references to liberation from the past and the incorporation of "ella" into himself (pp. 120–21). As he masturbates in front of a series of photographs of her, he seems momentarily to reestablish symbolic contact with her. He later undergoes a mysterious experience of spinning in time with the rhythm of the world itself; this produces a comforting vision. The end of the second section clearly marks a step forward in self-integration: he has, in a sense, re-found "ella" and (the narrator assures us) "llegará a buen puerto" (p. 131). Interestingly, this first step in his recovery is associated with "recognizing" Latin America for the first time. Reintegration with himself would bring reintegration with his origins.

By the beginning of section three "el que ya es yo empieza poco a poco a identificarse, a rejuntarse" (p. 135) and the upward movement gains momentum; but the process is far from complete. Now amid the mountains of Mexico, AZ undergoes a process of ritual purification that prepares him for a symbolic journey out of the abyss to the peaks "donde viven las águilas" (p. 143), a phrase which was to reappear as the title of a later book. It is suggested (p. 145) that the journey is from the abyss to greater awareness, or self-awareness, perhaps of "lo inconfesable en nosotros" (p. 146). But the object of AZ's desire, "ella," remains as yet "inasible." Indeed, after a visionary moment induced by peyote mushrooms, AZ appears to recognize that "la búsqueda reside en el rechazo" (p. 152), rather than in any solution based on love (human or divine), or on hope of happiness. A key sentence is that which defines his search interrogatively, as being for "¿una parte de sí mismo, la verdad, el conocimiento, la felicidad, el sumo acontecer, la desesperanza?" (p. 154). If this is relevant, his search is for self-integrating awareness of some form of absolute that may or may not be life-enhancing and that, it later transpires, may perhaps be glimpsed only at the moment of death. To Montserrat Ordoñez, speaking in general of the quest theme in her work, Valenzuela said, rather cryptically, "La búsqueda es la búsqueda de . . . lo que nadie tiene, la carencia absoluta. Es la búsqueda de una carencia."[34] At this point the text turns a sharp corner as AZ discovers that his quest seems to have reached an impasse. Love and death, the great abstractions that seem to have conditioned it, now give place to concrete problems of the here and now: hunger and oppression. He begins to approach the part of himself that "tenía conciencia de las cosas y luchaba por una causa concreta" (p. 162) and comes to see that (some degree of) "illumination" may perhaps be achieved through the collective struggle rather than through self-scrutiny. But we cannot overlook the fact that the guerrillas he meets are in fact a group of actors and that the performance they describe is one involving cannibalism. It seems that rebellion is an experience that must form part of the quest, but does not fulfil it. AZ moves on to Buenos Aires, his hometown.

The final section of *Como en la guerra* (a title that, as Magnarelli reminds us, refers to a slogan used by the military regime in Argentina to justify its barbarities[35]) is quite different in tone from the other three, though this does not seem to have attracted critical notice. It is linear and climactic, with few of the disconcerting contradictions or shifts of narrative voice characteristic of the other sections. It is not, for that reason, any easier to understand. In it AZ makes his way past multitudes of people waiting in line to pay homage to a saintly figure. Cordones-Cook is clearly correct in identifying this figure of popular devotion with Evita Perón.[36] AZ despises her worshippers as "trastornados," though expressing his love for them as fellow Argentines. As he approaches the fortress-shrine of the saint, he finds it under attack and, with joy at finally "belonging," participates "por defensa de algo que absoluta-mente lo trasciende" (p. 191). Unaware of why he is risking his life ("sabe para quién, y eso le basta," p. 193) he succeeds in dynamiting the walls of the building to reveal to the waiting throngs the glass coffin containing "ella."

Hicks asserts that "the semiotician . . . does not find his true iden-tity until he has sacrificed himself in an act of political commitment," whereas Maci believes that AZ's "voyage does not end in discovery but rather the opposite" and Magnarelli sees the ending in terms of "gratu-itous action based on ignorance."[37] It seems arguable that any attempt at interpretation that does not take note of the change in narrative tech-nique and the association of "ella" in some way with Evita must be inadequate. AZ appears to function symbolically on two levels: as a rep-resentative, like the protagonist of Carpentier's quest-novel *Los pasos perdidos*, of contemporary Western man, and as a representative of con-temporary Argentina. In both cases what is emphasized is split person-ality and the search for self-integration whether by means of analysis, mythic experience, or action involving some form of recovery of the ideal. Speaking to Cordones-Cook in 1990, Valenzuela made fun of a reader who identified the figure in the glass coffin simplistically with Evita. She asserted that at the end of *Como en la guerra* "hay un encuen-tro con el mito."[38] This suggests that the split personality of the protag-onist can be healed by a combination of self-sacrificing action and recognition of a "mythical" ideal capable of capturing mass support. In her earlier interview with Mull and de Angulo, she had mentioned that Evita had represented such a myth for her in her youth. Clearly, it is this, not the person, we are intended to think of. If so, the end of *Como en la guerra* reveals a certain distrust of the masses, and perhaps even of their leadership in some instances, as being beyond the reach of reason and needing to be dynamized by appeals to mythology.

*Libro que no muerde* (1980) need not detain us, since it merely con-tains selected stories from *Los heréticos* and *Aquí pasan cosas raras* together with a series of jottings that do not affect my line of argument.

During the 1970s in Argentina pressure on writers had become acute. Valenzuela writes: "Some writers suddenly disappeared; many were threatened by the paramilitary forces. Publishers' offices were bombed and thousands of books were destroyed. The threat became so intense that in 1973 when I completed the novella "Other Weapons" ["Cambio de armas"] which spoke about the torture and oppression so common at that time, I didn't even dare to show it around."[39] "Cuarta versión," the opening story of *Cambio de armas* (1982) begins with a superb Post-Boom image: that of the "Great Writer" (= representative of the Boom) at an embassy party reading from his latest masterpiece to the accompaniment of police sirens. The message is explicit: it is no longer the "angustia metafísica"[40] of the older generation of writers that is relevant now. It is oppression, symbolized by the people who have sought refuge in the embassy. But this is not expressed directly. As always in Valenzuela, ambiguities prevail, partly, no doubt, because of the censorship but also because of the aforementioned problem of expressing the horror of the real while recognizing that all accounts of the real are fictitious and that language is not an ideal expressive tool. Valenzuela, in "Cuarta versión" and elsewhere, tries to confront the problem by incorporating awareness of it into her narrative, so that what is called "demasiado real" in the second line of the story is balanced against "la llamada realidad" thirty-seven pages later. Language, it seems, can never really "express" reality directly; it can only "represent" it allusively. This is why the protagonist of "Cuarta versión" is an actress who at one point puts on a one-woman show abroad that alludes to the oppression and torture she may suffer if she returns home. "Lo represento y representando, soy" she comments (p. 41): it is an act, but also in some sense (her) reality. The analogy with what we are reading is clear.

A key to all the stories in *Cambio de armas* is Agustín's distinction, made later in *Novela negra con argentinos*, between "cápsulas de vida" (realistic accounts of lived experiences), which he rejects as belonging to a preliterary stage of creation, and "aquello que accede a la noble condición de metáfora."[41] Thus, one version of the events in "Cuarta versión" would have been a "novela testimonial" (p. 24) written first hand by Bella, the protagonist. But the final text rejects this possibility, not only out of fear of censorship or persecution, but also as impossibly crude. Instead, although it is plainly stated (p. 21) that the real theme is that of the political refugees in the embassy, they are now only mentioned in passing, in connection with one side of the dichotomy that governs all the stories in *Cambio de armas*. Magnarelli argues that the factors that unify them are the use of a female narrator and female protagonists.[42] But the deep themes of the book are love and fear, announced by the triple reference to them in "Cuarta versión" (pp. 10, 30–31, 53) and, as Cook maintains in her thesis, victimization, inherited from *Hay que sonreír*.

A feature of "Cuarta versión" is the strange ending in which Bella, having been shot by the regime's soldiers in an attack on the embassy, hears the start of her own story whispered to her by the ambassador, Pedro, her lover, who attributes it to "tío Ramón," a kind of imaginary Uncle Remus. Has Pedro stage-managed the whole sequence of events in order to get rid of the problem of the political refugees? Saltz notes that in all the stories in *Cambio de armas* the female central characters resist oppression and submission, but that Bella's strategy fails.[43] She does not explain why, but the answer must have to do with Pedro and his extraordinary response to Bella's last moments. Perhaps we should see in this tale an unconscious endorsement of Mora's complaint, à propos of Allende, that heroines often become involved with political activism only because of their entanglements with men.[44] Certainly, Bella is at one point (p. 13) described as falling into a trap. Although alerted from the first page to the fact that it is hard to see an "order" (a causal sequence) in events, we seem to be invited to read back from the ending and recognize, behind the self-deconstructing and obtrusively self-aware narrative, that from the moment the "Mensajero con mayúscula" brings her an invitation to the embassy, her fate is sealed: he is the Messenger of Death.

As she sets out, it is repeatedly implied that she is taking a false step. When she manages to persuade Pedro to accept two of her friends as political refugees, she is openly dscribed as "un peón en el juego." Whose game? There are ambiguities in Pedro's behavior, as well as in the narrator's confessed readiness to attach importance to some clues rather than others. But while abroad Bella seems to intuit "probables traiciones" and accuses Pedro of playing a murderous conspirator to her Julius Caesar (p. 41). The evidence is not conclusive, especially as Pedro seems to change in the later part of the tale. In the end we return to "el tío Ramón" as the clue to the meaning. He seems to represent fabulation, dream, an opening on to a new reality, perhaps Bella's temptation to rewrite her role on the stage of reality to become more active on behalf of the refugees. At all events, this is what she does, with tragic results for herself. If the answer to the story as a puzzle is not to be found in the role of Pedro, it is perhaps to be found in Bella's surrender to "el tío Ramón" who draws her down into quicksand. The story's message, in either case, would be a warning rather than a call to action. Martínez refers to the ending as a "final trágico que no involucra, sin embargo, una nota de desesperanza," but her account of the story ignores sundry details; this makes the ending more ambiguous than she implies it is.[45]

The same is true of "De noche soy tu caballo." Lagos Pope points out, a propos of the women in *Cambio de armas*, that this is feminine, not feminist writing: "la aparente centralidad del compromiso político es engañosa, ya que aunque militantes participan de la acción política, como mujeres su centro es la pareja, no la acción comprometida."[46] The central character here longs for love and togetherness with her guerrilla boyfriend, Beto. But it is clear that she is not going to get them on her terms. When she listens with him to the song that gives the story its

name, she interprets it in terms of possession by a spirit, magically uni-
fying the lovers. But he sees it in crude terms of male sexual domination.
She wants reassurance of love before the sexual act; he regards the act
itself as containing the reassurance. She submits, but the story is in two
halves: the first describes his visit, the second her arrest and torture as a
result. "De noche" owes its impact to the brutal contrast. Its climax is
not that of the heroic woman who refuses to betray her man; it is that
of a woman taking refuge in a dream in order to cling to what we as
readers recognize is an utterly falsified reality. The story can be read two
ways, but it is more probable that we should read it as about self-deception.[47]

By contrast "Ceremonias de rechazo" is a remake of the same situation seen from the opposite perspective. The central figure, Amanda,
this time is aware of her passivity, but also that the link with her lover
"el coyote" (who is perhaps an agent of the regime) is what she calls "lo
inconfesable en mí" (p. 88)—physical titillation derived from the possibility that he is cruel and treacherous. But his unexplained absence provokes her to "sacudirse las ideas" (p. 89), especially when he refuses all
real communication with her. Their relationship, which is now seen significantly in terms of "torturas" on his part and a struggle for control
on hers (p. 93), reaches a pivotal moment when she leaves him. During
the rest of the tale she undertakes a series of rituals designed to rid herself of his influence. They culminate in her throwing into the river a rose
he has given her and taking a flower to plant for herself in the balcony
garden that he had created. Cordones-Cook misunderstands the symbolism here; contrast Martínez.[48] We can see Amanda as Argentina shaking off authoritarian control (despite its attractions) or as a woman
rebelling against patriarchy, but in either case the happy ending is contrived and the story too symmetrical and overloaded with symbolism.

Searching is a basic theme in Valenzuela's work. The central character in "La palabra asesino" is from the first "en busca de una
respuesta" (p. 67). The tale is about her deepening self-awareness, especially of what Valenzuela calls "the deep unspeakable thing" in oneself,[49]
something we have already noticed in *Como en la guerra* and in "Ceremonias de rechazo." Here "ella" takes a black lover who turns out to be
a killer. We asume that the story will be about her coming to terms with
him, but it is her discovery about herself that provides the climax. Once
more the story is organized symmetrically around a pivotal moment,
when "ella" asks herself: "¿Cambia ahora la belleza, cuando la belleza
ha andado por ahí destruyendo la perfección de líneas de los otros?" (p.
74). Her lover's admission of the deaths in his past shatters her original
self-deceiving notion of offsetting with her loving care his earlier depri-
vations. How can she now identify his attractiveness with life-enhance-

ment and love, when he has destroyed life? She becomes aware, like Amanda in "Ceremonias de rechazo" and Roberta later in *Novela negra*, that fear can be a powerful component in sexual attraction. Fulks's dismissal of the murderer-lover as unimportant is, like her general interpretation of the tale,[50] debatable: both the lovers are questing. Near the end of the story a narrative voice that does not belong to "ella" remarks implacably, "El quería buscarse, buscarse en ella, ella en él, y ya no. Nadie se encuentra" (p. 80). So "ella" goes on with her own self-analysis. But if her conclusion is that perhaps she loves him because of his dark past, what then? In the final phase of her quest she realizes that she also has her own dark side and is potentially a murderer too "porque no hay orden" (p. 78): there is no objective moral order. By now she is trapped in contradictions that, as usual in Valenzuela, are not resolved but remain to challenge the reader. Finally "ella's" resistance breaks down, and with the assistance of her newfound awareness of her own inconfessable secret self, she is able to articulate the word *asesino*. As with psychological treatment, what matters is bringing the hidden problem into consciousness.

Metaphorically the story can be read as a call to Argentina to acknowledge that the "dirty war" expressed the dark side of the collectivity. "Cambio de armas," Valenzuela's most functionally effective and successful short story, is much more explicit. It is about Laura, an urban guerrilla, who has been captured and tortured by an army colonel, Roque. He now keeps her locked in an apartment in a state of drugged amnesia, using her as a sexual object. We can see this as a metaphor of the subjection of Argentina by the military and as about male domination of women. The story chronicles Laura's carefully graduated recovery of memory and the will to act. Roque's ambiguous personality is developed in parallel with hers. He shows, paradoxically, tenderness, but there are also hints of fear, remorse, and tension. The first stage of reassertion of Laura's will comes when she asks for a plant, which we subsequently identify with her: its growth and change symbolize her gradual evolution. At first this is rooted in the only part of her which is "active," her sexuality, which is soon not fully under his control. The pivotal moment in this story comes with the subsection "El rebenque," when he brings a whip to the apartment. It is closely associated with another symbolic subsection: "La ventana," a "window" that only he can open (as he does fully at the end) and that can throw light on the the dark pit of repressed memory inside her. Roque's personality oscillates between harshness on the one hand and the need for "alivio" on the other. Strangely, the narrator suggests that one purpose for his bringing the whip is to be beaten (or worse) with it himself. But the whip serves as a triggering device, accelerating Laura's recovery of memory.

After exhibiting her to fellow-officers and teasing her sadistically with the whip, he tries to force her to perform with him sexually while his bodyguards peep at them through a spy-hole. But now she takes over the situation: it is, not she, but he, who howls; not he, but she, who has the orgasm. Until the situation is resolved by the collapse of the regime, she only has momentary "accesos de rebeldía" (p. 193). But then the hubris he has sporadically shown at work in himself gets the upper hand: he brutally recalls to her memory her (and her former lover's) failed attempt to assassinate him and her capture and torture. As he does so, a blob of congealed paint on the wall becomes the symbol of what in her has resisted modification. With a final gesture of contempt and triumphalism, Roque offers her the loaded pistol with which she had tried to kill him. As, with her finger on the trigger, she has a last flash of understanding, we intuit that his fate is sealed. This is the story that most memorably combines an attack on the patriarchal structure of society with a metaphor of Argentina under the heel of the military, a point developed by Castillo from a strongly feminist standpoint.[51] However, we must not simplify the meaning of the stories in *Cambio de armas* so as to reduce it merely to this dual theme. Geisdorfer Feal reminds us in a lucid article that the characters in the collection, especially the women, are full of ambiguities. "Valenzuela," she writes, "refrains from assigning knowable, stereotypical roles to her female protagonists and their male partners; rather, she suggests a series of gender-based positionings that may or may not open up avenues of resistence or subversion."[52] A propos of "Cambio de armas" itself, she points out perceptively that, on a level below that of the tale's superficial impact, "what deeply disturbs us" is the combination of subversion and submission in Laura (pp. 169–70). Similarly she criticizes Amanda's rituals in "Ceremonias de rechazo" as containing a "psychological masquerade of femininity" (p. 180). Feal's insistence on the idea that a "fundamental ambivalence" subsists in Valenzuela's attitude to her themes in *Cambio de armas* and that "the battle between masculine and feminine desire, the fight for mutual recognition and equilibrium of power, is never definitively won, but merely reconfigured" (p. 181) must give future critics pause for thought.

*Cola de lagartija* (1983), which Valenzuela called "a mythicized and damning version of recent Argentine history,"[53] carries the political commitment of *Aquí pasan cosas raras* and *Cambio de armas* to a new level. Published just after Allende's *La Casa de los Espíritus* got the Post-Boom ball rolling, it confirms her important place in the movement. It evokes the presence in Argentina of a sociopolitical force that was essentially ambiguous, not only in itself, but also in its relationship with the military government. We are not here in the presence of a clear-cut conflict, as, for example, in Skármeta's *La insurrección* (in Spanish, 1982); rather Valenzuela creates an enigmatic allegory of events in modern Argentina, seen in terms of magic and charlatanism; this allows her to recycle features of Boom technique (fragmentation, shifting narrators, the use of a nonlogical, nonrealist approach), not, as formerly in *El gato eficaz*, to comment on reality, but to emphasize the irrationality of political events. The novel's "Advertencia" tells us that it is necessary to "intentar darle la palabra" to this irrationality "a ver si logramos entender algo de todo este horror."[54] In the light of this remark, Gwendolyn Diaz's treatment of the novel, though cogent, is ultimately unsatisfactory. If it reflects both disintegration of space, time, and the human personality as well as the deconstruction of language, how can it comment meaningfully on sociopolitical conditions?[55] A little later, the voice of a reasonable onlooker is heard to remark: "Son contingencias socioeconómicas. Contra las que hay que luchar. No contra brujerías inexistentes" (p. 18). One of the aims of *Cola de lagartiga* is to suggest that such a pseudorational approach is a simplification. There is what Valenzuela's narrator/persona calls "la cara oscura de la realidad" (p. 45), which transcends such concrete factors and plays a tragic role in her country's affairs. "Se trata," she writes, "de un perfecto juego especular con un superyó represor en superficie (el gobierno) y su contracara represora bajo tierra (el brujo)" (p. 45). The object of the novel is to bring to consciousness the terrible national id that underlies the repressive national superego. It is not just the latter, but rather the existence of the former, that explains the brutal exercise of arbitrary power together with the irrational admiration of, and submission to, the principle of authority.

El brujo was suggested by Isabel Perón's minister of social welfare, López Rega, who believed in and practised sorcery. He operates in the novel behind the scenes of the current military regime, where, like him, many people are nostalgic for the days of Perón ("el generalísimo" of the novel) and especially of Evita, the national icon. Described as "nuestra contracara" (p. 217), he represents the dark face of Argentine national life, a meta—or intra-historic force, which had manifested itself in the worst aspects of Peronismo and continues to reveal itself in the present. Suffering from alternate paranoia and delusions of grandeur, el brujo as co-narrator scribbles a delirious story in which Valenzuela parodies and satirizes the cruelty, self-interest, ignorance, and folly of the military leaders and the hollowness of their nationalistic rhetoric, but also the gullibility of the masses. His relationship with the regime, whose representatives he despises even as he advises them, while they in turn hate and fear him even as they accept his advice, derives from something in the national psyche. He is "la personificación de la histeria colectiva y sus miedos indefinidos" (p. 43) in a society in which the electorate is characterized by a "yo lábil" (p. 45) and normal political discourse has been replaced by irrational propaganda and violent intimidation. Valenzuela makes its plain that she is writing for a "país de avestruces" (p. 140), unwilling to face its deepest self. But aspects of the novel's ambiguous technique reflect not only the ambiguity of what el brujo represents but also Valenzuela's uncertainty about her role as author "como si una pudiera meterse así no más en otros pellejos cuando el propio se ha vuelto tan incierto" (p. 143). Her intervention at this point both plainly asserts the book's intention and puts the reader on guard against any simplistic account of Argentine political reality. Here as elsewhere she refuses to hide her awareness that writing is not an ideal instrument for the purpose in hand. On the one hand all "reality" is a (fictional) construct of the mind; on the other, the "horror" alluded to in the "Advertencia" demands a reaction.

A feature of the novel is that part of the opposition to el brujo and the military regime that (*faute de pire*) he supports comes from the *Pueblistas*, whose allegiance is ironically to old-style Peronismo and specifically to Evita whose mummified corpse figures significantly in the plot. Just as el brujo steals an index finger from the corpse in order to use its fingerprint to authenticate any document he may concoct, so the *Pueblistas* adore her memory and wish to place her body on public view in a basilica just outside Buenos Aires. They function symbolically in the novel as do the followers of el hermano Francisco in Vargas Llosa's *Pantaleón y las visitadoras*. They stand for a fanaticism that threatens any rational and moderate solution to the nation's difficulties. With el brujo himself they represent two faces of the same problem.

A disconcerting aspect of *Cola de lagartija* is its self-referentiality. We are regularly reminded that this allegory of the Argentine political situation in the post-Peronista period is merely a novel, one over which the narrator has uncertain control. On the one hand el brujo, as counter-narrator, is trying to take over. On the other Navoni, who heads a group of rebels against the regime, refers to the novel in which he figures and invites the narrator to kill off el brujo, as if by incorporating such an episode she could by some magical process affect reality outside the text. Inside the political allegory, in which "magical" (i.e., irrational) forces are highlighted, there seems to be a metaphor in terms of which "magically" writing can play a part in altering reality. This appears to be Valenzuela's answer to her own self-accusation as narrator: "farsante, por creer que la literatura va a salvarnos, por dudar de que la literatura va a salvarnos" (p. 200). In true Post-Boom fashion, the narrator confesses herself trapped between doubts about her understanding of the national situation she is allegorizing, as well as about the value of her writing even as she writes: "Algunos de mis amigos más queridos han sido muertos . . . y yo aquí bromeando, hablando de una telaraña que me atrapa, metiéndome en imágenes poéticas" (p. 217). Yet at the same time she sees the spiderweb image as truly referential to her country; in it the military have woven an immense web in which they and the whole population are caught.

None of this alters the fact that in *Cola de lagartija* Valenzuela, like Martínez Estrada before her, postulates a pathological condition in Argentina, symbolized by el brujo's "enfermedad psíquica" (p. 229). The therapy required is not clear. Navoni "cree en la fuerzas de un pueblo que habría que encauzar" (p. 230). But Valenzuela's narrator/persona seems to regard this as a dream. She refers vaguely to time (p. 238) and to faith (p. 240) and to the chance that her writing may one day bear fruit: "planto la palabra escrita y quizás algún día todo esto sirva de semilla" (p. 245). But in the end, like all those who perceive national problems in terms of mentality, she has no real solution. *Cola de lagartija* appears to contradict, on a basis of more recent experience, Eduardo Mallea's belief in the existence of an uncontaminated "Argentina profunda." The marshy country of the interior, with rottenness just under the surface, which is el brujo's stamping ground, symbolizes the nation, as el brujo himself symbolizes its murky, deluded, collective soul. The novel is overfull of other symbols, which impair its impact. They distract attention from, but do not disguise, its basic negativity. Although el brujo appears to die at the end, releasing only a trickle of blood instead of the river he prophesied, it is hard to disagree with Cordones-Cook's view that the conclusion of *Cola de lagartija* postulates a cyclic reappearance of violence and oppression in Argentina.[56] Similarly, Bruce Gartner asserts that "The novel is permeated by a frustrated resignation to self-perpetuating dictatorial regimes."[57]

Almost all the stories in *Donde viven las águilas* (1983) are of challenging complexity. In the preface to *Open Door* Valenzuela wrote that it took her "long years" to complete the collection and that it was characterized by her love for Latin America and her passion for reinventing its myths.[58] To Montserrat Ordoñez she explained that they were "mitos de generación, de creación, de renacimiento."[59] As such, they are myths, or rather metaphors, of and for our own time. As Martínez suggests, apropos of the title story,[60] they seem to deal with the way people in modern times need to recover the ability to integrate their lives. In "Crónica de Pueblorojo," "Donde viven las águilas," and "Para alcanzar el conocimiento," for example, tribes of people are characterized by some form of lack or loss, or by a false lifestyle or by the need to acquire some new and transforming awareness. In these stories, there tends to be an "above" and a "below" of some other kind of separation that has to be overcome. A paradigmatic story is "Leyenda de la criatura auto-suficiente," in which symbolically identical twins of different sexes finally discover "el cariño, la esperanza, el retorno a las fuentes"[61] and are fused to produce a new being with the attributes of both. The light-house keeper and the sea captain in "Unas y otras sirenas" exhibit a similar duality, but this time it remains unresolved. In the case of the people in "Generosos inconvenientes bajan por el río," what they lack is an object of veneration that, when found, links them to the town nearby. Other people in "Carnaval campero" and "Mercado de pulgas" seem to have lost *joie de vivre*. In "Los engañosos preceptos" what seems to be missing is the capacity to love. At the end of the collection a small group of stories allude to life under the military regime in Argentina during the seventies and early eighties; among them the best is "Los censores," a bitter satire on the thought-police with an impact as strong as any similar stories by Skármeta or Peri Rossi. The collection illustrates Valenzuela's disconcerting ability to shift from the abstract and existential to the horror or pity of the here and now.

*Novela negra con argentinos* (1990), begun in the middle 1980s just after the collapse of the military regime, was originally to be called *El motivo*, for as Valenzuela told Picón Garfield, "That's what is it about: the search for a motive to a crime . . . the assassin and the victim are known, but not the motive of the crime . . . Not even the murderer knows it."[62] But this is not simply a psychological investigation; the key word in the title is *argentinos*. Though set in New York, *Novela negra* is in large part about Argentina. Clues to this abound: at one point Agustín Palant, the killer, reflects after a visit to a *maison de supplice*: "¿Cómo quiere que me guste la tortura sexual consentida cuando vengo de un país donde se torturaba dizque por razones políticas, por el puro horror, con víctimas desesperadas y para nada complacientes? ¿Cómo quiere que me guste o me interese siquiera? Lo que necesito es saber por qué alguien se convierte en torturador, en asesino, saber por qué un ciudadano probo puede un día cualquiera y sin darse cuenta transformarse en un monstruo."[63] By setting the novel in New York after the fall of the military regime in 1983, Valenzuela achieves a distancing effect that allows her to comment metaphorically on the "horror" (p. 73)—once more—haunting her native land. New York is an appropriate setting "porque en ese simple hecho de caminar por las calles nos jugamos la vida" (p. 161), so that it parallels Buenos Aires under military rule.

Two exiled Argentine writers, Roberta and Agustín (who is her friend and occasional lover), set out to try to find an explanation for his apparent "acte gratuite," which is clearly related to the many acts of mindless cruelty and violence in their country's recent past. Alyce Cook, in an unpublished thesis,[64] points out that the novel is arranged symmetrically around part 3, subsection 1, in which the two leave Roberta's apartment, where Agustín had taken refuge after the murder. Up to that point, the novel is static: through the thoughts and words of the two protagonists Valenzuela develops a series of subthemes that extend and complicate that of the couple's basic quest for understanding. These include the relationship of the murder to Agustín's (indirect) experience of terror and torture in Argentina, his own reactions to the crime, and Roberta's reactions both to it and to him. At the same time (since the two appear to be collaborating on a pornographic story) the novel alludes to the relationship of writing to living and of imagination to reality.[65] A recurrent motif in the text is Roberta's pressure on Agustín, who is presented as a "razonador" to "escribir con el cuerpo" (p. 37); that is, apparently, not to write just with his mind but to act out, in some sense, his writing, to base it on life experience. He feels pleased with himself for having done just that, as he makes his way deep into the downtown area where he presently meets and kills Edwina. There is an implicit cause-and-effect here that is never explained. Was Roberta wrong to advocate a closer link with the real, or did Agustín misunderstand her? We never find out. Equally, several times the text seems to imply that what is presented as his action may have been a hallucination suggested by Roberta's urging.

At least twice, including once on the first page, the narrator uses (afresh) the term "la llamada realidad" (pp. 9, 111), which has a double effect. On the one hand, as Magnarelli points out,[66] *Novela negra* continues the Boom's tendency to problematize reality, so that we never can know what happened in Edwina's apartment, let alone why any possible murder might have been committed. The novel's prominent use of the theme of theatricality is clearly relevant to this. On the other hand, the undermining of the real in this case may be a metaphor of the way the military in Argentina had similarly manipulated the frightful reality that they had called into being. The reader is put on notice to read this work both as a conscious piece of fiction and at the same time as a metaphor of an unbearable reality. It is not clear how the two readings can be fully compatible, or what role language plays, when it is explicitly suggested that "la letra impresa lo embadurna todo" (p. 77) and that we can never perceive the frontier between lived reality and written accounts of it (p. 81). As with Skármeta and Allende, we have to read *Novela negra* "as if" it held a mirror up to the real and "as if" language were acceptably referential.

Agustín's evolving reactions to (what he regards as) his crime provide the main focus of interest. The third-person (pseudo?) omniscient narrator informs us on the first page that he had no motive for the crime. But this is followed by the suggestion that it grew out of

Roberta's notion of "escribir con el cuerpo," perhaps because she wanted to use Agustín as the basis for a fictional character. Certainly Roberta, who through her friend Ava Taurel has a suspicious interest in the *maison de supplice*, seems intended to bear some responsibility. The house itself is a fundamental symbol in the text. It stands for a level of order and control even in cruelty and pain that is totally lacking in the real world of antiterrorism. At the same time, while it is a theatricalization, it is based on a hideous reality that lurks in all of us, as the street vendor who sells whips as Christmas presents (p. 189) indicates. Initially Agustín seems to attribute his action to folly, chance, or even literary influences, and he refers to it as "mi tragedia en marcha" (p. 48) as if it were a play he were composing, using reality as its stage. Roberta follows suit (p. 52), and the narrator also appears ready to view the episodes she describes as part of a work of theater whose "second act" begins after Agustín has confessed to Roberta and sought her help. Killing, writing, and loving seem to be mysteriously related (pp. 64, 84).

However, we are perhaps on firmer ground when Agustín mentions that the theater production that preceded the murder "me removió tantas cosas de otros tiempos, Buenos Aires, sabés" (p. 57). A key-sentence in this connection occurs quite early, when Agustín and Roberta discuss the "guerra sucia" in Argentina, and the former asserts baldly "todos somos responsables" (p. 74). It is tempting to see this as the clue to the novel's deepest message: Agustín as an arbitrary murderer and Roberta as his accessory may represent the mass of Argentines who gave at least passive acquiescence to the military. But the question remains: Why did the murder in New York, which may or may not have taken place in reality and which may or may not be a metaphor of many other murders in Buenos Aires, happen? Particularly when the murderer is one who prides himself on his love of order and rationality (p. 93). Agustín remains baffled, aware only that in the depths of himself there are "indescifrables signos" (p. 100) and that his victim may have represented "la persona que es la otra parte de nosotros mismos, la parte que no podemos tolerar ni siquiera admitírnosla" (p. 64). Roberta also recognizes that both she and Agustín have phantoms from the past buried in their minds, connected with cruelty and oppression. By helping him to understand his crime, she also wants to find out something about her own inner self. She relates her willingness to help him to a horror-story she heard as a child in which a victim becomes a victimizer. Magnarelli perceptively interprets this as referring both to our own inconfessable selves and to Argentina.[67] We are back to Valenzuela's obsessive interest in the "dark side" of human nature. More recently María Inés Lagos has argued that "shaking [the two characters'] sense of identity and the belief in the independence of their culture" is the real theme of *Novela negra.* But her analysis minimizes the crime element. Lucille Kerr's assertion that the novel "produces a dialogue with recent Argentine history by calling up a host of horible images of historical violence from beneath the surface of its own quasi-criminal text" is nearer the mark. Cordones-Cook makes a similar point in Lacanian terms.[68]

The second half of the novel is less static. The quest undertaken by Roberta and Agustín continues via a succession of metaphorical episodes situated in unlikely places: a hostel for the homeless, the *maison de supplice*, a couple of strange studio apartments in which odd things happen. But, without reaching any firm conclusions, both the central characters begin to come to terms with their respective situations. Roberta, in true Post-Boom fashion, begins to approach an answer through the emotions, asking herself twice in a few pages, "¿Dónde está el amor en este extraño territorio?" (pp. 114, 137). Soon after, Agustín seems to move in a similar direction in episodes with Baby Jane, the receptionist at the *maison de supplice,* and a casual woman aquaintance who offers him friendship and perhaps more. The tone of the novel has changed. Presently, when the two writers go to a loft party, they are taken up to it in an elevator, accompanied by a "caronte en ascenso" (p. 150). The symbolism is obvious. Less clear are the scene in the loft and the visit to Eduard on the floor above. There is manifest influence of the Cortázar of *62, modelo para armar.* Both novels contain "una búsqueda superior a nosotros mismos como individuos y que nos usa para sus fines," and both illustrate the authors' desire to "intentar una visión diferente de la causalidad."[69] *Novela negra* is an important novel of the Post-Boom because it both affirms and challenges (as does so much of Valenzuela's work) some Post-Boom characteristics. Even as it deals metaphorically with the horror of Argentina's "guerra sucia" and reasserts the central value of human love in a story that alludes to a popular genre, the crime story, it questions the assumptions implicit in using such materials. Once more, the writer is seen as a "mistificador" (p. 179), reality as largely unknowable, causality and human motivation as inexplicable, and language as ambiguous. One could hardly find a better example of the Post-Boom's uneasy relationship with the Boom.

In *Cola de lagartija* Valenzuela's narrator/persona wrote: "Me gustaría meterme en cama por un buen tiempo, desaparecer bajo las mantas, pero la cama es el lugar menos seguro porque en la inmovilidad late el miedo de que tiren la puerta abajo y vengan a buscarme" (pp. 199–200). *Realidad nacional desde la cama* (1990) expands that thought. Originally conceived as a drama,[70] it is an absurdist allegory of what Valenzuela observed when she returned to Argentina in 1989 after ten years abroad. "La señora" returns from the United States and goes for a rest cure to a country club. However, the club adjoins a shanty town, and its golf course has been taken over by a crack regiment of the army as a place to practice maneuvers. Valenzuela's aim is clearly articulated. It is to remind readers of the ongoing threat of right-wing militarism. A key sentence occurs when "la señora," in her double role both as an onlooker whose powers of observation have been sharpened by her life abroad and as a representative of the Argentine middle class, realizes that outside her bedroom there is: "algo que tendría que ver y no quiero, o algo que no quiere ser visto y yo lo intuyo."[71] The sentence alludes both to the concealment of the authoritarian threat and to the unwillingness of the people to perceive it, each dangerously reinforcing the other. These two elements are both developed in a lighthearted but fundamentally serious way. We can never decide whether the danger is greater from a comic-opera military, under Major Vento (i.e., windbag) or from the civilians who are lulled by nationalistic propaganda and media manipulation. "La señora" is symbolically afflicted with a lack of willpower. She can neither get up nor resist the insubordination of her maid (representing the sector of the people who are corruptly in league with the military), the soothing blandishments of the television, or the invasion of her bedroom by the soldiers themselves.

Alongside her Valenzuela places Dr. Alfredi—physician, seducer, and taxi driver—whose shifts of roles imply the failure of the Argentine middle class to play its proper part in the reestablishment and conservation of democracy. His character combines cynical opportunism and trickery with that charm and self-serving guile so characteristic of a bourgeoisie that lacks traditional social values and whose economic wellbeing is under constant threat. We notice, however, that it is he who finally heads off the rebellion with typical deceit and effrontery. Meanwhile the common people, their numbers increased by the pauperization of the lower middle class, are too involved with the struggle to survive to do more than make fun of the major and his myrmidons. They, like their counterparts in Skármeta's *La insurrección*, force young men into military service, where they are abused morally and physically, subjected to mindless slogan-mongering and trained for use against their fellow citizens.

The novel would not have worked as real theater because there is no real element of conflict or suspense. It is dominated, not by clash of forces, but by "la señora's" ambivalent role as observing subject and potentially oppressed object. Throughout the novel she resists thinking or analyzing. By chapter 16, however, she begins to recognize that what she is seeing is a repetitive pattern in recent Argentine history, a pattern she and others have preferred to forget. The message of the novel is hinted at in the phrase "pensar es peligroso, rememorar es mortal, le

dice una voz interior y sabe que puede muy bien ser todo lo contrario . . .
La parte que no quiere pensar se solaza, pero no es ni remotamente su
mejor parte" (pp. 99–100). As elsewhere, Valenzuela is concerned with
her responsibility as a writer to bring to her readers' consciousness an
awareness that has been repressed. Writers cannot solve social problems, but they can keep them before the attention of the public. For that
reason, the novel ends with a question mark over the future of
Argentina.

Only the title story of *Simetrías* (1993) seems directly relevant to
our interests in this chapter.[72] As in "Cambio de armas" it deals with a
woman who is in the hands of a military torturer, who, however, falls
in love with her. The *simetrías* in question have to do with 1947, the
year after Perón's seizure of power in Argentina, and 1977, the year in
which the tale is set. Symbolic of 1947 is the episode of a colonel's wife
who conducts a love affair with an orangutan at the zoo, until her out-
raged husband shoots the animal. Thirty years later the "desaparecida"
in "Simetrías" is shot by the military during her lover's absence, to avoid
scandal. Though the two episodes are explicitly linked, the symbolism is
obscure. Gwendolyn Díaz explains it in Lacanian terms (each of the subjects is "trapped by the structure of its desire") and then in more under-
standable terms of ageless violence resurfacing in modern civilized surroundings.[73] Both the imprisoned victims, the ape and the woman, seem
to have triumphed over their captors and have to be eliminated. It is as
though love were seen to prevail even in the most unusual circumstances
and to threaten every oppressive status quo. In her discussion of *Novela
negra*, Martínez writes, "El amor es poder en tanto libera la 'verdadera
vida' . . . la que bulle más allá o más acá de la organización falagocén-
trico del mundo y que el autor interpreta en términos de 'crueldad.'"[74]
This seems to be the case here. If so, it illustrates afresh the Post-Boom
tendency to revalue human love.

At the deepest level of Valenzuela's work there is an aspiration
toward a positive "order," toward an explicable world in which ideals
of love, justice, beauty, reason, and human solidarity exist and are
meaningful. At the same time, she has an abiding suspicion that that is
not how things are, that "no hay orden," that "nadie se encuentra,"[75]
and that "Lo que no suele haber es eso que andás buscando: una explicación. Nunca vamos a saber exactamente cómo funciona el mecan-
ismo."[76] The quests of her characters to find something satisfying and
life-enhancing tend to fail. The real remains stubbornly resistant and
opaque. Literary activity can deal only in ambiguities. Yet the aspiration
remains, and with it the sporadic assertion that values survive that are
worth struggling for and that contact with some kinds of writing can
make us more self-aware. It is this that situates her in the Post-Boom.

# CHAPTER 6

# *Rosario Ferré*

Despite her rather scanty production in prose (and even some of this, her stories for children, is only marginally relevant for our purposes here),[1] Rosario Ferré (b. 1942) deserves consideration as a Post-Boom figure because of her initially militant feminism, her critical stance toward Puerto Rican society past and present, and her significant contributions to literary criticism from a Post-Boom standpoint. Indeed, an appropriate way to begin considering her as a Post-Boom writer is to glance at her criticism on Felisberto Hernández and Cortázar as short story writers. (Recall that, interestingly enough, Skármeta wrote his master's thesis on Cortázar). Hernández, whose period of production ran from *Fulano de tal* (1925) to *La casa inundada* (1960), belongs really to that crucial decade of the 1940s, which was the gestation period of the Boom. However, as suggested above, Cortázar is, for our purposes, a very significant Boom writer, since he can be clearly seen to move away from the questioning of reality typical of the Boom toward a greater degree of commitment to reality in some of his later work. In that sense he seems relevant to the shift to the Post-Boom. Now, as we have seen in the case of Skármeta, any kind of conscious reaction on the part of the Post-Boom writers to their predecessors is of cardinal importance. Ferré told García Pinto, "Felisberto Hernández was very important for me."[2] She began to study him with Angel Rama in 1971 and wrote her master's thesis on him. In 1986 this became her book *El acomodador*. The comments it contains are at least as significant as those of Skármeta, for instance, on Rulfo.

In the most important passage of *El acomodador* Ferré asserts, "estos cuentos no conllevan ningún mensaje, ni público, ni social, ni psicológico."[3] What this remark tells us is that Ferré was no less aware of the difference between her own work and Hernández's than Skármeta was with respect to Rulfo, or Allende with respect to García Márquez. When she writes in that same passage that Hernández "ordenaba los sucesos de la vida en una nueva secuencia, acomodándolos en una imagen original del 'misterio', que él le imponía al 'misterio' de la realidad," she is referring to that characteristic tendency, inherited by the Boom writers from the 1940s, often to prefer "created" (imaginary or mythicized) reality to the "observed" kind (p. 71). When she suggests that Hernández's "La envenenada" is about writing rather than about an incident (p. 38), she is similarly drawing attention to that greater awareness of the "writerly" quality of texts that reached its peak in the later part of the Boom. The assertion that Hernández's later tales function "sin intentar otra comunicación que la de la escritura misma" (p. 71) could be quoted as showing that Hernández in a sense prefigured Sarduy's ideas a generation later. The confidence with which Ferré discusses the characteristics that she attributes to Hernández's work shows the degree to which she internalized them. At the same time it indicates that she quickly made a conscious decision to move in a different direction. She sees Hernández, in the last analysis, as a writer who, (in contrast to the regionalists' primary preoccupation with exterior reality) was concerned with interior reality. What he discovered there was on the one hand a sense of mystery and on the other a sense of man's existential anguish. Moving away, that is, from the specific problems of Latin American man, Hernández was already writing about universal problems. But, according to Ferré, being "un escritor cobarde" (p. 25), he preferred simply to contemplate the spectacle of mystery and anguish rather than present them conflictively, that is, as things we must struggle to come to terms with. He eludes any attempt to resolve the mystery or attenuate the anguish, taking refuge in a purely literary response to them. At one extreme this leads to the theme of "la literatura como asunto de sí misma" (p. 35), so that some of his tales become, in pre-Boom fashion, aware of themselves as fictions. At the same time, Ferré interprets the neuroticism and even semi-insanity of some of Hernández's characters as responses to a "mundo cruel e inhumano, en el cual las categorías de los valores del espíritu han quedado subvertidas" (p. 59). In the end we can perceive *El acomodador* as a work in which Ferré pays tribute to the renovation of themes and techniques in fiction characteristic of the best writing of the 1940s and of the legacy of that decade to the Boom. As we recognize this, we also recognize the importance of the shift, visible in her own work, away from this earlier kind of writing.

Her *Cortázar: El romántico en su observatorio* (1990),[4] dealing with him significantly as a short story writer, not as a novelist, again has the double interest of being a systematic commentary on a Boom writer by a Post-Boom writer and of being implicitly connected with her own work as a *cuentista*. As she writes in *El árbol y sus sombras*: "Cuando un escritor de ficción escribe sobre una obra literaria que no es la suya, tiene siempre sus razones secretas para hacerlo."[5] What is important is her insistence, from the opening sentence, on Cortázar's evolution toward a more "committed" literary stance. Unlike Hernández's, that is, "un gran número de [sus obras] se encuentran dedicadas al estudio del subconsciente, de ciertos problemas del psique . . . mientras que otras, las de factura más reciente, se encuentran enfocadas hacia la denuncia y el enjuiciamiento de la realidad política latinoamericana" (p. 13). Ferré's whole book is dominated by her intention to see Cortázar as a writer who in a sense links the Boom to the Post-Boom. Thus even his more mysterious and enigmatic stories are seen not so much as designed to undermine our comfortable construct of reality but rather as "un desafío al orden social pequeño burgués" (p. 33).

Of signal importance for our interpretation of her own work is this determination to "relacionar lo irracional con lo social" (pp. 54, 70) in regard to Cortázar. With hindsight we can see that Ferré perceives some of Cortázar's stories as marking a certain shift away from the Boom (compared for example with Hernández's or later with García Márquez's) and thus as indicating the direction some of her own stories were to take. When she writes, for example, apropos of Marini in Cortázar's "La isla a mediodía" (*Todos los fuegos el fuego*) that "la integración a lo irracional, desvinculado de una concepción política e histórica de los movimientos sociales de la época, no es lo suficiente para su salvación" (p. 78), we can see behind the sentence her own awareness, illustrated in "La bella durmiente," of the possibility of integrating the irrational with the need for the liberation of women as one of the "movimientes sociales de la época." In a simplified sense, just as Ferré postulates that in Cortázar's "Reunión" "El desafío de lo irracional se integra ahora al socialismo" (p. 89), we might postulate that in some of the stories of *Papeles de Pandora* (1976) the same challenge is integrated with feminism. Similarly, as we about to see, when Ferré turned toward a set of writers quite unlike Hernández and Cortázar, the shift may have been due in part at least to a certain disappointment with the latter, who in *Octaedro* (1974) turned away again from sociopolitical commitment and what he called "el signo afirmativo"[6] toward pessimism and preoccupation with death and the abyss.

Important as was the impact of Hernández and Cortázar on Ferré, it was not these authors who were uppermost in her mind when she began writing. In "La cocina de la escritura," added to the second edition of *Sitio a Eros* (1986), she refers to "mi debut como escritora" and affirms: "Virginia Woolf y Simone de Beauvoir eran para mí en aquellos tiempos algo así como mis evangelistas de cabecera."[7] The rest of the book makes it plain that these two were not the only women writers she admired or was soon to admire. Others include Mary Shelley, the author of *Frankenstein*, Georges Sand, Silvia Plath, and Julia de Burgos. The very title of the volume echoes the Russian feminist Alexandra Kollentay's *Sitio a Eros alado* (1923). What *Sitio a Eros* makes clear is that it was feminine and feminist writing that was important to Ferré during the 1970s. As is already clear from even a superficial reading of the work of Allende and Valenzuela, feminism is a prominent aspect of the Post-Boom, in line with its general tendency to allow expression to groups (homosexuals, Jews, etc.) that previously had little or no presence in literature. Without restricting consideration of Ferré's work only to her feminism, we must regard her as a particularly prominent representative of the movement's impact on Post-Boom fiction.[8] Jean Franco writes:

> Like French feminists, many Latin American women writers understood their position to be not so much one of confronting a dominant patriarchy with a new feminist position, but rather one of unsettling the stance that supports gender power/knowledge as masculine. This "unsettling" is accomplished in a variety of ways, through parody and pastiche, by mixing genres and by constituting subversive mythologies. The writing of Rosario Ferré, Luisa Valenzuela, Cristina Peri Rossi, Griselda Gambaro, Reina Roffé, Ana Lydia Vega, Albalucía del Angel, Carmen Boullosa, Isabel Allende—for example—corresponds to this project.[9]

Under the influence, then, of a new range of women writers, Ferré rejected the kind of uncommitted approach she associates, as we have seen, with Felisberto Hernández and turned, in a typically Post-Boom way, to a kind of writing which depended on what she called "una voluntad de hacerme útil."[10] Although she insists that this impulse was not consciously present at the moment of writing, we can see that "la voluntad de hacerme útil, tanto en cuanto al dilema femenino, como en cuanto a los problemas políticos y sociales que también me atañen" (p. 22) was a major factor affecting her early work. To this end, she, like Allende, was prepared to incorporate into her work whatever elements were necessary to get her ideas and feelings across. "Como todo artista en fin," she wrote, "la mujer escribe como puede, no como quiere, ni debe. Si le es necesario hacerlo rabiando y amando, riendo o llorando, con resentimiento o irracionalidad, al borde mismo de la locura y de la estridencia estética, lo importante es que lo haga" (p. 39). It is her willingness to accept, if necessary, this "aesthetic stridency" to get her point across that marks Ferré as diverging from the more "writerly" ideals of the Boom writers. It is for this reason that she defends the work of the photographer Tina Modotti from the "juicios estetizantes" of Carleton Beals and praises the "anger" and "ferocity" of Sylvia Plath. Her essay on Plath allows her to clarify the differences she saw between feminine writing in the 1950s and the more openly feminist writing of the 1970s with which she can be associated. For Ferré, the 1970s brought to women (and to women writers especially) a clearer vision of the struggle for sexual freedom, a stronger adhesion to militant feminism, greater mental balance in the face of hostility and adversity, a franker use of direct and even obscene language and the incorporation of humor and optimism into the struggle for womens' rights. These are plainly the characteristics she wished us to see in her own work. They both situate her in the central current of the Post-Boom and provide a good introduction to her first collection of short stories, *Papeles de Pandora* (1976).

Ferré describes the book as "sin duda un libro iracundo, que cae dentro de la categoría de esas obras que pertenecen a la primera avanzada de la lucha feminista."[11] But, she argues, it was precisely her anger that unblocked her and stimulated her to start writing. A version of how she first began to write is contained in the aforementioned essay "La cocina de la escritura." She explains that the first story she ever wrote, "La muñeca menor," was intended to be one that "trataba de la ruina de una clase y de su sustitución por otra, de la metamorfosis de su sistema de valores basado en el concepto de la familia, por unos intereses de lucro y aprovechamiento personales, resultado de una visión del mundo inescrupulosa y utilitaria." However, she tells us, when the story was written, it turned out to be an angry story "sobre la realidad interior de la mujer."[12] In her interview with Wolfgang Binder in 1988 she even went so far as to say: "Lo primero que escribí fue 'La muñeca menor', que podría ser la historia de mi mamá y de sus hermanas. Ellas podrían ser muñecas rellenas de agua y miel."[13]

"La muñeca menor" illustrates the fact that Ferré had already absorbed from Felisberto Hernández the lesson that what is important about fantasy is what it can tell us about reality. In other words, the best fantasies contain a symbolic or allegorical element that transmits meaning. She had found confirmation of this in Todorov and Rabkin's work on the fantastic, while writing her master's thesis (if the published version is a reliable guide) and had also discovered that this meaning was related to "la vertiente nocturna y perversa de la naturaleza humana."[14] At the same time, Hernández's *Las Hortensias*, which contains references to a life-size symbolic doll, may well have suggested the central symbol here. Ferré's story tells of a maiden aunt, a member of the family of a wealthy sugar planter, who is bitten while bathing by a river-prawn. Unable to get the wound to heal, she remains single, making life-size dolls for her nieces, especially on the occasion of their marriages. The youngest niece, unhappily married, turns into a doll, inhabited internally by the symbolic prawns. López's article on the tale explains most of the meaning.[15] The dolls, at one level, clearly refer to the "cosificación" of women by men and their relegation to a merely passive, decorative function. They represent, semi-ironically (since they are filled with honey) a symbolic warning of the destiny which awaits the girls. But in the case of the youngest niece, the situation is more complex. The key statement is that the artificial eyes intended for the dolls must be left in the river so that they can detect the least movement of the prawns.

What these last symbolize is not completely clear. López asserts in a footnote that the original bite represents a violation of the aunt's body and is therefore sexual in nature. But it is possible, in light of the ending, that what the prawns symbolize is painful awareness of the position of women. Equally, they may symbolize female castration, since the bite in question occurs while the aunt is experiencing sensuous feelings while bathing.[16] It is the bite that converts the aunt into a passive, immobilized, decorative "doll" prefiguring the fate of her nieces. Her exploitation by the family doctor, who could have healed the bite but preferred to go on charging his fees, prefigures the exploitation of the youngest niece by his son. When, at the climax, we realize that the prawns have multiplied inside the wife/doll and that now their antennae protrude from her eye sockets, we might conclude that they symbolize her rage at his multiple "violations" of her, financially and morally. This would harmonize López's interpretation with that of Rivera.[17] Alternately, they could symbolize the aunt's revenge on the (implicitly masculine) order of things which "castrates" women, condemning them to unfulfilment. Skinner puts it very well: "In the end his [the husband's] abuse causes his wife to turn into the object he has also wronged—the doll made by her aunt, whose eyes he has gouged out and from which prawns swarm to engulf him in the story's final frightening image. In this way both aunt and niece avenge themselves upon the doctors, father and son, who have professionally and figuratively mistreated them."[18] We notice that whereas in Allende's *La Casa de los Espíritus* the women gradually become more emancipated as the class structure of Chile evolves, in Ferré's tale the youngest niece is even more deliberately exploited by her middle-class husband than her aunt had ever been, since the latter's planter aristocracy family had permitted her to choose her own role and hobby after being bitten. Although the tale clearly looks back to Hernández, its use of fantasy and the doll motif to figure forth angry protest against the role formerly assigned to women in middle- and upper-class Puerto Rican society is totally different from anything in Felisberto and marks afresh the mid-1970s as the moment of the shift to the Post-Boom.

There are, to be sure, elements of ambiguity in "La muñeca menor" that challenge the reader, but the new tone is unmistakable. It illustrates that "acercamiento ético a lo irracional" which Ferré was later to attribute to part of the later work of Cortázar.[19] Once the "ethical" approach (that is, the element of overt social or moral commitment) appears, it tends, as is commonly the case in Post-Boom fiction, to create a certain tension between the "writerly" aspect of the texts and the authorial intentionality. The outcome, as we have seen in Skármeta and Allende, tends to be the production of works that are more reader-friendly.

That this is also true of Ferré can be recognized if we glance at "Mercedes-Benz 220 SL" also in *Papeles*. Probably the most important single statement by Ferré that marks her as a Post-Boom writer is her remark to García Pinto, after mentioning that she had learned what she knows of fictional technique from Boom writers like Onetti, Vargas Llosa, and Cortázar, that "I'm interested in pieces whose narrative structure is anecdotal . . . what I'm doing now [in the mid-eighties] and what I've done in *Papeles de Pandora* is a logical linking of cause and effect."[20] This is in total contradiction to Cortázar's famous assertion in "Algunos aspectos del cuento" that his tales were specifically intended to undermine our confidence in being able to interpret reality in terms of "relaciones de causa a efecto."[21] It amounts, like Skármeta's endorsement of "esta realidad que por comodidad llamamos realidad," to a return (in some degree) to referentiality, so that one can comment on it from a Post-Boom "ethical" standpoint. "Mercedes-Bentz 220 SL" is a clear example. It is completely linear in structure; its central symbol, the expensive car, is wholly unambiguous; and the cause-and-effect approach is not merely obtrusive but (as often in Allende) actually melodramatic.

On the one hand the story contains a savage attack upon the wealthy Puerto Rican bourgeoisie, with its "unscrupulous and utilitarian" outlook, which Ferré refers to in "La cocina de la escritura." To that extent it is a characteristically "committed" Post-Boom story, similar to others we can readily find in Skármeta, Allende, or Valenzuela, one primarily involved with its own time and place. The couple at the center of the story, Papi and Mami, are similar to the parents of María de los Angeles in "La bella durmiente" as we shall presently see: he, full of the arrogance of newly acquired wealth; she, worried about his outlook (in this case) but ready to accept the benefits of his success, symbolized by the luxury car he has just acquired. On the other hand, however, the epigraph to the tale, taken from Apollinaire, alerts us to its second theme, which is that of separation and togetherness: the son of the couple in the car has left them, rejecting both their lifestyle and the parents themselves, but he has found fulfilment living in poverty with a young woman of the people. For her part, Mami herself recognizes a barrier between herself and her husband, reflecting that she was "siempre a su lado y siempre sola"[22] until her son was born. In the central episode, Papi, driving too fast, runs into and kills his son, who was on his way to visit his parents. The vengeance of the son's young partner is to inform Mami of the death and burial of the victim, without revealing his identity. Thus the impact of the story changes after the accident, which divides it into two parts. Both halves are ironic. But whereas the irony of the first half (that the outward sign of Papi's success and the source of his infantile happiness, the car, causes the death of his son) is cheap and obvious, the irony of the second half, which leaves the parents once more enjoying the car and their way of life, unaware of what has happened, is much more effective.

Like "La Bella Durmiente," *Maldito amor*, and "El libro envenenado," discussed below, "Mercedes Benz 220 SL" illustrates Ferré's ambivalence about the work ethic: she recognizes in it the dynamic of change in the new Puerto Rico but also tends to associate it with greed, *gringuismo*, and dehumanization. Like Trueba in Allende's *La Casa de los Espíritus*, Papi instinctively accepts a kind of social Darwinism: the survival of the fittest through their own efforts: "este carro es del fuerte dondequiera que vayamos nos dará la razón por eso lo compré, Mami, porqué pendejos te crees que trabajo como un burro de ocho a ocho" (p. 46). This he combines with disdain for the undeserving masses of his fellow-countrymen: "esta chusma," "pueblo de cafres." Mami endorses his outlook: "la verdad que trabaja tanto, el pobre, se lo merece no hay derecho a matarse trabajando sin tener una recompensa" (p. 47). Similarly, after the visit of her son's lover, Mami refers to her merely as "la tipa" (and to her son, unwittingly, as "el tipo," pp. 61–62), suspects her of intending blackmail, and finally dismisses the visit from her mind with the reflection "este mundo está lleno de canallas" (p. 62). Here, as elsewhere, we perceive Ferré's biting contempt for the newly enriched bourgeoisie of Puerto Rico. By contrast, the son is described by his father as "una primadona que no da un tajo" (pp. 41–42) and we learn from Mami that he left the family because of disgust with his parents' exclusive dedication to wealth and social prestige.

At one level, the young couple, presented through the thoughts and actions of the girl, offer a refreshing contrast to the parents. The passages that evoke the life and love of the two young people are focalized on the girl, and their tone is carefully tinted here and there with poetic emotion in order to stress (perhaps, as so often in Ferré, a shade too explicitly) the different outlook of the young people: "Fíjate en la diferencia entre ellos y nosotros floreciendo ahora debajo de tus manos cultivando anémonas ocultas en los orificios de tu cuerpo cultivando corales en tu piel cada pétalo sedimentando lento supurando púrpura afelpada en los oídos . . ." (p. 51). Once more, as in Allende and Skármeta, we are immediately conscious of the Post-Boom's neoromantic rehabilitation of the love ideal.[23] But the tale's ideological thrust demands that the idyll be destroyed. Ferré's problem here is to avoid the sentimentality and bathos that constantly threaten the treatment of love in a movement part of whose objective was to recapture a slightly less sophisticated audience than that to which Boom writing often appealed. She achieves this avoidance by incorporating into the presentation of the son's partner and her thoughts a high level of symbolic foreshadowing of the unhappiness to come. The blue (not red) roses on the cup the girl is washing prefigure the blue and red color-symbolism of the window panes in the room where the girl wreaks her vengeance on Mami; the sinister green detergent liquid is (again overexplicitly) associated with the girl's unexplained "miedo"; her burial of beloved objects during her childhood contains an obvious allusion to her burial of her lover; above all, the symbol of a wall of crystalline ice at first enfolding the lovers, preserving their love for ever, then separating him from her, is highly effective. So, too, is the tale's tendency to slip easily from third-person narration to interior monologue and reported speech. But, like the use of fantasy in "La muñeca menor," the effect created is intended not to undercut our sense of the "reality" of the events but rather to figure it forth more effectively.

What links "Mercedes-Benz 220 SL" to the more feminist stories in *Papeles de Pandora* is, of course, the theme of power, whether expressed in terms of social relationships or of individual ones. The two most powerful feminist tales in the collection, "Cuando las mujeres quieren a los hombres" and "La bella durmiente," deal with the power of a patriarchal society to affect in a negative way the lives of women. As in most feminist writing, the aim is to sensitize readers of both sexes to the fact that patriarchy is not something inherent in the way things are but a sociohistorical phenomenon, susceptible of being changed. To bring this point home Ferré takes over from Hernández and Cortázar (and from fantastic literature in general) the motif of the double, putting it into a different context. Lagos-Pope comments à propos of "Cuando las mujeres": "A través del uso del doble Ferré ilustra la alienación que produce una relación totalizadora y dependiente en la que la mujer centra su vida en el hombre hasta el punto de olvidarse de sí misma."[24] The story tells of the two women, wife and mistress, of a wealthy Puerto Rican, each of whom is a kind of "double" of the other, as they discover after his death. The theme is that individual personality is largely socially constructed and a function of one's class situation and (in Puerto Rico and elsewhere) of one's color.[25] This means that in the upper echelons of (white) society certain aspects of female behavior, especially sexual behavior, are repressed but do not for that reason disappear. At the same time, in the lower echelons of (black) society there is a repressed desire for respectability and social status. Both may produce effects that threaten the status quo. The key quotations are close to the beginning of the tale: "Nosotras, tu querida y tu mujer, siempre hemos sabido que debajo de cada dama de sociedad se oculta una prostituta . . . nosotras hemos sabido que cada prostituta es una dama en potencia, anegada en la nostalgia de una casa blanca como una paloma que nunca tendría . . ." Later in the same paragraph we read: "nos habíamos estado acercando, nos habíamos estado santificando la una a la otra sin darnos cuenta, purificándonos de todo aquello que nos definía, a una como prostituta y a otra como dama de sociedad" (p. 27). The two quotations imply a balance. But what critics of the story have overlooked is that it is not maintained.

We must, as always, look at the technique if we are to perceive how the story's ideological thrust tends to simplify the issues and to compromise the values of ambiguity and irony we learned to prize in the work of the Boom writers. The central symbol, the house in which the wife, Isabel Luberza, has always lived, turns from virginal white to sensual pink as it ceases after her husband's death to be an upper-class mansion and becomes an expensive whorehouse. In addition, the interior monologues of the two women, which make up the bulk (but not all) of the text, are not "spoken" at the same time. Those of the wife belong to the period after her husband's black mistress, Isabel la Negra, a famous whore and whorehouse madam, has come to share the house, under the terms of the husband's will. But those of the mistress belong to a moment after the wife's death. That is, Isabel la Negra (who symbolizes women's power over men exercised through her sexuality) outlives Isabel Luberza (who symbolizes conventionality) and triumphs over her. We, as readers, especially as feminine readers, are expected to draw the appropriate conclusion.

The opening of the tale establishes the ambiguous love-hate "doubling" relationship between the two women. But then we notice that their eventual meeting is told from the viewpoint of the mistress, who is next developed as a representative of female power in contrast to male sexual timidity and weakness. Only after this do we gain insight into the marriage relationship of the Luberzas and the gradual ousting of the wife by the mistress, not only in terms of sexuality but also in terms of male social standing (Isabel la Negra becomes president of the Junior Chamber of Commerce!). The interpretation proposed by María Solá, is that the two women, at the end of the tale, "se unen mágicamente, quedando una sola persona donde antes hubo dos" and that this represents the triumph of Isabel Luberza, the wife, over Isabel la Negra, the mistress. This hopelessly misreads the text.[26] Clearly we are not in the presence here of a "realistic" story, but in that of a satire designed to encourage us to withdraw our allegiance from conventional and moral values. The point is that expressed by a character in Gustavo Sainz's *Obsesivos días circulares*: "Si no podemos hacer la revolución social, hagamos la revolución moral."[27] If one can undermine acceptance of conventional bourgeois values, one has taken a major step toward changing the power-structure of society. But as in all satire, the tendency is toward exaggeration. The two Isabels are myths: the society lady and the black whore, brought into an artificial relationship in order for one to put down the other through a kind of feminized version of *machismo*.

"La bella durmiente," perhaps Ferré's most famous story, is altogether different. Niether of the two Isabels in "Cuando las mujeres" is really rebellious or liberates herself from servitude to men, and the situation which triggers the story is set up by a man. Even the self-assertive Isabel la Negra, empowered by her sexuality, needs men to operate on and must have learned from a man initially. But María de los Angeles's determination to be herself is expressed through dance, an autonomous activity needing no partner. However, it is incompatible with a conventional marriage and with motherhood. As in "Cuando las mujeres," the story is based on the contrast betwen upper-class proprieties, as they affect women, and female self-assertion. María and her double and role-model, Carmen Merengue, a high-wire circus performer, both represent the story's theme: rebellious female self-assertion. The other characters—her parents, the mother superior of the convent school María had attended, her husband, the local gossip-columnist—all stand for repression.

The story begins with a triggering device, a couple of poison-pen letters about her behavior, dated late September 1972,[28] to María's husband. Then follows a series of flashbacks to the time when María's scandalous attachment to dancing first became apparent, to her engagement and marriage, and to the birth of her child. Then we have a flash-forward to 1973, when, as a result of the letters (apparently written by María herself in order to precipitate the situation), her husband finds her in a compromising situation, kills her, and dies himself. A letter from María's father to the mother superior fills in details and reveals a cover-up, but the tale ends with a stream-of-thought excerpt revealing that María had brought about her own death as a final act of defiance against a repressive, patriarchal society. Apter-Cragnolino writes: "la protagonista, desesperada entre el ser y el deber ser que le imponen, busca su propia muerte en un acto que expresa además la ira y el deseo de venganza contra aquellos que se ensañan contra ella para obligarla a un estilo de vida que choca con su vocación."[29] Unlike Isabel la Negra, who in "Cuando las mujeres" refuses to compromise and fights men successfully both by exploiting her sexuality and by becoming a wealthy business woman, María accepts a compromise when she marries but hopes to salvage her ideal of self-expression. But the male world, symbolized by her husband backed by the rest of society, rejects the compromise and forces María to destroy both her husband and herself.

Three features of the tale call for comment. First, the supporting women characters: Apter-Cragnolino points out that Carmen Merengue was the same age as María when she broke off her liason with the latter's father to put her vocation first. It is seeing her perform that provides the pivotal moment in the tale as it stimulates María to rebel against her husband. Opposed to Carmen is María's mother, who accepts the traditional role of wife and mother (and its rewards in terms of wealth and social position). They represent the two options between which María seeks to find a compromise. Alongside them, the mother superior perceives ultimate self-fulfilment only in conventional religious terms, whereas María achieves an implicitly more fulfilling, semireligious extasy through dancing. She refuses to have her son baptised and uses religious practices to enhance her erotic pleasure while committing adultery just before her death. The male characters, for their part, are treated rather reductively as examples of a patriarchy that in reality has found subtler ways of exercising its power than they do. Second, a further aspect of the technique: we notice the marked contrast between the "splintered mirror" effect created by the nonlinear narrative together with the shifts from conventional forms (letters, articles) to stream-of-thought, on the one hand, and the story's unambiguous message, on the other. Vélez suggests ingeniously that "The contrast between the din of the voice of patriarchy . . . and the muffled cry of the protagonist is made possible by a narrative strategy that provides access to both." She goes on to suggest that beneath "the use of multiple narrative structures to undermine the validity of any one message," we find "a multiplicity of possible readings."[30] But this is simply not true. Not for nothing does Ferré mention Vargas Llosa as having taught her things about narrative technique. As in his *Pantaleón y las visitadoras* (1983), which had used a similar variety of narrative devices, there is really only one way to read the story. We are not in the presence now of a multifaceted reality; if we were, the point of the story would be lost. What is valid, on the other hand, is Vélez's observation that the stream-of-thought technique expresses the fact that María is mute: she has no public voice (p. 76). Finally we must notice the very effective use of references to Hans Andersen's *The Red Shoes* and the ballets *Coppelia*, *The Sleeping Beauty*, and *Giselle* as part of the symbolic commentary that figures forth (ironically in the case of the title ballet) María's situation.

The story that, Ferré tells us in *Sitio a Eros*, she would have liked to write, but that was supplanted by "La muñeca menor," eventually became her historical novella, *Maldito amor* (1988). It was to be about, she asserts, "lo que significó para nuestra burguesía el cambio de una sociedad agraria, basada en el monocultivo de la caña, a una sociedad urbana o industrial; así como la pérdida de ciertos valores que aquel cambio había conllevado a comienzos del siglo."[31] A glance at the second chapter of her *Cortázar* makes its clear, however, that behind the social implications of the story lies a line of development that reaches back through Cortázar's "Casa tomada" (*Bestiario*, 1966) to Poe's "The Fall of the House of Usher." "En ambos cuentos," Ferré writes, "la casa es vista como símbolo de un orden social absoluto, condenado a desaparecer, y el incesto de los hermanos es una segunda prueba de la necesidad de un cambio social que elimine a las familias 'decadentes.'" In each case, she points out, there exists a "doble transgresión social (el vivir de acuerdo a una clase social cuya existencia no tiene ya razón de ser, porque no contribuye al futuro de la sociedad, y el vivir una relación malsana)" (p. 48). The relevance of these remarks to *Maldito amor* is patent.

In her interview with García Pinto, Ferré explained that the administrations of Luis Muñoz Marín in Puerto Rico (1948–64) "initiated a series of key social reforms and changed the island's economic structure. It was transformed from a feudal agricultural society to an industrial one, because of American influence."[32] In the course of this process, her mother's family of sugar cane planters became impoverished because of their refusal to sell their land despite their inability to compete with North American companies. *Maldito amor* is a brief saga of family collapse, in which Ferré draws on her memories of her family's history. Her feelings about what happened are deeply ambivalent: "Perhaps," she told García Pinto, "deep down what I'm trying to do is recover a world that has disappeared, even though its a world based on such tremendous injustice that I'm glad its changed" (p. 87). We should notice that this ambivalence is not concerned with the reality or otherwise of what is described, as is so often the case with Cortázar or other Boom writers in the wake of Borges. Nothing could be further than *Maldito amor* from the "vacío histórico" which Ferré complains about with respect to some sectors of Cortázar's work. It is a novella that is deeply, but not exclusively, concerned with rapid social change at a particular time and place in Spanish America, not unlike elements in later chapters of Allende's *La Casa de los Espíritus*. This is precisely what marks it as a Post-Boom work. The ambivalence lies in Ferré's feelings toward the process of change, which she saw happening in part in the "real" reality of her own family, and which she incorporated into the thematic content of the three short stories ("El regalo," "Isolda en el espejo," and "La extraña muerte del capitancito Candelario") that were published along with *Maldito amor*. Thus the narrative strategy is intended to cast doubt not on the story of the family's collapse but only

on any simplistic interpretation of it. We should also notice her comment
to Binder that "*Maldito amor* es una reescritura de una novela romántica,
la parodia de *María* de Jorge Isaacs."[33]

The text begins with a pair of inverted commas that are easy to
overlook. But they tell us something crucial: the magniloquent description of the district of Guamaní, where the action is situated, and the
novelesque account of the courtship and marriage of Doña Elvira and
Don Julio, together with the admiring references to their son Ubaldino,
("nuestro egregio procer," "nuestro procer patrio")[34] are extracts from
an exaltedly romantic and idealized *novelón*, in the process of being
written by Don Hermenegildo, the family lawyer.[35] We later learn that
that his narratives are not just passion-filled romances but that in each
"siempre defiende la patria a brazo partido" (p. 38). For him, therefore,
Don Julio's defence of his sugar plantation against the Americans is not
merely commendable but even heroic. Similarly when Ubaldino succeeds
in hanging on to the property for another generation, Hermenegildo
regards his action as representing "el momento más glorioso en la vida
de Ubaldino de la Valle" (p. 52). Chapters 1, 2, 4, and 6, all extracts
from the *novelón*, represent one (falsified) face of the family's history.
But the remainder of the text, narrated by a series of different voices
with Hermenegildo providing continuity, deconstruct this account and
present a quite different one. It is one in which Don Julio, far from being
a romantic Prince Charming, is a mulatto on the make; his son Ubaldino
is a political hack, a syphilitic, and the seducer of his son's wife, Gloria;
while the son in question is (perhaps falsely) accused by his younger
brother Arístides of being a passive homosexual, reduced to purchasing
sexual favors from his father's employees. At the novella's climax we
hear the version of Gloria as she symbolically burns down the plantation mansion. Hermenegildo emerges as a liar whose novel exalting the
family has been brought to nothing; Arístedes has calumniated his
brother and perhaps (along with Ubaldino) brought about his death;
and the lovely Guamaní evoked originally is populated by peasants who
die like flies from tuberculosis, hookworm, and undernourishment. The
love between Don Julio and Doña Elvira, far from being an idyll, was,
in every sense, a "maldito amor." All Hermenegildo's traditionalist values are subverted (but not necessarily replaced by better ones). An interesting footnote to the novella is provided by an interview in which Ferré
asserted that the *maldito amor* referred to in the title is in fact "el que
siente el puertorriqueño por su patria."[36] If that is the case, we should
have to interpret the story's deep theme as being the disenchantment of
Puerto Ricans when their patriotic vision of their homeland comes into
contact with its political and social realities and is demythified.

More explicitly connected with modern Puerto Rico and the question of its independence from the United States is "La extraña muerte del capitancito Candelario" published along with *Maldito amor*. Part of the inspiration for the tale is clearly René Marqués's famous essay "El puertorriqueño dócil" (1962). There Marqués sharply criticizes his fellow Puerto Ricans for passively accepting their dependence on the United States. He argues that, while sporadic violence erupts amid the resignation that characterizes most Puerto Ricans, it is usually directed against the wrong people and (since what it expresses is frustration, not real commitment to independence) it may even take a suicidal form. Ferré imagines a Puerto Rico from which the United States has decided to withdraw. News of the decision divides the islanders into rock-music supporters and salsa supporters, the former attempting to cling to the United States connection, the latter committed to independence. Between the two groups, Ferré situates the commander of the special police corps, Candelario, who, influenced by family tradition and training, has accepted his post from the pro–United States party that controls the corps but rejects the party's authoritarian and repressive mentality. Ambushed by the independence faction and deserted by his own men, he pays with his life for his refusal to embrace the ideology of either party.

This is clearly a classic example of the "national allegories" that Fredric Jameson, as we shall see in the final chapter, regards as typical of Third World writing. What is interesting about it, in contrast to that of cognate works by Skármeta or Allende (but not Valenzuela: cf. *Realidad nacional desde la cama*) is Ferré's sarcastic tone. Unlike Cuba, which seized its independence by force of arms from a United States dominated dictatorship, Puerto Rico is presented as having independence forced upon it. But the result is the same: a shift from one oppressive regime to another, and from economic dependence to economic collapse. The key to Candelario's representativeness within the tale's allegorical structure is his "convicción profunda respecto a la naturaleza tímida y apocada de su pueblo" (p. 174) borrowed from Marqués. Apart from this, Ferré presents Candelario as essentially a brave and honorable man and an idealist, albeit an "idealista triste" (p. 175), saddened by what he regards as the constitutional unwillingness of his people to fight for independence instead of waiting for it to be thrown to the island contemptuously by Congress in Washington.

At first sight, therefore, what we seem to have here is an example of political melodrama that reminds us of Allende's early novels. Candelario appears to be a scapegoat for the greed and cowardice of the upperclass Puerto Ricans from whom he stems. When he is murdered at the end of the tale by his former friend and subordinate, Lieutenant Fernández, the latter reproaches him for his refusal to take sides in the conflict and suggests that the factional violence now flaring in the island indicates that "el pueblo no era tan manso como parecía" (p. 201). Read this way, the tale would imply that Candelario's class allegiance and inherited cultural prejudices blind him to the realities of the Puerto Rican problem and lead him to his death. But there are difficulties with such a reading. Candelario is shown as ingenuous, but not by any means uncritical of the pro–United States party on whom his job depends. He despises the industrialists who transfer themselves and their capital to the United States instead of trying to make independence work. Equally, he opposes the use of force to maintain order among a divided and panicky population. His secret antagonist, Fernández, is cast as a devious, rather coarse-grained, and treacherous figure whose organization of a massacre—the first victim of which is Candelario—is the prelude to the establishment of a one-party, dictatorial regime.

One more we are confronted by an essentially ambiguous tale. Candelario (like Ferré) belongs to the upper class, Fernández to the slums. The former, until just before his death is all but impotent, while his lieutenant has no sexual inhibitions. Fernández enjoys salsa; Candelario regards it as nonmusic and preferes the classics. It appears that Candelario's characteristics are those of an effete, overcivilized oligarchy, with little capacity for practical political action. Fernández's seem to be those of a working class prepared to use any methods to attain its ends. Only with a working-class girl does Candelario recover his virility. But we are not in the presence here of a text like Skármeta's *Soñé que la nieve ardía* in which virility is identified with political activity on the Left. The cold-blooded murder that begins the rebellion and the illiberal regime to which it leads make it clear that Ferré, while realizing that Puerto Rico must work out its own salvation, fears that in the process some ideal values will be trodden underfoot without a corresponding gain in liberty.

The effect of her allegorical intention is to make the tale structurally ill-proportioned, with a long thematic introduction on Puerto Rican independence and a brief reference to Candelario's murder followed by an extended central section establishing the contrasting roles and representative significance of the two central figures. After an interlude concerned with Candelario's impotence, the murder of Candelario and the massacre of the rockmusic supporters suddenly bring everything we have been told into dramatic focus. Not enough of the thematic content is expressed in action. Not only is everything prior to the climax simply build-up, but the build-up itself sends mixed signals to the reader. Ferré does not quite succeed in harmonizing her endorsement of Puerto Rican independence with her reservations about the means of obtaining it and the subsequent objectives. Even so, *inter alia* because of its political theme and its use of pop music to express contrasting allegiances, this is a clearly recognizable Post-Boom text.

A similar ambivalence is visible in a much later story, "El libro enve-nenado" from *Las dos Venecias*.[37] Once more the tale is concerned with a landowning family, now impoverished, represented by Rosaura and her father Don Lorenzo. The latter, to improve the family's lot, marries his dead wife's dressmaker, Rosa, whose hard work in fact restores financial independence to her thriftless husband and stepdaughter. On this showing, she ought to be the heroine; but this is not at all the case. On the contrary, she is depicted by the main narrator in a generally dis-agreeable light, not so much as mercenary but rather as one whose coarseness and materialism stands in contrast to the literary culture and tastes of the other two. Like the mansion in *Maldito amor,* Don Lorenzo's house in "El libro envenenado" is a symbolic space. It stands for the island's past and lost independence "porque sobre sus almenas había tomado lugar la primera resistencia de los criollos a la invasión hacía ya casi cien años" (p. 136).

In the novella, Gloria burns the house down, symbolically attempt-ing to destroy a past, the memory of which she finds unbearable. There, we seem to be intended to endorse her action. Here, on the other hand, when Rosa sells off Lorenzo's family heirlooms and insists that he sell the plantation house to the local (we assume *nouveau riche*) mayor, instead of turning it into a museum dedicated to the island's sugar-pro-ducing past, we seem to see another example of her insensitiveness. For this she is punished, ironically through contact with a book whose pages are poisonous. We are evidently in the presence of an allegory: Don Lorenzo, who holds out as long as he can against selling the family prop-erty and sets out to write a book lamenting the lost national identity of Puerto Rico, but who is presented as inept, though warm hearted, stands for unreconstructed, traditionalist Puerto Ricans. His daughter, denied a suitable education because of her poverty, who takes refuge in literature (reading, instead of struggling against her situation), stands for a younger generation that prefers dreamy passivity to action. Rosa, mak-ing money, but making it by flattering the vanity of a tasteless bour-geoisie rather than in a more productive way, stands for wealth-creation that is not socially beneficial and demeans the maker.

At first sight, then, "El libro envenenado" seems more pessimistic than *Maldito amor*. But once again we must take into account the tech-nique. The epigraph (from *The Arabian Nights*) is a clue: Scheherazade, we recall, at a certain point begins to tell her own story; here Rosa, pick-ing up by chance a book of stories given by her husband to Rosaura before he died, begins to read her own story. It all seems very Borgesian. But in fact it is quite different. What delighted Borges about Scheherazade's suddenly beginning to tell the story of *The Arabian Nights* in *The Arabian Nights* itself is the idea of circularity and the notion of *mise en abîme* that undercuts our sense of reality. Ferré, on the other hand, is concerned not with the mystery of the real but with re-cycling this Borgesian motif so as to grant Rosa the possibility of com-menting on the account of her actions as she reads it. It is her comments that create the story's ambiguity and, by providing (as in *Maldito amor*) another version of the events, express Ferré's own ambivalence. At first, surprised by and indignant at what she is reading, she soon reacts criti-cally, contradicting the presentation both of her behavior and that of Lorenzo and Rosaura. As she does so, she not only comes alive as a character, partially (though not completely) justifying her own actions but also questioning, for example, Lorenzo's longing for Puerto Rico's independence and his anti-Americanism, as well as drawing attention to the passivity and indolence of Rosaura.

Nonetheless, handling and reading the book brings about her death, presumably from licking her finger that has touched the poisoned ink of the pages containing her story, ink that is the color of the guava preserve that Rosaura had earlier spilled on her stepmother's dress. How are we to understand this? Not, surely, in terms of the kind of "magical" ele-ments that we find, for instance in some of Fuentes's stories. This is not a wierd story concerned with undercutting our comfortable presupposi-tions about the real; it is an allegorical story about modern Puerto Rico. The "magical" ending is designed to fit the specificity of the theme. Rosa, despite making some shrewd remarks in her own defence, remains a disagreeable figure. Her only acceptable qualities are her practicality and her capacity for work. Apart from these she is greedy, unscrupu-lous, manipulative, and self-pitying. That is to say: however much at the allegorical level Don Lorenzo incarnates regrettable aspects of the past of Puerto Rico, and his daughter a disappointing response to the pre-sent, Rosa does not represent an appropriate future. This is not only because her work is a luxury occupation that panders to the vanity and self-importance of a parasitic class, the wives of the *nouveaux riches*, on whom Rosa is dependent even as she scorns them; but also because her "practical" outlook causes her to reject her own roots. When she forces Don Lorenzo to sell his property, having previously sold off his family heirlooms, when she scolds Rosaura for wasting her time on literature and even refuses to cook traditional Puerto Rican dishes, she is turning her back on a time-honored way of life, with its own pattern of values, without having anything more valid to put in its place.

Ferré does not idealize the Puerto Rican cultural tradition and even makes gentle fun of Puerto Rican nationalism, but she is not prepared to advocate abandoning the former (as so many have done) merely for personal gain. When Rosa is poisoned by one of the books she had viewed with contempt, while in the process of reading it primarily for what it might suggest as a means of satisfying her own vanity (styles of dress borrowed from the illustrations), we are intended to see culture—especially literary culture—taking its revenge on *mere* practicality with selfish ends. The ending of the tale, that is, illustrates the very process that is taking place as the reader reads it: literature reacts against those forces that underrate its influence. The key element in the allegory that the tale contains is the book, symbolizing the writer's task, which is seen in mainstream Post-Boom terms as (ideally) acting at the social and national level to destroy deleterious elements in outlook and values. Jean Franco's suggestion, that the ending might symbolize "the conspiracy of the old aristocracy that traps the entrepreneur Rosa in its deathly web,"[38] offers another possible interpretation.

Long ago Henry James wrote to Edith Wharton: "There it is around you. Don't pass it by—the immediate, the real, the only, the yours."[39] It is clear from her critical writings that Ferré consciously chose to strike out in a different direction from Felisberto Hernández and Cortázar, who were early influences, toward areas of "the real" that she, like other writers of the Post-Boom, felt were more "immediate," more "hers": Feminism and the situation of Puerto Rico in particular, though, particularly in the case of the latter, she is careful to avoid taking a simplistic stance.[40] Like Skármeta and Sainz, she inherits the Boom's quasi-obsession with language, though never to the extent of seriously questioning its referential function. Like Valenzuela, she sporadically continues the Boom's experiments with narrative technique, but again, never to the point at which fragmentation or allegorical structure seriously compromise her grip on what is, in the Jamesian sense, "around" her. María Solá correctly situates her among the group of women writers in Puerto Rico, and by extension in other parts of Latin America, who have brought a new vision to fiction in the continent. If, as seems to be the case, she has in middle life taken to writing in English, one may be forgiven for contemplating this development with regret.

# CHAPTER 7

# *Gustavo Sainz*

It is appropriate to conclude this brief survey of representative Post-Boom writers with Sainz for three main reasons. With *Gazapo* (1965) he, along with Skármeta and others, was influential in introducing the important new Post-Boom theme of youth and urban adolescent outlook into Spanish American fiction. With *La Princesa del Palacio de Hierro* he endows the Post-Boom with its finest piece of comedy. Finally, with his most extensive novel so far, *A la salud de la serpiente* (1988), he offers a novel that is in some ways a compendium of Post-Boom characteristics and stands as an exceptionally representative work of the movement.

In 1960 Sainz was twenty years old and had already begun the first draft of what was to become *Gazapo*. Looking back some years later, he declared that around that time, with the emergence of Fuentes, "Desde luego y de golpe la novela representativa del país se volvió obsoleta."[1] Later he was to repeat that that it was Fuentes's early work that made him decide to become a writer,[2] though it is important to recall (in the light of what was said about him in chapter 2) that David Viñas was also an important influence.[3] We should notice that Fuentes and Viñas are more than a decade older than Sainz, who is an exact contemporary of Skármeta. Like Skármeta, he began publishing in the 1960s, the decade par excellence of the Boom, but did not fully develop until the next decade, that of the beginning of the Post-Boom.

*Gazapo*, which the author/narrator describes in *A la salud* as "una novela que él [Sainz] tildaba de ensayo narrativo"[4] and whose original title, perhaps in homage to Dylan Thomas's *Portrait of the Artist as a Young Dog* (Thomas is mentioned in the text of *A la salud*) was *Los perros jóvenes*, marks in some important respects a turning point in modern Mexican fiction. It is, in Sainz's own words, "un reportaje vívido del sistema de vida de jóvenes de la clase media de esta ciudad de México," whose chief merit was "haber incorporado a la literatura mexicana el lenguaje cotidiana de la gente común y corriente, con todas sus expresiones características, sus matices, sus significados."[5] Sainz's fellow novelist José Agustín writes: "the story . . . basically deals with the initiation rite of a young man into maturity. Sainz was in his early twenties when he wrote the novel, and was, in Mexico, one of the first authors to write about youth while still being young himself . . . he displays a freshness, a vitality, an authenticity that is almost impossible to reproduce as an adult." But he goes on to point out that the novel's funniness and irreverence produced a sense of outrage among older people.[6] It was an outrage Sainz was to satirize mercilessly in *A la salud*, still thumbing his nose at the middle class a quarter of a century later.

It was conceived and perhaps begun in 1958 under the stimulus of Fuentes's *La región más transparente*, which appeared that year, and was largely rewritten and completed in 1962–63 when Sainz had a fellowship at the Centro de Escritores in Mexico City. In February 1966, a couple of months after its appearance, Sainz explained to Emmanuel Carballo that it has two plotlines, which are closely connected: the first concerns the unsuccessful attempt by the central character, Menelao, to break away from his family and live on his own; the second, equally unsuccessful, is "la crónica desenfadada de una seducción"[7] involving his girl-friend Gisela. Sainz's remarks and Carballo's comments situate *Gazapo* very close to Skármeta's early work. Both writers portray the lives of young, relatively carefree and irresponsible, but highly intelligent, lower-middle-class protagonists. Those of Sainz reject the stifling, hypocritical, moralistic, and repressive world of adults in Mexico, just as Skármeta's young people reject it in Chile. But, crucially, along with this goes what Sainz calls "a degree of faith in the availability of reality";[8] this corresponds closely to Skármeta's cautious endorsement of "esta realidad que por comodidad llamamos realidad."

The word *gazapo*, we are told on the flyleaf, means a tall tale, a piece of intentional deceit. It refers both to the novel as a whole, which is a fanciful, fictional account of aspects of Sainz's late adolescence, and to the stories that Menelao and his friends tell each other, many of which contain elements of male adolescent sexual fantasy. To Rodríguez Monegal, Sainz asserted, "mi novela se desarrolla de un viernes a un miércoles,"[9] and to Carballo in his autobiography he explained that the implied moment of writing was the Monday in between: "Hacia el primer viernes Menelao maneja un tiempo real. Hacia el segundo se complica al hablar de un tiempo creado, lleno de posibilidades y variantes." Gyurko, interpreting the novel as if it were a typical product of the Boom, heavily stresses the fantasy element, asserting that "The enchantment of *Gazapo* lies in the fact that its apparent realism is constantly dissolving into fantasy . . . *Gazapo* does not contrast reality and fantasy, it fuses them" so that "the narrative as a whole affirms the liberty of the author to create his own universe with its own laws and its own language."[11] This is an overstatement. Although Sainz in his autobiography recognizes that everything in *Gazapo* is presented obliquely instead of directly and that there exists a certain ludic element in the novel, he emphasizes the fact that Menelao is recording his own experiences (and fantasies) because he "sabe que esos diálogos, esas consideraciones van a regir su vida futura."[12] Gyurko is much closer to the real thrust of the novel when he writes: "Through their re-creating of the past the adolescents attempt to impose order on experience and to penetrate the mystery of the ever-changing self."[13] For this reason, we can agree with Brown that "el verdadero meollo de *Gazapo*" is Menelao's adolescent crisis.[14] It is this that the novel's earliest readers recognized: what Sainz called its fictional "authenticity,"[15] its convincing picture of an age group that so far had not figured in Spanish American fiction, both in terms of its speech-patterns, outlook, and behavior and (in the case of Menelao, the only one with real inner life) in terms of his reactions to a process of sometimes painful self-exploration. Brown's approach to *Gazapo* is very convincing because it fulfils the requirement to relate the content of the novel to its technique and formal arrangement. He contends that there are really three axes to the narrative, each of which is psychologically significant for the protagonist. First, his timid attempts to seduce Gisela; these function as a kind of rite of passage leading away from his more youthful past, for which the "symbolic space" is his family home. Second his aspiration to a more adult future, for which the "symbolic space" is the apartment he has taken over from his partially estranged mother. To the third axis belong the episodes of his quarrel with Tricardio, during which he oscillates between modes of behavior which are now more mature, now quite immature. In each of these areas of the novel Menelao is trying to come to terms with a situation that tends to generate anxiety and unhappiness. The fantasy elements in the text are not there, as they would be in the Boom, to challenge our confidence in reality; they are functionally related to Menelao's inner tensions. In the same way, the uses of the telephone, a tape recorder, diaries, and reported (rather than scenically presented) events are not, as Gyurko suggests a "demolition" of reality.[16] Sainz explained to Rodríguez Monegal that Menelao used these devices to preserve his experiences: "el personaje quiere aislar, fijar, fotografiar, grabar, describir, con el fin de anclar en él años más tarde."[17] What we should notice here is how strikingly similar in his frustration, his ambition to sleep with Gisela, and his interest in writing, Menelao is to Skármeta's young protagonist in "Basketball," except that he is less successful. Certainly the complexity of experimentation in *Gazapo* illustrates Sainz's allegiance to the Boom's elitist conception of fiction, as he later makes explicit in *A la salud de la serpiente*. But, as we also see in the later novel, and as the verbs just quoted—"fijar," "fotografiar," and so on—proclaim, reality, the notion of a causal universe, the idea of

Menelao's crisis as something actually and painfully there, stand unchallenged. We are a long way from, say, Cortázar's "Las babas del diablo," which at one point Sainz considered quoting from to open *Obsesivos días circulares* (ODC).[18]

While writing *Obsesivos días circulares* (1969), Sainz told Rodríguez Monegal: "es una novela sobre los abusos del poder, sobre la violencia urbana, sobre la educación en México, sobre la aniquilación de la pareja en pro del grupo erótico, sobre obsesiones de toda índole y desde luego sobre el problema mismo de la novela, la validez de la belleza literaria y la inutilidad de la denuncia."[19] Twenty years later the narrator in *A la salud*, which in part describes and comments on the writing of the novel, refers to it as a "novela social" (p. 472). Elsewhere he affirms: "intentaba violentar ciertos hábitos perceptivos, digamos que al seguir a un personaje no representar solamente su mente pensando, sino lo que miraba, lo que leía automáticamente al pasar la vista sobre un periódico . . . lo que oía . . . y los olores . . . [etc.]" (p. 20). But one of his fictional correspondents in the same novel remarks: "Yo creo que vas a dar desde el punto de vista de la novela una visión de lo que está sucediendo en el país" (i.e., in Mexico) (p. 175). This duality deserves attention: on the one hand the novel is seen by its author in terms of perception, but on the other its theme is presented in terms of social and political commentary. In a further comment, the narrator affirms:

> me gustaría que en mi novela, digamos, la lengua fuera un personaje . . . por otro lado me gustaría que mi novela no dejara ver detrás de sí un significado total y rotundo pero por todos partes chorrea sentido, no puedo escapar del simbolismo, de la información, de la tradición de las palabras, o sea como si las palabras terminaran diciendo lo que ellas quieren a pesar mío, o sea que la novela terminara por contarse a sí misma" (p. 509)

and describes the book as being written with the author

> "casi de espaldas a la realidad, aunque por otra parte, sin intentar para nada describir la realidad . . . erigiendo una interrogante sobre la realidad, e incluso desenvolviendo, desarrollando una especie de discurso sobre el poco de realidad que lo rodeaba." [It is] "un libro que no perseguía hacer el retrato de ningún personaje, ni contar ninguna historia, sino que más bien trataba de plantear un problema mediante su propia escritura y de resolver ese problema . . . *Obsesivos días circulares (años fantasmas)* resultaban entonces tortuosos, intelectualoides, espesos, oscuros, casi ilegibles, pero a la vez le provocaba escribir así, perseguir texturas narrativas a partir de un lenguaje narrativo, o volver narrativo un lenguaje por tradición anti-narrativo . . . terminar su proyecto . . . una novela inacabada, afásica, o casi inacabada, casi afásica, ligeramente incomprensible." (pp. 644–45)

It is clear from these and other remarks in *A la salud* that Sainz in *ODC* was bent on writing a more experimental novel that *Gazapo*, one that returns to the Boom's obsession with language and uses the "splintered mirror" technique, which García Márquez was to allude to later in *Crónica de una muerte anunciada* when he writes of trying to "recomponer con tantas astillas dispersas el espejo roto de la memoria."[20] Decker's complaint that *ODC* is difficult to read is due to Sainz's awareness that reality is fragmentary, hard to fit together, even contradictory.[21] Fiction, it seemed, in the sixties, had ceased to be able to hold up a mirror to nature and to reflect a simple, unbroken image, because nature, reality, had ceased to seem to present a clear, simple, and comprehensible image to reflect. Hence both the theme and the plot of *ODC* are difficult to define. The novel deals with a couple of months in the life of Terencio, the author of two novels, in whom we recognize much of Sainz himself. He lives with his second wife, Donají, in a Catholic girls' school in Mexico City, where he earns a modest living as a janitor, thanks to the influence of Papá la Oca, a political boss who owns the school. Papá la Oca uses it both as a hideout for one of his *pistoleros*, Sarro, and as a locale where a select male clientele can be invited to spy on the schoolgirls' changing room through a one-way window. Thus they can later be blackmailed. In the course of the novel, Sarro suffers a stroke and is hospitalized. Terencio, as narrator, explains in detail his physical attraction both to Sarro's wife, Yin, and to her younger sister, Lalka, as well as his inability to shake off the memory of his first wife Leticia, to whom he writes incessantly and who appears at intervals to torment him erotically. There is a brief trip by Terencio, Yin, Lalka, and Donají to Acapulco, with beach scenes and parties. Finally Terencio is sent by Papá la Oca back to Acapulco, along with a group of sinister *pistoleros*, ostensibly to report on their intimidation of a group of insufficiently submissive Indians. Terencio is uneasy, since the mission may include his own liquidation for allowing Yin to escape Papá's clutches and because Lalka has broken the glass of the one-way window and may have compromised his operation at the school. However, the novel ends enigmatically, with a phrase running obsessively through Terencio's head as the plane lands. We do not learn what becomes of him.

The role of Papá la Oca, the descriptions of Sarro's life and activities, the presentation of the nuns' school as part of Papá's turf, with some of the pupils used as sex objects, the tale of police brutality told to Terencio as he shares a taxi with an acquaintance in chapter 3, and the final scene on the plane justify up to a point Sainz's assertion to Dwyer that "*Obsesivos días circulares* es donde más directamente se trata de la coerción o de la represión que ejerce el núcleo en poder sobre el pueblo."[22] This is the most immediately recognizable Post-Boom element in what is otherwise a novel more in line with late Boom fiction. Along with it goes the generally unfavorable picture of Mexican middle-class society, symbolized by the furtive voyeurs who patronize the gatherings at the school, the architects and their friends with whom Terencio and his group party in an expensive hotel in Acapulco, Terencio's former wife, who loans her flat to friends for casual sex only to surprise them maliciously in the act, and even the nuns at the school itself, who inflict barbarous punishments on the girls and of whom one, at least, is carrying on an erotic relationship with a man. But, just as in *La Princesa del Palacio de Hierro*, this portrait of a Mexico rotted by violence, greed, crime, hypocrisy, and self-indulgence is presented by Terencio with a surprising insouciance that tends to soften its impact.

It would be imprudent, therefore, to regard this as primarily a social novel. The main thrust of most of Sainz's fiction is semi-autobiographical and reflects a certain self-obsession, most prominent in *A la salud*. Here this characteristic takes the form, as Decker suggests, of an ongoing attempt by Terencio to "dar orden a la experiencia sicológica" (p. 99), to make some kind of sense out of the ambiguous reality around and inside him. Glantz remarks insightfully: "el Menelao de *Gazapo* se ha transformado en Terencio y la parodia evidente lo convierte en moralista apócrifo que se autocontempla con disgusto."[23] The novel begins with Terencio spying on Sarro and Yin as they make love and ends with him contemplating the possibility of his own imminent death. At one point we hear that Leticia's son is mentally handicapped. Thus love, death, and failure to comprehend are all symbolically present. But once more, what gives the novel its disconcerting tone is the apparent casualness with which Terencio reacts to their presence. Decker writes of "paranoia" and "angustia," presenting Terencio's life in terms of struggle and questing. But the facts that Terencio, a well-published writer, has accepted a humdrum job that includes cleaning toilets and emptying garbage, that he does not do that job very responsibly, that he collaborates with Papá la Oca, that he frequently finds refuge in humor and fantasy, and above all that his obsessions are mainly erotic do not suggest fear and despair.

Terencio's real problem is a vague dissatisfaction with his situation, his drab and at times shaming lifestyle, and his own behavior. He refers to periods in his past as "años fantasmas" (which was to have been the novel's subtitle). It is clear that he is still living out "años fantasmas," full of immature physical desire ("en la locura de seducir a todas las mujeres deseables," p. 122), jealousy, frustration, drunkenness, nostalgia for his first wife, voyeuristic activity on behalf of himself and others, and degrading dependence on the goodwill of Papá la Oca. At the end of chapter 3, he describes himself as "Inútil, cansado, sucio de remordimientos . . . Insatisfecho . . ." (p. 160). At the same time he is aware that human destiny is symbolized by his ex-wife's (presumably adulterine) son, who "empezó a morir un segundo después de haber nacido. Y brotará en él, recité, el egoísmo, la crueldad crecerá, las mentiras. Y guerreará a su hermano, provocará mucho dolor, será injusto y pocas veces bueno" (p. 146). Beyond that, life seems to him incomprehensible. As his sits among the *pistoleros* at the end of the novel, he asks himself a key question: "¿De qué dependerá mi arribo a esta máquina ronroneante? ¿De qué insignificante, pinche movimiento, decisión, chingadera? (p. 247). There is no response. The chains of causes and effects in which our lives are enveloped are beyond our ken. The image of the retarded child, trapped in a life which he is incapable of comprehending, but "sin inquietudes" (p. 249) significantly recurs. But, unexpectedly, Terencio refuses to be intimidated. Like Molly Bloom, at the end of Joyce's *Ulysses*, a novel that has accompanied him like an amulet in his recent experiences, he is finally able to say yes to life, to overcome his fears and achieve a brief moment of tranquility and confidence: "No siento nada, ni siquiera el miedo de un accidente: sólo sosiego . . . Sé que esta tranquilidad es temporal. Experimentaré aún la obsesión de los monstruos y el miedo a catástrofes abstractas que no llegarían nunca . . . Pero siento que el mundo absorbe, consume, disuelve mis miedos, los priva de toda verdad" (pp. 252–53). This is not an epiphany of the sort enjoyed by some of Skármeta's characters, but it is a momentary yea-saying, which marks Sainz's movement away from the pessimism of the Boom. The repeated phrase with which the novel ends does not, as Decker suggests it does, denote desperation. It is not a comment on existence but a tongue twister taken from a comic film, and as such it should not be taken too seriously.

The facts that *ODC* is told partly in the form of fragmentary letters to Terencio's friend, Tobías, and occasionally to Leticia, and that it constutes a long series of monologues in which "reality" and "fantasy" are not always easy to distinguish, or the time frame clearly established, complicate the text. But by and large it is conventionally linear. Though open ended, it moves toward a recognizable conclusion that marks a moment of insight for Terencio. The problem is not really one of narrative devices. It is that so much of what happens in the novel is banal and hard to invest with meaning. If Terencio were as anguished as Decker contends, our interest in him might be greater. As it is, we feel reactions ranging from amusement to a certain irritation and impatience, mitigated only by Terencio's own honesty and self-awareness. Fortunately, in his next novel, *La Princesa del Palacio de Hierro* (1974), Sainz, using much the same basic technique, this time of telephone monologues, avoids the banality through much greater reliance on humor and (melo)drama to produce what seems destined to stand as the comic masterpiece of the Post-Boom.

Refreshingly unlike Menelao and Terencio, the Princess is not an intellectual. Though she is often endearingly a little confused, especially about herself ("me identificaba más con la gente seria . . . Este . . . Me gusta más la gente profunda, la gente que tiene más cosas adentro . . . y los hombres, bueno, me gusta que sean un poquito cabrones").[24] She is nobody's fool, but she frankly admits that university studies were not for her (p. 30) and deflates attempts by a couple of her many boy-friends to perceive her as possessing unusual levels of insight and culture. When she presents herself initially, at the age of fifteen, she describes herself candidly as "una escuincla" (p. 51), as "pendeja" (p. 34) and as "payasísima" (p. 30), as indeed her behavior, especially her sexual behavior, soon illustrates.

At this time, she is still taking Communion every morning and emphasizes her traditional Catholic formation, referring to "el criterio que tenía de mosca, de minipiojo, de ancianita decimonónica, de Madre Abadesa" (p. 92). Beneath both her featherheadedness and her rigid upbringing, however, we recognize, with her, her fundamendal goodheartedness ("me consideraba, y creo que ahora también me considero, bueno, que era buenísima, que era una niña de lo más bueno que hay en el mundo," p. 78). She is in fact an innocent, growing up as a member of a group of people, both young and old, for the most part much less innocent, representing upper-class beneficiaries of the (failed) revolution. Philip Swanson, in an illuminating article, argues that the novel's theme is, yet again, self-discovery, "the processes of construction of the individual in an urban setting," and notices that we sense, beneath the hilarious surface of the text, the Princess's growing frustration and unhappiness, even as she achieves marriage and security. It leads him to conclude that the events of the novel may in fact constitute a fantasy, "a fictional alternative" to "the underlying banality of her life" as a young woman married to a rich yuppie whom we do not meet. In his view, she is subjected to a process of "socialization into acceptance of patriarchal structures and subservience to a male implied author."[25] This perhaps overstates the case. But certainly, if we were to take the episodes and characters wholly seriously—which would be to forget that this is above all a comic novel—we should find our credulity strained.

Even at the time of writing, this was almost a historical novel. The Princess was born apparently in 1938, so that the action covers the period from about 1953 to the middle sixties, the success of the Cuban Revolution in 1959 and the murder of President Kennedy (1963) being mentioned as contemporary events. The text consists of twenty-one chapters, each of which is a telephone monologue delivered by the

Princess to an unknown friend, who never intervenes in the narrative. The monologues evoke autobiographical episodes from the Princess's past in broadly chronological order, beginning in adolescence and ending when she is perhaps in her mid-twenties. The events are narrated in a richly vivid and highly amusing oral style, with frequent digressions, flashbacks, and loose ends, and they involve a large cast of rather larger than life characters (boyfriends, girlfriends, relatives, and acquaintances), whose chief characteristics are immediate self-gratification and in some cases self-destruction. Drugs, sex, violence, and an obsession with often dangerous or criminal forms of "fun," centering on fashionable clubs, bars, and restaurants, dominates the lifestyle of the younger set, while the older generation combine hypocrisy with the exploitation of their social, economic, or political position, again largely for self-gratification. The merest glance at the way they live (and sometimes the way they die) seems to suggest serious, though never explicit, criticism of the section of Mexican society to which they belong.

The leading older members of the Princess's family, her father and uncle, belong to the in-group of unscrupulous and corrupt wheeler-dealers, closely connected to the president, who exercise power without responsibility. Significantly, her father is murdered in a gambling affair, while her uncle comes to a similarly violent end, after raping her best friend (who afterwards lives with him, although she does break one of his legs in a quarrel). The uncle in question is avenged by one of his bodyguards, who shoots two of the police responsible for his employer's death. The Princess's mother looms rather large in the text as an abusive and unloving parent who, after her husband's death, relapses into mental confusion; while her sister, the Princess's aunt, becomes the lover of a Nazi war criminal. The Princess's other aunt, the wife of the murdered uncle, takes up shoplifting as a form of self-therapy. To complete the picture of this highly disfunctional family, the Princess's brother is described as quite incapable of handling the practicalities of everyday life and is reported to have smashed up no fewer than six cars in driving accidents.

Of her friends of her own sex, the Princess casually remarks, "una de nosotras iba a cometer un crimen, y otra a abortar cuatro veces, y otra a volverse loca" (p. 11). Among her numerous boyfriends (with the exception of "El monje," who is hard working and cultured, but emotionally unstable), drug addiction is virtually universal and crime a hobby. Like Terencio in *ODC*, however, the Princess remains for the most part unjudgmental, at most referring sarcastically to her catalogue of episodes of violence, lawlessness, irresponsibility, and moral squalor as illustrating "pequeños defectos nacionales" (p. 242). However, the contrast between, on the one hand, her own innate decency of character and, on the other hand, the scenes and people she is involved with after rebelling against her parents's restrictions, does mean that on occasion her reactions function as a form of implicit moral commentary. Thus, for example, she is in the drug scene, but not of it, and indeed shows a panic fear of the drugs, casual crime, and irresponsible violence in which her friends indulge. When her friend, La Tapatía Grande, invites her to an apartment and proceeds to sleep with the owner in return for a hundred pesos, the Princess feels "una profunda y manifiesta repugnancia hacia ella y hacia mí misma" (p. 94). Equally, when she herself is propositioned by a government minister who had earlier molested her physically, she alleges that she reacts by recording his proposition and turning it over to the president of Mexico, her father's schoolfriend, who quickly puts an end to the problem.

In the course of this last episode the Princess describes herself as having "unos problemas muy serios" (p. 202), a complaint she repeats later (p. 257), but it is never made clear what exactly they involve. Julie Jones correctly suggests that they derive ultimately from lack of parental love.[26] Since throughout the novel she is speaking retrospectively from after her wedding, the problems must be emotional and psychological ones, initially deriving from her rejection by her mother. Near the end of the text she asks plaintively, "¿Por qué no soy feliz? ¿Por qué no?" only to answer her own question in part by asserting, "Yo no soy una gente estable" (p. 251). She spends much of the novel searching for love, but settling for sex, and at the end seems as far away as ever from stability and serenity. The interest of the Princess as a character, in other words, derives from the increasingly evident contrast between what she seems to be to others, "una gente muy abierta, muy extrovertida, cautivadora y además muy bonita" (p. 226), and her own inner dissatisfaction. One of the basic messages of Sainz's fiction is that "todo es ambiguo" or, as he remarked to Rodríguez Monegal, "Cada cosa con su contraria, como todo el arte de nuestra época."[27] This is certainly true in the Princess's case; she is by turns rebellious, thoughtlessly imprudent, frivolous, and promiscuous and yet at the same time sporadically self-aware and not without moral principles.

But it is not the evolution of her personality that is the primary source of the novel's interest. What makes it so readable is the remarkable combination of the Princess's wonderfully lively narration and the rich variety of horrific, dramatic, and hilarious incidents she describes, together with the gallery of extraordinary figures whose behavior gives rise to them. There are no normal, everyday people in the Princess's circle. The headwaiter at the restaurant where the opening events of the novel take place bullies the customers, runs a vice ring, and before long disappears with compromising documents and a fancy mistress, before turning up again as a very unlikely kind of taxi driver. The Princess's main boyfriend, el loco Valdosiera, alias "el guapo guapo," is an ex-convict, smuggler, murderer, and drug addict. Another, Alexis, is also a gangster. Gabriel, a failed suicide, is "loco y borracho," and the list could be continued. Not surprisingly, the episodes include drunken driving, fatal accidents, fights, incidents with the police, drug use, rape, theft, and general destructiveness, illustrating an utterly antisocial lifestyle. But these are described by the Princess in a usually funny and and uninhibited way that contrasts with what would be their usual impact.

There is a certain distance between the reader's reaction to what is going on and her entertaining, noncritical description of events that distracts us from their seriousness. It is only when we count up the number of violent deaths, criminal actions, cases of grossly selfish and infantile irresponsibility, that we break the spell of the Princess's absorbing and hilarious narrative, which rests on two elements: one, an alternation of melodrama, slapstick, and breakneck pace; the other, the Princess's enchanting oral style. In chapter 5, for instance, the Princess treats us to accounts of a momentary attempt by Valdosiera ("traficante de drogas" and "el golfo más golfo que hayas conocido en tu vida," pp. 59, 60) to adopt a more socially acceptable lifestyle; her uncle's threat to have him shot; her father's gullible reaction; her failure as a salesgirl; Valdosiera's infidelity reported by a friend, Tito; her angry reproaches when Valdosiera next sees her; his fury with Tito; their speedy reconciliation, and the Princess's rage at men's solidarity with one another. All such events are breathlessly reported to the accompaniment of droll exclamations ("¡Tortugas ninfómanas!" "¡Prepucios de elefante!," pp. 18, 28) and vividly humorous touches of description ("teníamos una cara que pregúntame si de indigestión con chayotes"; "La gente se apartó para dejarlo pasar; como la vagina de una puta deseosa de terminar aprisa"; "Ni siquiera sabía masturbarme, así que me quedé llorando como estúpida, gris y desabrida, lánguida, moquienta, pesimista. ¡Changos depravados!," pp. 9, 26, 29). This is vintage Post-Boom: emphasis on youth, on easy-to-read, rapid-paced narration, on entertainment value, on a specifically Spanish American urban here-and-now setting, emotion, sexuality, spontaneity, exhuberance, colloquiality—in fact, virtually all the characteristics identified by Skármeta in "Al fin y al cabo." Along with his *Ardiente paciencia* and Allende's *La Casa de los Espíritus*, *La Princesa del Palacio de Hierro* takes its place as one of the defining novels of the movement.

*Compadre Lobo* (1977)[28] continues the pattern set in Sainz's first two novels. Like them it consists of an episodic series of events, hardly amounting to a plot, centering on a group of streetwise young people growing up in Mexico City during part of the 1950s and 1960s. The story is told by a narrator who occasionally intervenes in the text to remind the reader that s/he is reading a novel, but who for rest writes omnisciently, except for two pages (pp. 215, 250) on which he hints that Lobo's confidences to him may have provided some of the data. The episodes take place predominantly in the streets, bars, and nightspots of the city center and once more contain an alluring mix of sexual activity, drunkenness, and violence, spiced now and then with petty crime and other kinds of antisocial activity. The same ambiguity that was present in the earlier novels and peaks in *A la salud del serpiente* is visible here: the outward behavior of the two male protagonists, the narrator and Lobo, is in total contrast to their inner disquiet, verging on despair. One is irresistibly reminded of the novels of Roberto Arlt, especially his first, *El juguete rabioso* (1926). In it, the young central character, Silvio (the ultimate predecessor of all the young fictional characters of the Post-Boom), tries to come to terms with his developing insight through cruelty and self-degradation. What it is crucial to bear in mind while reading the novel, therefore, is that its main characters are not just young punks: the narrator develops (against all expectation) into a professional writer and Lobo into a successful painter. Both of them, that is, are in process of becoming creative intellectuals. Sainz's problem, like Arlt's, is to resolve the contradiction between what they do in the novel and who they are at its end.

For that reason, *Compadre Lobo*, unlike its predecessors, begins on a note of anguished introspection. As his drunken companions vandalize the street, Lobo "pretendía comunicar con lo desconocido de él mismo, con los misterios que se oponían y dominaban *eso* que a veces era él" (p. 13). The central symbol of the novel is the night, the abyss of darkness attenuated by pinpoints of light, which stands for awareness on the part of Lobo and of his alter ego, the narrator, of dark forces inside themselves and surrounding them, including a characteristically Mexican sense of death. In Lobo's case, the key pages occur in the sixth chapter. They clarify the fundamental ambivalence within him:

> Cada noche amenazaba constantemente hundirlo en el absurdo, donde ninguna relación era posible, donde toda fórmula carecía de sentido, donde no había misiones que cumplir ni fines que alcanzar. La cultura, el trabajo, la gente, eran las fuerzas que querían arrastrarlo, construir su existencia coherentemente, imponer orden, cifrar su pensamiento y su conducta en lo claro y lo distinto. Lo queríamos lúcido y eficaz, y él se negaba a traicionarnos, pero no podía negar a la vez la potencia oscura que lo gestó. (p. 232)

In the novel Lobo is specifically called "un hombre de la noche" and "un habitante de la noche" (pp. 233, 251). Four times on one page the narrator refers to his "pasión por la noche" (p. 233). This is explained as referring to his attraction to total nihilism, his sense of *la nada*, the appeal of self-surrender to his own vicious instincts, and his need for a "traición absoluta a la existencia." But, as the earlier quotation illustrates, Lobo is incapable of taking a plunge without returning to his own inner abyss. The text refers to a "doble traición: haber traicionado el mundo en su entrega a la pasión por la noche y traicionar la noche en la impotencia para abandonar el mundo" (p. 233).

Behind this melodramatic rhetoric lie the metaphysical preoccupations prominent in some of the novels of the Boom and in some sections of Western fiction generally. These Sábato had earlier praised in his *El escritor y sus fantasmas* and advocated as suitable themes in his essay "Para una novela novelesca y metafísica." But we are now in the Post-Boom and there are significant differences. The first is concerned with the age and social class of the relevant characters, in this case Lobo and the narrator. They are quite different from, say, Onetti's Jorge Malabia in *Juntacadáveres*, Sábato's Castel, or (to mention a figure whom Skármeta regards as archetypal) Vargas Llosa's Zavalita in *Conversación en la Catedral*. They are much more like the central figures in Skármeta's "La Cenicienta en San Francisco," "A las arenas," or "Basketball": young, intelligent, sexually liberated, anti-conformist, and not noticably middle-class. The background to their disquiet, in other words, is quite different from what we are familiar with in Boom fiction, and it now includes sport, film, pop music, and adolescent devilment as part and parcel of a worldview that is nonetheless characterized by "un residuo permanente de angustia" (p. 41).

A second difference concerns, as elsewhere in the Post-Boom, the role of love and sexuality. Although once or twice the narrator asserts that he cannot compete with Lobo's extreme reactions to life, at bottom their outlook and problems are similar (perhaps too similar). So that when he refers to his "necesidad inquietante de amar y de ser amado" (p. 33) he speaks for both. Sexuality is explored at various levels by both young men. In chapter 3, for instance, the narrator has an Arlt-like experience with a cheap prostitute that seems intended to indicate self-degradation as a source of self-insight, a recurring theme throughout the text. Later he marries his girlfriend, Amparo, partly to escape his "desesperación por no haber hecho nada, y peor aún, por no tener nada, pero nada que hacer en este mundo" (p. 120). The marriage quickly degenerates into mutual infidelity. But an essential section of chapter 4 vividly describes how, despite the narrator's sense of the otherness and fundamental incomprehensibilty of his partner, they manage to achieve through love and sex a moment of plenitude in which "el mundo y nosotros somos una misma cosa" (p. 150). The experience will be repeated by the lovers in *A la salud*. Lobo, for his part, enjoys a homosexual affair with a fellow painter and apparently finds in it a sense of liberation and a source of motivation for practicing his art. Here, as much as anywhere else in the Post-Boom, love is a vital ingredient in the mix of experiences that help the protagonists to come to terms with life. Lobo reflects in chapter 6 that love is the chief source of his sense of life's contradictions, his sufferings, and his moments of self-deception; and yet "de lo que se trataba en la vida era precisamente de enamorarse" (p. 260). Like Skármeta, Sainz sees love and sex as what contradicts "las leyes de la noche" and as where "la dignidad última de la vida" resides, even though it produces only sporadic fulfilment and its deepest effect is to "revelarnos nuevas facetas de nuestro aislamiento" (pp. 259, 262, 279).

The fundamentally contradictory nature of love and sexuality is for Sainz the ultimate manifestation of the contradictions inherent in the human condition. The mindless rebelliousness of the young people in *Compadre Lobo*, their need to experience "toda clase de excesos" and to "transgredir todas las prohibiciones" (p. 66), is chiefly a response to a world in which, as in Valenzuela "no hay orden," a world in which the narrator feels "Siempre la misma ausencia de armonía" (p. 148) both in himself and in his surroundings. Less melodramatic than the symbolism of the night is Sainz's affirmation, once more, that "La ambivalencia es la ley de la vida" (p. 248). It is not so much fear, solitude, or *hastío* that surround these young people as it is confusion and awareness of "diferentes niveles de realidad" (p. 277) that they cannot fully bring into focus: "Nuestra vida," the narrator complains, "no podía cerrarse hacia algo, no podía orientarse" (p. 306).

But even as he writes these words he is aware that his life and that of Lobo are changing for the better. This is the final difference between the situation of the protagonists in *Compadre Lobo* and that of, for example, Onetti's Jorge Malabia. Despite all the references to night and the abyss, these young people are in process of moving away from their much trumpeted *angustia* toward integration both with society and with themselves. We have just seen that, as usual in the Post-Boom, love in its various manifestations, and despite its terrors and ambiguities, is a major factor in the process. There are two others. One is humor, as in *La princesa*. For all their unhappiness and frustration, these young pople live life ludicly, in the power of "el demonio desenfrenado del juego" (p. 56). Part of their youthful, wholesome attitude to life is to see it as a game, symbolized by Lobo's antics at the museum where he works. Behind the novel's evocations of despair and futility, there is a recurrent lightheartedness rarely if ever found in the Boom, a new, joyful sense of "la risa y sus victorias cotidianas" (p. 100). The young people's ability to respond to "el absurdo cotidiano" by living life to some extent as a game, to enjoy love and laughter spontaneously, can be seen as prefiguring the novel's final situation, in which the narrator is a success and Lobo, through art, has found "una nueva corriente de vida" that "rompía la costra de la rutina y transformaba su conflictivo presente y el ritmo mecánico de sus días en una suerte de música distinta, de impulso mágico y alegría *otra*" (p. 212). With this Lobo (unlike the Princess in the earlier novel) rediscovers the missing harmony of existence at the personal level, while in the final pages of the novel the narrator evokes a political march attended by thousands of people (probably a reference to the events of 1968 at Tlatelolco) to suggest the rediscovery of collective values that justify struggle and rebellion. *Compadre Lobo*, then, like a typical Post-Boom novel, ends positively, despite the narrator's awareness that the march will end in the "crucifixion" of the participants.

The last relevant element in the novel is the narrator's attitude toward language. It, too, is ambiguous. We are clearly in the presence of a writer for whom the exterior world exists. The specifically named streets, bars, and cinemas of downtown Mexico City at that time are totally realistic and the language evoking them is unequivocally referential. Yet, like Valenzuela, Sainz is fully aware that, in the aftermath of the Boom, problems of language subsist. They arise not so much in relation to events and places (though the narrator recognizes that these have disappeared into the past and are now no longer real, p. 95) as in relation to the inner lives of the characters. On the one hand, the narrator's confessed aim is to "escribir todo esto que veo," so that "los amigos de la calle hablarán a través de mí" (pp. 43–44), to produce "este texto que intenta rescatar sus toscas maldiciones, su espontánea sublevación, su irrupción en mitad del mediodía" (p. 145). At the same time he realizes that to write about the group is in some sense to affirm the specificity and the authenticity of its lifestyle and, in so doing, to explore it (pp. 134–35). So far, so good; the difficulty at this level is to give his language the sharp, cutting edge of a scalpel (p. 44). But at a deeper level the narrator recognizes that the personalities of Lobo or Amparo are in the last resort incomprehensible and communication with them, largely nonverbal. In any case language itself is problematic: "un misterioso tráfago de símbolos y de símbolos de símbolos" (p. 177). Thus the ever present sense of ambiguity pervading *Compadre Lobo* extends to language itself. On the one hand, the narrator wishes to fix his life and those of his friends at a particular moment in time; on the other, he complains that "era en vano escribir" (p. 185). For this reason the idea of silence plays an important role in the novel. Both the narrator and Lobo, writer and painter, perceive art and literature as linking the silence of the creative mind to the silence of the mind of the reader or viewer (pp. 178, 346); but in some mysterious way, the link produces "palabras nuevas" (p. 346), new insights. Something is communicable even via silence. Hence the importance of the silence of the marchers at the end. To the narrator it brings the recognition that "de su silencio podía manar otro orden moral" (p. 369). For all his doubts about the efficacy of language, the narrator pursues his vocation as a writer and ultimately produces the novel we are reading. Out of the silence of his remembered past comes a communication we receive into the silence of our consciousness.

In Boom fiction, with its frequent emphasis on innovation, "verbal construct" often replaced "narrative line." We have seen that Valenzuela, for instance, pays tribute to this tendency, notably in *El gato eficaz*. Similarly Giardinelli turns somewhat in that direction in *Santo Oficio de la memoria* (1991). Evidence of its attraction for Sainz was seen above in his remarks a propos of *ODC* and reappears in his praise of the elitist stance of the Boom writers in *A la salud de la serpiente*. It reemerges in *Fantasmas aztecas* (1982, but copyrighted in 1979), in which he hints at the problem (which R. L. Williams regards as central to any understanding of postmodernism) of the relation of linguistic signs to "truth." One of the characters, Claudia, is "como privada de algo que hallaría en cualquier otra parte, es decir, de una realidad que le ofreciera signos, pruebas objetivas y compartidas con los demás de la realidad de sus percepciones."[29] The hint seems to be connected to Sainz's (possible) definition of *Fantasmas* as "mi novela: una especie de aventura de la percepción" and as "una novela incomprensible, inacabada, afásica y consternadora" (p. 179), a definition not unlike what he was to write about *ODC* in *A la salud*. *Fantasmas* bears as its subtitle "un pre-texto" and is referred to in the dedication as "estos ideogramas." Among the epigraphs is a quotation from Borges that contains the notion of history as composed of "imágenes discontinuas."

All of this suggests that what we are reading is the record of a series of fragmentary perceptions that have to do with (Mexican) history but are neither objective nor consensual, and may constitute a "rompecabezas" (p. 102) for the reader. In chapter 4, however, the narrator refers to "el principal paralelismo, justamente la historia que puso en marcha este relato" and to the Aztec practice of allowing a victim to live like a god before sacrificing him ("mito que muy bien podría ser el principio de este texto," p. 84). The victim in question is the symbolically named Reyes Moctezuma, a professor of archeology who is supervising the excavation of the Aztec Templo Mayor in Mexico City. This site is seen by the narrator as an "espacio mágico, punto fijo, fuerte y significativo, centro del mundo e hito y frontera entre dos mundos . . . uno amorfo y vacío de sentido [i.e., modern Mexico and the West in general] . . . y otro sacralizado" (p. 101). Moctezuma, in turn, is seen as "microcósmico en relación con la historia de ese lugar" (p. 161).

At the center of the text, then, is Moctezuma, surrounded by a group of adoring women students with whom, in spite of his successful marriage, he has passionately sexual affairs. However, in what is now a familiar fashion, he is at bottom frustrated and unhappy, seeking deeper self-knowledge and a fixed point around which to construct his life meaningfully. He does not find it and at the end of the novel is trapped "como los antiguos trasuntos de los dioses que se encerraban en una jaula de madera" (p. 206), unable, that is, to escape the parallelism with an Aztec victim. Beside him, the narrator, making notes for a future novel, also perceives that reporting his own experiences may produce a "sincero autorretrato" (p. 75) and lead him, through a "descenso a los abismos" (p. 70) to greater self-awareness. In chapters 3 and 4 there is a significant repetition of the same sentence that refers to the narrator's and Moctezuma's joint aspiration to replace "las incoherencias de la vida diaria" with "un estado de ánimo donde la vida volviera a la calma" (pp. 71, 87). But in the case of the narrator this is frustrated by his awareness that any attempt to overcome the incoherence of experience will be foiled by the fact that our memories are of disorganized perceptions, mere "imágenes y vestigios de imágenes" (p. 75) and that behind these again there are only words, verbal signs that have no necessary relationship with any possible reality. This explains why the strands of narrative half-hidden in the text never form a clear pattern, which in turn also means that the postulate of a link between the Mexico of today and that of the Aztecs is never really clarified. *Fantasmas*, that is, leaves the reader with the impression that it is not only unfocused, but deliberately unfocused. It has veered away from Post-Boom reader-friendliness and specificity of theme toward what looks like mere contingency.

Something similar is true also of *Paseo en trapecio* (1985); this may explain why both novels have received little critical attention. The protagonist, a young zoologist (but in fact the same ultraliterary, name-dropping intellectual we have become familiar with), asserts that he wants to make a gift to his wife of "un animal hecho de palabras" (a book? this book?) that will "incarnate" "toda esa confusión que parecía ordenarse al llegar ella, al caminar a su lado."[30] He has returned to Mexico City from their home in New Mexico, with a high fever. The bulk of the novel consists of his feverish and at times delirious thoughts and memories, which essentially center on the themes of love, time, and death. We are again faced with a fragmentary narrative suspiciously similar to the novel that the protagonist is reportedly writing and that is described variously as "atemporal" (p. 62), "implacablemente experimental" (p. 76), "nueva, extraña y provocadora" (p. 91), and as a "novela-río" (p. 104). This time, however, rather than expressing insecurity with regard to the word as sign, as in *Fantasmas*, the technique seems to be intended to reflect insecurity with regard to the reality of the self (in this case as observer/narrator) and hence of perception. At one point the zoologist imagines himself trapped behind a pane of glass, seeing through it, but cut off from life on the other side. At a later point he imagines himself transformed into a dog. The first words of the novel: "como si" recur constantly throughout the text as though casting doubt on the congruence of what is being described to any external reality. There is even a hint that the protagonist may in fact be already dead. *Fantasmas*, *Paseo*, and Sainz's next novel, *Muchacho en llamas*, are—and are intended to be—disconcerting to the reader. They represent a parenthesis in Sainz's work before his ideological and literary stock-taking in *A la salud de la serpiente*.

In *Muchacho en llamas* (1987) Sainz returns to the theme of *Gazapo* and *Compadre Lobo*, that of growing up in Mexico City in the early 1960s. According to Sefamí,[31] it is a remake of one of his earliest writings: "Fue producida en forma inicial en el Distrito Federal en 1961 y después afinada y retocada en Albuquerque en 1987." The first person narrator and protagonist, Sofocles (without an accent), is once more largely autobiographical and reflects the young Sainz trying to write his first novel and hoping for a scholarship, which he ultimately obtains, to the Centro Mexicano de Escritores. In the meantime he lives with his feuding father and step-mother, neglects his education, runs up debts, and, predictably, spends much of his time in highly sexual affairs with sundry girlfriends. Although at one point he reflects, "Nada más insoportable que un libro con confesiones adolescentes,"[32] this is what the novel is. Written in semi-diary form, it consists of miscellaneous jottings that record the narrator's reflexions, activities and experiences in the period between his failure to obtain a scholarship to the Centro (presumably in 1960) and his success in 1961. Like Menelao in *Gazapo* (and, indeed, as we have seen, like all Sainz's protagonists), Sofocles is chiefly seeking greater understanding of his own personality. A key section occurs when a second narrative voice intervenes to comment on the elusiveness of Sofocles's real identity and, by juxtaposing comments on the novel we are reading ("Se debe volver a hallar en estas páginas ese difícil estado de libertad que es propio de la creación sin límites" [p. 85]), seems to suggest indirectly that the form of *Muchacho en llamas* (*MEL*) is related to his tendency to slip through the reader's fingers.

With hindsight, it seems possible to argue that in *MEL*, as earlier in

*Fantasmas* and in *Paseo*, Sainz got into a blind alley. The sense of possessing a sufficient knowledge of reality to cope with its ambiguity, which we found sporadically in his earlier work, seems to have receded. In *MEL* the narrator exclaims: "¡Basta ya de novelas realistas poseídas por el ánimo de reflejar! . . . [Q]ue mi novela sea vida ella misma, riesgo y aventura" (p. 35). He rejects the notion of an art whose objective is to "tranquilizar al hombre sobre el mundo" (p. 96) and affirms categorically "Estoy harto de historias, que continúan obedeciendo los principios de la causalidad y el efecto" (p. 111). But the three novels that culminate in *MEL* do not seem to offer a satisfactory alternative to comforting, old-style realism. Sefamí's comment on *MEL* that "la dispersión que se proclama como meta en este tipo de escritura no se consolida completamente. Las mismas discusiones en torno al proceso creativo ya dan un hilo distinguible al libro. El juego entre unidad y disparidad ofrece un sentido nuevo a la estructura que sirve de base al volumen" (p. 131) remains simply an assertion, unsupported by any analysis. *MEL* is quite unlike *Gazapo*, to which its first draft is historically related. There, as Peña has pointed out, the seduction of Gisela offers a clear "hilo conductor." "La seducción de Gisela," he writes, "se vuelve el eje referencial y el acontecimiento aglutinador en donde coinciden o del cual se desprenden los diversos bloques narrativos."[33] Here, by contrast, there is no definable development in Sofocles's quest. Significantly also, from the point of view of this study, he receives two warnings. One is from his fellow novelist Carlos Monsiváis, who describes his narrative experiments as "completamente innecesarios" (p. 26). The other is from his father, who recommends that he read earlier Mexican prose writers and learn from them to produce a "relato coherente": "Porque lo que tu escribes es demasiado complicado, yo incluso diría que hasta innecesariamente confuso, o predominantemente caótico" (p. 217). The results of these warnings to himself become evident in the later stages of *A la salud de la serpiente*.

*A la salud de la serpiente* (1988) is fascinating—to the critic, at least—when looked at both as a homage to the Boom (notably to Borges, Fuentes, and Donoso) and to its conception of the novel, and at the same time as an archetypal Post-Boom work. The protagonist corresponds to Sainz as he remembers (or imagines) himself to have been[34] twenty years earlier in 1968 while he was writing *Obsesivos días circulares* in the International Creative Writing Program of the University of Iowa. The novel describes, through third-person narrative interspersed with letters attributed to Fuentes, Donoso, and other friends, his life and activities in Iowa City among other writers and graduate students, aspects of his earlier life in Mexico City; the impact on him of the massacre at Tlatelolco; his reflections on fiction; his exploration of the worlds of pop music and film in the 1960s; and the response on the part of journalists, students, teachers, and parents in the provincial town of Mexicali in Baja California to the alleged use of *Gazapo* as an academic text. There is much in *A la salud* that smacks of self-indulgent reminiscence, given the length of the text and the fact that its only theme is what the narrator vaguely calls "la conciencia [i.e., his own] en constante evolución" (p. 279). But there are certain key elements for our purposes, and these include a remarkable and obtrusive tendency to praise the Boom novelists. Initially Sainz defends them for having created "difficult," totalizing novels like *Rayuela*, *Paradiso*, *Cambio de Piel*, or *Conversación en La Catedral* that appeal to a cultured minority rather than to "la clase media idiota de América Latina" that prefers Irving Wallace or trashy North American best-sellers (pp. 23–24). It becomes clear that the notion of reality as ambiguous and unpredictable (not to say chaotic) that surfaced in *Compadre Lobo* was influenced by the Boom writers and by their contemporaries elsewhere. From them Sainz inherits the idea enunciated here that any attempt to impose a tidy plot-structure on a reality that is random is a falsification dictated by attachment to nineteenth-century (bourgeois) illusions, by mental idleness, or by simple stupidity. The great novelists of our time, it is urged (the narrator mentions among others Butor, Barth, Semprún, and Juan Goytisolo), "ven el mundo desarticulado, permanentemente mentido, contradictorio, inaprensible, excesivamente complejo e imperfecto, pleno de vacíos y roturas" and at best can only present a parallel reality that is essentially verbal and will be "ciertamente infiel" to any possible reality outside itself (p. 26). We are here on completely familiar ground. It is confirmed when the first two letters inserted into the text purport to come from Fuentes and Donoso, while the third is attributed to that Grand Panjandrum of Boom criticism, Emir Rodríguez Monegal. Under these influences, of Borges (who is mentioned about a dozen times) and more remotely of certain nineteenth-century novelists like Melville, all of whom emphasized the bewildering complexity of reality, Sainz envisions the writer's task as that of exploring, through the written word, oneself and the world around one, attempting to "rescatar lo irreparable que había sido" (i.e., the past, p. 69) and "para volver verosímil la realidad [of the present], para ordenarla, para creer que se le entiende" (p. 75). We are at once reminded of Isabel Allende's stance, indicated above (p. 59), according to which the order that the novelist imposes on reality is not inherent in reality itself but a projection of the author's mind. However, what matters in both cases (and in the Post-Boom generally), is the shift of emphasis from reality as incomprehensible, which, Sainz recognizes, dominates whole sectors of Boom fiction, to reality as subject to the writer's ability to invest it with a semblance of intelligibility.

In common, that is, with others of his generation, Sainz inherits from the Boom "esa desconfianza que lo asaltaba con tanta frecuencia frente a la 'realidad', lo que los demás llamaban 'realidad', 'cronología', 'tiempo', 'verdad'" (p. 87). But like them he is now ready to see in the novel a verbal construct that is capable, within certain limits, of containing a reassuring metaphor of man's power to cope with this lack of confidence. The novel that thus emerges will be in this case a "historia personal," a micro- or infra-historia, in which the narrator's own reactions will be reinforced by those of his correspondents. In itself, as a fiction, it will be no more than "un tejido de mentiras," but it will comprise "la trama de la acción social, las complejidades de los sistemas intelectuales, la tramoya del conocimiento, el indescifrable sistema político mexicano . . . la textura del amar," and numerous other elements. These are intended to provide on the one hand "la posibilidad de una lectura infinita" but on the other "un laberinto de luz y oro" with the hope that one may "encontrar la salida" (p. 158). We notice the contrast between social commitment, political commentary, love, and a positive outcome to the narrator's preoccupations at one level, and his awareness of more abstract issues (chiefly connected with the problem of cognition) at another. But it is clear that the balance has shifted in favor of the former.

Nevertheless the role of cognition is crucial. The narrator, writing in New Mexico in 1988 (p. 488) looks back to himself writing in Iowa in 1968, where in turn he sporadically looks back to the past in search of "las causas que tenían que haberlo llevado a ese efecto" (p. 173) (i.e., his being who he is, where he is and doing what he is doing—writing a different novel: *Obsesivos días circulares*). The narrator thus situates himself (symbolically perhaps) at two removes from any possible contact with whatever the notion of an original "cause," leading to any other events alluded to, might mean. The basic object of cognition in *A la salud* is the narrator's own personality: the novel, as an interlocutor points out near the end, is a vast exercise in self-scrutiny:

> cada una de estas anécdotas que ha contado es una especie de respuesta a su propia vida, ¿cómo decirlo? es el drama del yo que unas veces por medio de la imaginación, de la lectura, del cine, del contar historias, trata de hundirse en una realidad que le permita dilatarse

to which the narrator assents, confessing that while "podía moverse con libertad en el interior de su propio yo," "el mundo de afuera casi siempre resultaba hostil" (p. 754). Only insight into the self can attach us to others and overcome the radical isolation of the individual. This whole, elephantine, loose, baggy monster of a novel is fundamentally an attempt to see the world reflected in the self, through subjective experiences. But there is no desire to call into question the existence of the world outside the self. The narrator specifically quotes the words of Henry James to remind us that the world is neither an illusion nor a dream, and that we cannot forget it, deny it, or do without it (pp. 685–66). The real exists, the narrator seems to affirm, but it exists primarily for each of us separately as individuals. Our private experiences are the springboards from which we make the leap to contact with wider areas of reality, just as the narrator's experience of seeing a policeman on horseback jump over his car during a student demonstration in Mexico City prepared him to understand the behavior of the police and the army at Tlatelolco. In *A la salud* personal experience joins hands with imagination and offers the possibility of reaching out beyond the self to loving contact with others and to (often indignant or tragic) awareness of collective experience.

Nor is the notion of the novel as primarily a verbal construct less crucial. Recognizing, under the influence of Borges above all, "las limitaciones de nuestra escritura," the narrator accepts that words are powerless to reproduce, for example, our mental states and thus can at best be only approximately referential (p. 232). For the rest, an obsession with language, as we see equally in Valenzuela, is one of the main links between the Boom and the Post-Boom. Echoing similar remarks by Skármeta, Sainz's narrator reflects that "los novelistas han dado en la novela de hoy profundas estocadas a la poesía, procediendo como el poeta para conocer la realidad, dieron el salto de la intuición y han caído en medio de unas estructuras del lenguaje que abarcan prosa y poesía al mismo tiempo" (p. 481). In terms of novelistic structure, Sainz's work from the beginning illustrates his endorsement of the need to break away from the tradition of old-style realism and authorial omniscience. Here he explicitates his stance, accepting experimentalism, but with an important qualification: "se podían festejar todos los esfuerzos para convertir los libros en acordeón, o tubo, o servilletas, pero no se podía romper la progresión [i.e., minimal linearity] que representaban, y mientras no se lograra romper esa suma, que era un problema de nuestra concepción del espacio y el tiempo, consideró que se engañaban al romper la forma que la contenía" (p. 627). Readers will recognize in this quotation a classic formulation of the Post-Boom's aspiration to strike a balance between tradition and innovation.

Despite its length and complexity, then, *A la salud de la serpiente* is in no sense an attempt to rival the "totalizing" novels of the Boom writers, however much Sainz admires some of them. In the first place, its tone is completely different. Once more in words similar to those of Skármeta in "Al fin y al cabo," one of the main manifestos of the Post-Boom, Sainz writes of himself: "él estuvo a favor de lo cotidiano, de la sencillez, del coloquialismo, del buen humor, de la informalidad, de la intranscendencia" (p. 79). He makes no bones about his use of anecdote and of his own lived experience (p. 321). Equally, as we perceive from the important roles played in the novel by the narrator's girlfriend, Ambrosia, and by the evocation of the massacre at Tlatelolco, he was also in favor of high-lighting love and social protest. For if, in abstract terms, as we noted above, the world seems to Sainz "desarticulado" and ungraspable, there erupted in Mexico in 1968 a reality that "era inverosímil y al mismo tiempo real, dolorosamente real" (p. 96), as real and concrete as the Dirty war in Argentina was for Valenzuela, and the Pinochet regime for Allende and Skármeta. In the face of it, any "desconfianza" about perception, cognition, and language gives way to the imperative of expressing indignant and horrified testimony, to the need to emphasize, as the narrator states twice over, "la comunicación, la solidaridad" (pp. 279, 293). For Sainz, the tragedy of Tlatelolco is no banana-worker massacre that can be concealed from the people and provokes from the village priest in Macondo merely the the reflection that everything, including ourselves, is probably unreal. Once more we see how the pressure of terrible events from Mexico and Nicaragua to the Southern Cone compelled the writers of the Post-Boom to shake off, in significant areas of their work, the Boom's doubts about the referential function of language and to refurbish an older tradition of "civic" writing. Sainz's sense of guilt (p. 103) for not having participated in the Tlatelolco protest can only be (partly) assuaged by incorporating the event into his novel, with all the anguish which it implied for his generation and which triggers "ese deseo casi insoportable de hablar, de denunciar, de acusar" (p. 226) that is shared by Skármeta in *Ardiente paciencia*, by Valenzuela in *Cambio de armas*, and by Allende in *De amor y de sombra*, all central Post-Boom novels. In the middle of *A la salud* the narrator reflects that "el arte no era nada en sí mismo, sino que siempre entraba en relación, y al entrar en relación empezaba a alterar criterios morales, estéticos, políticos, y empezaba a ser utilizado por los espectadores, por los lectores, por el poder intelectual, por la mercadotecnia, por el poder económico y finalmente por el poder político" (p. 336). This conscious sense of art as an agent of change, social and otherwise, links Sainz, as does so much of what I have been commenting on, with the mainstream of the Post-Boom and, by the same token, would surely invalidate any attempt to associate him with what Raymond Williams (for instance) regards as postmodernism.

Alongside the stress on social commitment is the emphasis on "solidaridad y amor" at the individual level. *A la salud* stands squarely within the Post-Boom's neoromanticism. The narrator's love affair with Ambrosia, in which "el amor no parecía tener para cuando acabarse"

(p. 327) and in which the two, like the narrator and his wife in *Compadre Lobo*, find themselves "armónicos con el universo" (p. 342), strikes a chord seldom if ever heard in the Boom. It is specifically love that reconciles the narrator to life (p. 380) and indeed gives him the intuition of his own existence (p. 481). He is fully conscious that the "plenitud" he feels can collapse at any moment. But the novel emphasizes repeatedly "la comunicación, la risa, el abrazo, la penetración, la complicidad, la solidaridad." "Era como si se decubriera el uno al otro en pleno paraíso terrenal," the narrator continues, "sin árbol de manzanas ni serpiente" (p. 304). The novel's very title, as the previous quotation indicates, contains a reference to the Genesis myth. The narrator toasts the serpent who tempted Eve, because her fall was a fall into sexuality, through which, at the moment of orgasm, there can be a return to "la unidad adámica" (p. 664), an overcoming of otherness.

A final Post-Boom feature of *A la salud* is its ending. The narrator is constantly aware that his stay in Iowa is merely an interlude in which chance has allowed him to "dar la espalda a México y sus problemas mexicanos" (p. 471). But, as one of his feigned correspondents reminds him, he cannot evade his responsibilities for long: "debes regresar a tu país y hacerle frente al subdesarrollo, al canibalismo intelectual, a la estupidez y la ignorancia de la clase media idiota, a la corrupción, y a todo ese folklore de un país como México" (p. 386). The same correspondent warns him later: "tú no puedes desdeñar las ideas del nacionalismo porque precisamente estás envuelto en él, a tu pesar . . . precisamente los latinoamericanos, y los otros países tercermundistas, estamos inmersos en esas situaciones" (p. 495). When at the end the narrator packs his bags and returns to Mexico City, he is returning to a writer's task, which he perceives rather differently from the way most of the Boom novelists, with their tendency toward greater universalism, were inclined to perceive it.

*A la salud de la serpiente* brings home to us once more one of the central ambiguities of Post-Boom writing. All the authors I have discussed in this survey, by the very fact of being what they are, belong to the cultured intelligentsia. Both Skármeta and Sainz are professional university teachers. Whatever their class origins (and in the cases of the two novelists just mentioned they are relatively proletarian), all these writers reflect the mental behavior patterns of the group to which they belong. Skármeta's young student in "La Cenicienta en San Francisco" carries poetry of St John Perse in his pocket; the protagonist of Valenzuela's *Como en la guerra* teaches pyschology; the victim in Ferré's "Mercedes Benz 220 SL" leaves his luxurious home because he cannot stand his parents' materialism and anti-intellectualism; Allende's Eva Luna, like Sainz's narrator in *Compadre Lobo,* becomes a professional writer. Thus when the narrator in *A la salud* describes himself and his cronies as "seres que eligimos ser antes que otra cosa, altamente intelectuales" (p. 280), he is running perfectly true to form. Yet this same narrator, who drops the names of fellow writers and intellectuals from all over the Western world (not, alas, always correctly spelled) with wearisome regularity, at the same time avidly and largely uncritically consumes pop music and Hollywood films and spends part of his time playing pinball. On occasion his interest in popular entertainment seems justified, when (as in the case of the play *Hair*) middle-class conventions are denied. But what are we to make of his attraction to the Beach Boys, The Beatles, Dusty Springfield, *Hello, Dolly! Dial M for Murder, Rosemary's Baby*, and the like, while at the same time pillaging the university library for works by writers like Butor, Gadda, Sollers, Broch, Guimaraes Rosa, and Roussell? To be sure, the narrator aspires to produce a kind of fiction in which "triunfaba la vida, una vez más, y su juventud, su fuerza, su belleza, terminarían imponiéndose" (p. 302) and much of the pop culture he enjoys may be taken as symbolizing in its freedom, its anticonventionality, humor, sentimentality, and frank eroticism, the kind of life-enhancing outlook he would like to incorporate into his work. But it seems inconsistent to belabor the bourgeois reader in Latin America for enjoying Harold Robbins while one is at the same time listening to Mary Hopkins.

*Retablo de inmoderaciones y heresiarcas* (1992), a short novella, is Sainz's contribution to the Spanish American New Historical Novel. Based on research in the National Archive, it is offered as a composite picture of the mentality and behavior of some Mexicans on the eve of the Wars of Independence. Written in the form of fragmentary memories and reflexions, it evokes the experiences of a provincial professor of mathematics after his arrest and condemnation by the Inquisition on charges of irreligious words and writings, charges that have been trumped up by sundry fanaticized women in his life, including his mother. A student of the Latin and Spanish Golden Age poets, as well as of the natural sciences and recent critical philosophy from Locke to Helvétius, the unnamed central character stands for the Mexican intelligentsia at the end of the colonial period. Half-in, half-out of a culture still dominated by obsolete religious assumptions, he is a victim of the clerical establishment because of his awareness of new ideas and his opposition to the systematic exclusion of native-born Mexicans from positions of power in society.

As the novella unfolds we realize that he is seeking to protect a friend, fray Francisco, who is under attack from the Inquisition for a funeral oration which is held to contain heretical matter. The silly accusations that have led to the professor's trial; the details of his arrest, imprisonment, interrogations, and sentence; fray Francisco's grotesque funeral oration and his obsession with Columbus's nationality; and the description of the social gathering after the funeral oration all convey implications of the ignorance, superstition, vanity, moral corruption, obscurantism, and hypocrisy rampant in Mexican society just before the outbreak of the independence movement.

This is not a text whose content is easily accessible to the reader, compared (say) with García Márquez's *Del amor y otros demonios*, which also evokes a late-colonial, clerical atmosphere. We have to struggle to fit the fragments of the text into meaningful sequences. But Sainz's critical and semi-satirical intention is clear. This is the tainted mentality out of which grew the revolt against the Spanish colonial establishment, and the taint (as we saw in the absurd reactions to *Gazapo* chronicled in *A la salud de la serpiente*) survives. Despite its form, what makes this a Post-Boom work is its acceptance of history as real and all-too-comprehensible, so that we can trace in the past the origins of an oppressive social situation (and its attendent mentality) in the here and now of contemporary Mexico.

To conclude: developments in recent fiction in Mexico help to bring into focus the situation elsewhere in Spanish America. As we look again at Margo Glantz's well-known essay "Onda y Escritura en México,"[35] we are inevitably struck by the similarities between the characteristics she ascribes to "La Onda" (generational rebellion, reaction against the Boom writers, interest in urban youth culture, "lenguaje desenfadado," the influence of pop music, "un nuevo sentido al humor," antisolemnity, emphasis on sexual behavior, etc.) and those listed by Skármeta in "Al fin y al cabo." At the same time, however, and with greater insight, Glantz recognizes that, alongside these features, which clearly link "Onda" and Post-Boom, there also existed "La Escritura," with its greater emphasis on linguistic and formal experimentation, which equally clearly link "Escritura" with the high Boom and possibly with postmodernism. With her usual lucidity, she points out that, although a dividing line seems at first sight hard to draw, in fact "'escritura' negaría Onda. La negaría en la medida en que el lenguaje en la Onda es el instrumento para observar un mundo y no la materia misma de la narración" (p. 108).

This is a crucial distinction. As Raymond L. Williams's selection of writers suggests, in other parts of Spanish America a similar duality is visible. The point of differentiation is the degree to which language is seen as instrumental rather than as something to be explored and experimented with for its own sake, independent of its more referential function. It is, of course, important to recognize that we are dealing here with tendencies within approximately the same generation of writers and not with two clearly separate groups. In fact, in Sainz's case, as our survey of his work implies, he has never made up his mind which tendency he really belongs to and, like Valenzuela, has wavered between the two. But as the author of *Gazapo*, of *La Princesa del Palacio de Hierro*, and of *A la salud de la serpiente*, arguably his major works, he must figure prominently in any attempt to discuss the Post-Boom.

# CHAPTER 8

# Conclusion: Post-Boom and Postmodernism

As we review the more accessible and often-quoted books and articles about postmodernism in general and about its relation to Spanish American literature, we tend to be both intimidated and confused. Intimidated, because the requirement to relate it to contemporary writing in Spanish America seems increasingly inescapable. Confused, because approaches to postmodernism are constantly proliferating. Simply to understand approximately where things stand in the debate, let alone how we can proceed to apply what we have understood to the complex and changing patterns of literary production in Spanish America, is quite daunting. There is no obvious consensus about the meaning of postmodernism as a term in itself, and there is no agreement about whether and how it could be applied to—in our specific case—the Post-Boom (assuming we know what that term means). The best that can be hoped for is to present a tentative and provisional examination of some of the issues, while remaining aware that we are trying to explain one mystery (the Post-Boom) in terms of another (postmodernism).

Among the problems to be faced is that postmodernism is commonly not seen as a term that applies primarily to the arts (and literature in particular), but rather as one that has to do with the whole of the contemporary human condition and derives perhaps more from philosophy and cultural sociology than from criticism. Thus, to quote only obvious examples, Lyotard relates postmodernism to the inability of modern Western man to formulate and accept any kind of global or totalizing explanations of how things are, or to what Yudice calls "La incapacidad de representarse las condiciones de la existencia."[1] On the other hand, Jameson associates postmodernism with the current phase of late capitalism, which has somehow dehistoricized our worldview and sapped our capacity to advocate meaningful projects for the future of humanity. A third position, that of Hucheon, owes its popularity among literary critics to the fact that she tries to present postmodernism in terms of art and literature, that is, in terms of certain attitudes and techniques that stand in opposition to those which we think of as belonging to modernism. But her position is open to the criticism that it restricts itself to mere surface effects of postmodernism, without inquiring adequately into their economic, social, or political causes.

One of the consequences of this is that much of the debate takes place against a background of philosophical, political, or sociological considerations without specific reference to literature. When such reference is made, whether in passing by writers like Hucheon and Jameson, or more systematically by critics like Colás, Raymond L. Williams, or Sommers and Yudice,[2] there is usually no convincing attempt to integrate the notions of modernism and postmodernism with what we think of as the Boom and the Post-Boom. Yudice, indeed, seems at times to imply that literature and other forms of art may well have lost any formerly privileged status they may have enjoyed and are in danger of being elbowed aside by the mass media.[3] The real focus of interest in much writing about postmodernism in Latin America seems to be rather the question of transculturation, the alleged loss or fragmentation of Latin American "identity" and the expression of plangent regret for the recent failure of insurrectionary left-wing politics in that region in the face of the new network of power bases established by contemporary capitalism under the guise of neoliberalism. The tendency seems to be to postulate unprovable correlations between cultural movements and selected social, economic, and political forces. We learn from Canclini, for example, that modernism in Latin America, while not explicable in oversimplistic terms of socioeconomic modernization, is nonetheless to be seen in terms of "the mode in which the elites manage the intersection of different historical temporalities in order to incorporate them into a global project."[4] Correspondingly, Yudice appears to argue that postmodernism in Latin America is related to "the different ways in which local formations engage the colonizing tentacles of transnational capitalism."[5]

While no one would wish to deny the existence of a relationship between literary and artistic activity on the one hand and their social, historical, and cultural context on the other, it needs to be recalled that we do not know with any exactitude what that relationship is. If, for example, Colas's *Postmodernity in Latin America* shows anything, what it shows is that his critique of those who "inadequately interpret Latin American literature and culture . . . by excluding the specific social and political conditions out of which that culture has emerged" is not met by simply trying to situate individual works within this sort of context.[6] When he is not making useful, but quite conventional, points about the texts he analizes, he is engaged in the familar reductive practice of presenting the Boom as "the elitist aesthetic expression of a petit-bourgeois liberalism wedded more to the foreign values of modernization than to those of the revolution" and postmodernism (interestingly, he never refers to the Post-Boom) as a heterogeneous movement that arose in opposition to the consequences of "the restructuring of global capital in response to the crisis of 1973–75."[7] The fundamental shortcoming of such attempts to deal with literary and artistic production in Latin America by applying methods and assumptions drawn from cultural sociology is that they tend to be too deductive from broad, overarching notions, and thus their conclusions are difficult to apply in detail to individual authors or texts. It is significant, for example, how many writers on postmodernism simply ignore this difficulty. Typical are Nelly Richard's pompously entitled "The Latin American Problematic of Theoretical-Cultural Transference: Postmodern Appropriations and Counterappropriations" or Ticio Escobar's "The Furtive Avant-Gardes,"[8] neither of which contains a single reference to an illustrative text or work of art. The methodology and conclusions of cultural criticism, like those of the modern literary theoreticians, amplify the traditional inductive approaches to literature and art based on the comparative study of relevant works, but they do not supercede them.

More specifically than the writers mentioned above, R. L. Williams, in a preface to a collection of essays on the Boom, argues that we must distinguish between the "new novel" in Spanish America, which began in the 1940s, and the Boom itself, which he seems to associate conventionally with the sixties. He asserts that mainstream Spanish American fiction from Asturias's *El Señor Presidente* (1946) to Vargas Llosa's *Historia de Mayta* (1984) "including the fiction of Carpentier, Yañez, Marechal, Rulfo, Onetti, Viñas, Otero Silva, Roa Bastos and Sábato" was modernist. "These Latin American Modernists appropriated from the United States and Europe the techniques of Modernism (fragmentation, collage, multiple points of view etc.) and have used these techniques to seek order and express the ineffable in a world lacking order and waiting to be named." However, heralded by *Rayuela* in 1963, a postmodern thread of fiction appeared "and is evident in the fiction of Sarduy, Cabrera Infante, the early Sainz, José Agustín, Salvador Elizondo, Enrique Lihn, Alberto Duque López and others." Postmodernism, in his view, "subverts rather than seeks order, and has language as its primary object." Fuentes, García Márquez, and Puig, he continues, began as modernists but occasionally stray into postmodernism.[9]

It is difficult to imagine a better illustration of the pitfalls surrounding attempts to apply the notions of modernism and postmodernism to Spanish American fiction. To include Viñas and Yañez alongside Rulfo and Onetti, suggesting that all four writers belonged to a movement that sought order amid a chaotic surrounding reality, is to run counter to the bulk of mainstream critical opinion. How Viñas, who is a progressive left-wing writer can be lumped together with Onetti, who is a philosophical nihilist, is unclear. Nor is it easy to perceive how techniques of fragmentation, collage, and multiple points of view can be used in a search for order. That there is a difference between Carpentier, Onetti, Rulfo, and Marechal, on the one hand, and Cabrera Infante and Sarduy, on the other, is self-evident, but it is not based primarily on the notion of order versus the subversion of order. In *The Postmodern Novel in Latin America* (1995) Williams develops his earlier affirmations, this time placing "the possibilities of articulating truths" at the center of the debate.[10] For him, the Boom was "the culminating moment of Latin American modernism,"[11] because the Boom writers "still believed" in the notion of expressing truths in fiction. Postmodernism, by contrast, is for Williams a much more complicated, even contradictory, phenomenon, but it seems to be related (even in Latin America) to some kind of "crisis of truth."[12] In contrast to the kind of characteristics of the Post-Boom postulated in chapter 1 of this book, Williams offers other, rather less specific, ones for Latin American postmodernism. These include: indeterminacy, problematization of the center, marginality, discontinuity, simulation, and precariousness. By the same token, his choice of precoursors of postmodernism in Latin America—Cortázar, Cabrera Infante, Néstor Sánchez, Sarduy, and Puig—points to the fact that, rather than associating the new movement with reader-friendliness, plot-centeredness, and more directly referential language, he tends to relate it to "radically experimental novelists" like Ricardo Piglia, Reina Roffé, Héctor Libertella, Salvador Elizondo, Carmen Boullosa, José Emilio Pacheco, R. H. Moreno-Durán, Albalucía Angel, José Balza, and Diamela Eltit. Significantly perhaps, the names of Valenzuela and Skármeta are never mentioned, and the term Post-Boom is not used. What this might suggest is that the Post-Boom, in the sense in which the term has been used here, is a segment of postmodernism in Spanish American fiction; and any differences between the lists of characteristics elaborated by Williams and those that I have provisionally listed, or between the writers whom I regard as characteristic of the Post-Boom and those whom Williams sees as typically postmodern, merely illustrate the rich contradictoriness of the wider movement. I have to state frankly, however, that Williams's bland acceptance of "inherent contradictions" as part of the essence of postmodernism seems to me critically unacceptable. All cultural movements tend to contain inner contradictions. Indeed it is usually out of these that the next movement grows, by a gradual shift of emphasis. It is possible to argue that this is exactly what happened with the Boom and the Post-Boom. But, if this is the case, one of the tasks of the critic is to try to show how, when, and possibly why that shift took place, rather than squashing down on top of the new movement a grid of notions borrowed from elsewhere.

J. S. Brushwood, in "Two Views of the Boom: North and South," is more cautious. "There is no clear alignment," he writes, "between the Boom and Modernism or postmodernism, a condition that is hardly surprising given the vagueness of these concepts even in North American criticism."[13] He also makes the crucial point, which I developed in chapter 2, that there is an unbroken line of non-innovative, conventionally realistic narrative running right through the Boom period and linking with a less experimental strand of fiction in the Post-Boom. This greatly complicates the application of postmodernist criteria to the Post-Boom. A critic who attempts to face this difficulty is Roberto González Echevarría in "Sarduy, the Boom and the Post-Boom."[14] As in *La ruta de Severo Sarduy*, he does not see postmodernism as an ironic and parodic extension of the conventions of modernism, in line with Charles Newman, for instance. Instead he turns rather to John Barth and a rather different vision of postmodernism. Here the accent is heavily on reader-friendliness ("accessibility") and return to plot-centered writing ("narrativity"). Metadiscourse, the quest for the "total" novel, experimental, nonlinear techniques of storytelling, ironic reflexivity: these belong to the Boom. In place of them we find the centrality of the story itself, deliberate rejection of assumptions of portentous profundity or privileged insight, and loss of authorial authority. Once more, González Echevarría is careful to insist that all this "does not in any way mean that there is a return to the traditional novel"[15] and cites Sarduy's *Colibrí* (1984) as the most radical example of a break with the pattern of writing established by the Boom. This is an enlightening essay in many ways, but it seems to adopt a rather simplified notion of postmodernism, one tailored to fit some aspects of the Post-Boom. In addition, it fails to confront the basic question: Does Sarduy's alleged "recovery of conventional forms" in the early 1980s reflect a different view of reality from the one which is apparent in his earlier novels? What González Echevarría shows is that Sarduy has (in common with mainstream Post-Boom writers like Skármeta, Allende, Giardinelli, and Valenzuela) turned away from obtrusive experimentalism. But it is not clear that in doing so he has regained the confidence in the writer's capacity to observe, report, and interpret reality, a capacity that seems to typify the central group of Post-Boom novelists.

This raises the whole question of the Post-Boom's specificity to Spanish America and its prominent social vision. There are problems in the sense that, as a movement, postmodernism is often connected with a situation of economic, military, and political power on the part of developed societies in the West and thus could arguably be irrelevant to less developed ones. Similarly, at least one central current of postmodernism, its emphasis on the collapse of the hopeful grand narratives of human progress originally formulated in the Enlightenment, runs counter to much Third World writing. Ihab Hassan said as much in a discussion with Terry Eagleton, pointing out that if we accept as postmodernist the view according to which "any kind of general attempt to understand and so change the conditions of human suffering would be a fiction," then postmodernism is irrelevant outside the developed world's cultures.[16] In this he is generally supported by Jameson, who, however, asserts that the Third World can contribute what he calls an "input into the whole postmodernist debate on presentation." He continues, "In situations of economic or cultural subalternity there always tends to be a reference to the national situation that is always present and always felt in a way that it cannot be in the dominant culture of the superstate." For Jameson, Third World postmodernism must strike a balance between what he regards as the global postmodern cultural style and the needs of the national situation.[17] How far this is possible remains to be seen.

One is tempted to see Jameson as one of the few theorists of postmodernism to have attempted to think through the applicability of the term outside the developed West. His essay "Third World Literature in the Era of Multinational Capitalism" begins with the perception that all over the Third World there has been "an obsessive return of the national situation itself," which contrasts with the "long since liquidated" nationalism of the developed countries. It challenges, in his view, "our imprisonment in the present of postmodernism" by producing works that, while they often strike us as "conventional and naive," have "a freshness of information and a social interest that we cannot share." His argument is that Third World texts "necessarily project a political dimension in the form of a national allegory" and that this makes them "alien to us at first approach." Despite his disclaimers, there is a certain condescention in this approach, but its relevance to novels like Valenzuela's *Cola de lagartija*, Eloy Martínez's *La novela de Perón* or Allende's *La Casa de los Espíritus* is self-evident, especially because, in contradiction to his opening put-down of much Third World literature as old-fashioned, on reflection he is compelled to recognize that the defence of cultural specificity against cultural imperialism "seems to demand the invention of new forms."[18] Puig is one of his examples.

Jameson's article smacks, like the bulk of his writings, of his desire to relate postmodernism negatively to the current phase of late capitalism, an approach that, though sometimes illuminating, is ultimately reductive. Pushed to its extreme, it would in the end approximate to those of Viñas, Loyola, and others already mentioned. That is, it would condemn those aspects of the Post-Boom that remain strongly aesthetically orientated as merely prolongations of the Boom, which in turn is interpreted as a manifestation of Spanish American cultural dependency. By contrast, it would tend to exalt writers like Allende, Skármeta, Eloy Martínez, Posse, and Poniatowska as creators of "national allegories" that reflect the experience of the collectivity and represent a kind of counterdiscourse. Such a discourse, Jameson would like to think, the developed countries, sunk in "the illusions of a host of fragmented subjectivities . . . dying individual bodies without collective pasts or futures bereft of any possibility of grasping the social totality" have not only lost but are now incapable of comprehending. Notions of this kind, which perceive Third World cultural manifestations as largely unmediated products of infrastructural realities, cannot do justice to the complexities of the Post-Boom and must be viewed with caution.[19] But Jameson's postulate of a distinction between "two cultural logics" is of fundamental importance when we approach the question of relating the Post-Boom to postmodernism. For it is quite preposterous to write (as some commentators of the Lyotardian current in postmodernism do) as if confidence in the great explanatory or dynamizing myths and ideologies of modern society has been eroded everywhere. Certainly in Latin America there are far fewer indications that they have withered away than is supposed to be the case in the developed world.

The Post-Boom is, in part at least, a counter-project. It challenged the Boom at the point where the Boom had come to be a power-sytem legitimizing certain kinds of writing (and reading) while inhibiting or invalidating others—witness the negative reception of Puig's early work and the open resentment he expressed to Gazarian Gautier against a literary establishment that gave him no support. But its challenge to the Boom was in the name of ideas and values that were the reverse of word games. The Post Boom does not in general articulate the experience of a disorderly, directionless world in which our awareness of meaning is no more than an unstable and shifting construct with no purposiveness and no ultimate validation. To that extent, that is, to the extent that some form of collective project survives strongly in it, it cannot be easily fitted into mainstream postmodernism. Good equivalents are feminism and black culture in the United States. The former, for obvious reasons, remains committed to an ideal of equality and justice that is evidently incompatible with some prevailing conceptions of postmodernism that advocate or take for granted total ideological disintegration and cultural relativism (what Martin Hopenhayn in an illuminating essay calls "the disqualification of ideologies").[20] With regard to black culture, Cornel West, one of its advocates, insists that the authority of current conceptions of postmodernism must not remain uninterrogated. From a black perspective, he argues predictably that postmodernism is not a homogenous phenomenon and that its parameters must be widened to include the recognition that "political contestation is central." He goes on to criticize "the surfacelike character of a postmodern culture that refuses to speak to issues of despair" and that also attempts to ignore the brutal realities of areas of experience that the black underclass in the United States (and by extension the underclasses in Latin America) "cannot not know."[21] While in the developed countries opposition to the system has tended to become ever more muted since 1968 with the exception of certain black, gay, and feminist groups (themselves in process of deradicalization) and of course, in the United States, the religious Right, this is not the case as yet in Latin America to anything like the same extent. However, as Peter Brooker cogently remarks: "The challenge facing a progressive postmodernism committed to the possibility and necessity of 'basic political change' is how to articulate this commitment with postmodern dislocation and difference; how to achieve common political aims compatible with diverse social groups and agencies."[22] The potential conflict between an awareness of certain postmodernist assumptions and a desire for ongoing political commitment is a prominent feature of the current debate. Laura García-Moreno points out that some Latin American commentators have shown concern about the danger that the postmodern "crisis of legitimation" may include a tendency to delegitimize ideological agendas and to exert a paralizing effect on political militancy.[23] Certainly in the later work of writers like Skármeta and Valenzuela we can perceive indications of what Beverley and Oviedo call "the crisis of the project of the Left in Latin America."[24] But one might argue that this is a crisis of the radical Left, which still leaves room for advocating the kind of moderate democratic progressivism we now perceive in the outlook of the two writers in question and in that of Allende.

The fact is that over large areas of Post-Boom narrative in Spanish America we simply cannot postulate a loss or flattening of the distinction between signifier and signified or between the text of a novel and the world that surrounds it, as it has sometimes been alleged that we can do in some sectors of European and North American narrative. Thus we are driven back to recognizing some form of mixed coding that avoids old-style reflexionism, that is, to a nonconventional realism of the kind that Skármeta has referred to as "hiperrealismo," though not in the Baudrillardian sense. It is perhaps relevant to note that both Raymond Williams and Fredric Jameson (though for quite different reasons) have called for some sort of rehabilitation of realism.[25] One of the principal reasons we tend to see the Boom as allied to Modernism is its rejection of old-style mimesis, for as Lukács pointed out: "The negation of outward reality is present in almost all modernist literature."[26] It follows that to link the Post-Boom to certain aspects of postmodernism should not prevent us from recognizing that, in reaction against the Boom, it incorporates a form of "new realism" conditioned by a new sense of how and when and at which public it is directed. Similarly it tends toward what Eco, following Hayden White, has called "the rediscovery not only of plot but also of enjoyability"[27]—but not necessarily involving, as it tends to do in North American postmodernism, the problematization of representation, or any attempt to dehistoricize fiction (the sort of attempt of which Marxist critics sometimes complain).

When Linda Hutcheon writes that "What Postmodernism does is to denaturalize both realism's transparency and modernism's reflexive response while retaining (in its typically complicitously critical way) the historically attested power of both,"[28] she is saying rather portentously something that is applicable only in a more simplified way to the Post-Boom. That is, the Post-Boom writers, to the extent that they want to rehabilitate "realism's transparency" (in the cases, for example, of Skármeta, Allende, Giardinelli and Valenzuela, at various points in their work), wish to do so without wholly abandoning the legacy of the Boom, if that is possible. It is not a pretence of transparency, in contrast to real transparency, so much as a conscious foregrounding of uncomplicated representation that does not exclude elements that modify its realistic impact. Hutcheon in fact, like Jameson, is vaguely aware of this and, for all her references to Latin American texts, she is clearly uncomfortable with the application of North American concepts of postmodernism to Third World cultures. She writes defensively: "The ex-centric 'Other' itself may have different (and less complicitous) modes of representation and may therefore require diferent methods of study" (p. 38). The uncertainty in this statement bears underlining. It reminds us that the concept of postmodernism fits the Post-Boom only where it touches. In other words, as with feminism and black culture, we have to recognize that certain aspects of it (which may be the major ones) are not really compatible with postmodernism.

In reality, postmodernism, however we view it, tends to be uneasy with the concept of change (and especially of progress). Everything, for instance, that Hutcheon proposes about postmodernist "historiographic metafiction" in the end comes down to a "postmodern challenge to historical knowledge" in which "the undecidable" is paramount.[29] Despite the recognition, said to be part of postmodernism, that systems of meaning are "socially produced and historically conditioned,"[30] the kind of postmodernism Hutcheon postulates is remarkably reactionary. As such, it would not be endorsed by writers like Allende or Skármeta, though it is clearly relevant to other figures like the Vargas Llosa of *Historia de Mayta* and Posse.

One way to deal with this is to decenter postmodernism itself and think in terms of a plurality of postmodernisms, varying with different geographical contexts that are not all affected in the same way by political, social, and cultural change. This is clearly what underlies Colás's attempt to arrive at "a revised understanding of the multiple meanings of postmodernity when viewed globally" (p. xiii), that is, when an attempt is made to apply them to a specific literary or artistic culture, in his case, that of Argentina. His conclusion is that we must perceive "the various local postmodernities as related, but not therefore homogeneous or identical. As critics, we must retain, not pretend to resolve, a tension between what will remain as an unsatisfactorily homogenizing term: postmodernism, and the heterogeneous local forms produced within and sometimes against its logic" (p. 17). What this seems to imply is that the Post-Boom, in some of its aspects, could be considered a "local form" of postmodernism. But this does not dispose of the problem alluded to above. To accept, as Colás does, that we cannot understand postmodernism in Latin America unless we take on board the idea, underlying the texts he analyzes, that "historical representation" is "a site of social struggle"[31] is to postulate the survival in Latin American postmodernism of some valid form of collective project. In fact Colás explicitly refers on the concluding page of his book to "the project of remaking history, of reconstructing the future."[32] How can this be made compatible with what is alleged to be mainstream postmodernism's rejection of ideology?

Another way to approach the problem might be to borrow the distinction between postmodernism and postcolonialism used by Simon During and Helen Tiffin, and applied to the work of Eduardo Galeano by Diana Palaversich.[33] The value of this distinction is that it places the Post-Boom in a wider world perspective, one that foregrounds the ideological difference between a metropolitan movement (which is sometimes alleged to reflect the current late phase of capitalism through a crisis of cultural authority and of epistemological confidence) and a peripheral movement that, being more closely connected with the sociopolitical problems of the Third World, is apt to be more testimonial and militant. Palaverich does not hesitate to set the two terms in direct contrast to one another. Postmodernism is characterized by fragmentarism, self-referentiality, subversion of the literary canon, and scepticism about ideology and simple referentiality. Postcolonialism is seen as resisting postmodernism, accepting ideology and referentiality, and responding to an ongoing need in Third World nations to discover their identity. It is possible to argue that the process by which European and North American writers have sometimes tended to become estranged from society and to disassociate themselves from "objective" reality is not so prominent in Latin America, where social reality still often hovers between the contemporary and the traditional, has more clear-cut problems of injustice and oppression, and is in a sense a more *shared* reality than that of metropolitan nations.

However, Laura García-Moreno offers an important caveat. "For lack of a more substantive definition," she writes, "postmodernism is often placed in oppositional juxtaposition to postcolonialism. The challenge to the representability of the real crucial to postmodernism tends to be perceived as conflicting with the urgency felt by some writers and intellectuals to engage in social and political concerns." However, she goes on to argue that "An either/or perception of postmodernism/postcolonialism problematically assigns the need to produce realist representations of social/historical concerns to certain contexts and limits formal experimentation to advanced societies. It pushes the discussion towards exclusionary directions."[34] This is no doubt true, in the sense that a simplistic notion of postcolonialism would lead to our associating it with the work of writers like Benedetti, in which, as we have seen, formal experimentation is at a certain discount. But the existence in the Post-Boom of works like Valenzuela's *Como en la guerra* or Skármeta's "El ciclista del San Cristóbal" reminds us that there is no rigid separation between formal experimentalism (and the use of fantasy or myth), on the one hand, and commitment, on the other. We are concerned with trends and tendencies, not with "exclusionary directions." Bearing this in mind we may provisionally argue that the Post-Boom seems closer to postcolonialism than to postmodernism.[35]

At the same time we do well to keep in mind that *postcolonialism* is a term related particularly to countries that attained independence much later than Latin America. In them, on the one hand, the sense of postmodernism as a form of reinforcement of European and North American cultural hegemony might be expected to be more pronounced (though, as we have seen, it is not absent from some areas of Spanish American literary criticism). Similarly, the relation between postcolonialism and the search for national identity might be expected to be stronger in more recently independent countries. Finally, while it may be the case that writers in Africa or India have acquired familiarity with the outlook and techniques of recent Western fiction, Spanish America is unique in having experienced the Boom. Hence when Post-Boom writers in Spanish America react against certain features of the Boom, their reaction is more complex. It is not just against foreign models, but against a homegrown movement, and one that brought Spanish American fiction world attention. Postcolonialism, therefore, despite Palaversich's contrary opinion, means something slightly different in Spanish America. But is is a highly relevant term. Postcolonialist writers from Mexico to New Zealand to a greater or lesser degree tend to write nowadays with an adequate awareness of the heritage of modernism and the thrust of postmodernism. But they often choose to write consciously "as if" the ongoing evolution of Western literary outlook, and the changes in technique which go along with it, have a diminished relevance in postcolonial contexts, where pressures on the writer are different.

Whetever tentative conclusion we may reach, it seems inescapable that, as Geeta Kapur suggests apropos of postcolonial cultures generally,[36] Latin American culture probably should be seen to enter the postmodern age to some extent on its own terms, and that these include acceptance of the notion of the aesthetic as subversive. The problem of linking postmodernism to the Post-Boom is that the whole notion of postmodernism is in essence a critique of the modernist position and of all-encompassing explanations of the collective social and historical process. It postulates a crisis rather than formulating a doctrine, and it is therefore short on normativity. While there are works by Post-Boom writers, such as Valenzuela's *El gato eficaz*, that exalt the "ludic individualism" which some critics regard as forming part of the postmodernist outlook, they seem to lie wide of the movement's mainstream. Postmodernism's delegitimation of ideology, in other words, threatens the social agenda of some Post-Boom writers and would in fact tend to promote the idea of complete heterogeneity in the literary arena, with no dominant tendencies. By contrast, use of the term *Post-Boom* implies emphasis on the importance of a separate group of writers, identifiable by reference to a set of (loose) criteria. In this book we have deliberately embraced such an emphasis, but in the full postmodernist knowledge that there are no wholly reliable master narratives in literary history.

# NOTES

## CHAPTER 1. THE POST-BOOM

1. See, for example, David Viñas et al., *Más allá del Boom*. Buenos Aires: Folios, 1984. Roberto González Echevarría, "Sarduy, the Boom, and the Post-Boom." *Latin American Literary Review*, 15.29 (1987): 57–72. Ricardo Gutiérrez Mouat, "La narrativa latinoamericana del Post-Boom." *Revista Interamericana de Bibliografía* 38 (1988): 3–10. Donald Shaw, "Towards a Description of the Post-Boom," *Bulletin of Hispanic Studies* 66 (1989): 87–94. Gerald Martin, "After the Boom," *Journeys through the Labyrinth* (London: Verso, 1989) 309–58. Philip Swanson, "Conclusion: After the Boom," *Landmarks in Modern Latin American Fiction* (London: Routledge, 1990) 222–45. Peter G. Earle, "Back to the Center: Hispanic American Fiction Today," *Hispanic Review* 58 (1990): 19–35. Elzbieta Sklodowska, *La parodia en la nueva novela hispanoamericana* (Amsterdam: Benjamins, 1991). It should be noted that Charles Rossman, *After the Boom* (Madison: Wisconsin UP, 1987) is not on the Post-Boom.

2. Julio Cortázar, "La literatura latinoamericana de nuestro tiempo," *Argentina: Años de alambradas culturales*, ed. Saúl Yurkievich (Buenos Aires: Muchnik, 1984) 108–20.

3. David William Foster, *Alternate Voices in the Contemporary Latin American Narrative* (Columbus: Missouri UP, 1985) 2.

4. Donald L. Shaw, *Nueva narrativa hispanoamericana*, 5th ed. (Madrid: Cátedra, 1992) 218–24.

5. Noe Jitrik, *El no existente caballero* (Buenos Aires: Megalópolis, 1975) especially 82–92.

6. J. Ann Duncan, *Voices, Visions and a New Reality* (Pittsburgh: U of Pittsburgh P, 1986) 9.

7. Sklodowska, *La parodia en la nueva novela hispanoamericana*, xii–xiii. Sklodowska does not attempt to distinguish between Boom and Post-Boom. For the full texts of the lists given by Duncan and Sklodowska, see too my "Which was the First Novel of the Boom?" *Modern Language Review* 89 (1994): 362–63.

8. Carlos Fuentes, *La nueva novela hispanoamericana* (Mexico City: Mortiz, 1969) 20.

9. Carlos Alonso, *The Spanish America Regional Novel* (Cambridge UP, 1990); Roberto González Echevarría, *Myth and Archive* (Cambridge: Cambridge UP, 1990) especially 142–61.

10. Angel Rama, "El Boom en perspectiva," *Más allá del Boom*, ed. Viñas (note 1 above) 51–110, especially 61: "¿qué es el Boom sino la más extraordi-

naria toma de conciencia por parte del pueblo latinoamericano de una parte de su propia identidad?"

11. Julio Cortázar, "Literatura e identidad," *Argentina: Años de alambrados culturales* (note 2 above), 71–75.

12. Gabriel García Márquez, "La soledad de América Latina," *La soledad de América Latina* (Bogotá: Corporación Editorial Universitaria de Colombia, 1983) 8–9.

13. Inca Rumold, "Independencia cultural de Latinoamérica," *Plural* (Mexico City), 241 (1991): 21.

14. Alejo Carpentier, *La novela hispanoamericana en vísperas de un nuevo siglo y otros ensayos*, 2nd ed. (Mexico City: Siglo XXI, 1981) 157.

15. Carpentier, *La novela hispanoamericana*, 14–15, 25.

16. Mempo Giardinelli, "Un retorno a la espontaneidad." *Clarín* (Buenos Aires) Suplemento: Cultura y Nación, 2 January 1986: 2.

17. Gutiérrez Mouat, "La narrativa Latinoamericana del Post-Boom." I had not seen this article when I wrote my own "Towards a Description of the Post-Boom," on which the present chapter is based. The arguments, arrived at independently, are extremely similar.

18. Respectively in *Avances del saber*, vol. 9 of *Enciclopedia Labor* (Barcelona: Labor, 1975) 753–71; *Revista de Literatura Hispanoamericana*, Maracaibo (Universidad de Zulia) 10 (1976): 9–18 (also in French in *Europe* [Paris] 570 [1976]: 191–98); and Raúl Silva Cáceres, ed., *Del cuerpo a las palabras: La narrativa de Antonio Skármeta* (Madrid: LAR, 1983) 131–47.

19. See Jorge Ruffinelli, "Antonio Skármeta, la embriaguez vital" (an interview), *Crítica en Marcha* (Montevideo: Premia, 1979) 143.

20. Antonio Skármeta, "Suprarrealidad e hiperrealidad en los cuentos de Juan Rulfo," *Spanien und Lateinamerika*, ed. Carlos Segoviano and José M. Navarro (Nuremberg: Deutscher Spanischlehrer Verband, 2, 1984) 791.

21. See in this connection the last chapter of my *Nueva narrativa hispanoamericana* (note 1 above), 218–19.

22. "Isabel Allende" (anonymous interview), *Nuevo Texto Crítico* 4.8 (1991): 75.

23. Isabel Allende, "Mis raíces están en los libros que escribo," *Cambio 16* (Madrid) no 1048 (22 December 1991): 121.

24. Isabel Allende, "La magia de las palabras," *Revista Iberoamericana* 132.3, (1985): 451.

25. Isabel Allende, "Por qué y para qué escribo," *Araucaria de Chile* (Madrid) 41 (1988): 158.

26. Isabel Allende, in Shannon Jones and Bill Prillaman, "Interview with Isabel Allende," *Virginia Advocate* (Campus Magazine, University of Virginia) 3.2 (October 1987): 13.

27. Isabel Allende in Michael Moody, "Entrevista con Isabel Allende," *Discurso Literario* 4.1 (1986): 44.

28. Sergio Ramírez, *Las armas del futuro* (Managua: Editorial Nueva Nicaragua, 1987) 323, cit. Ross, "The Politician as Novelist" 170.

29. Jaime Mejía Duque, *Literatura y realidad* (Medellín: Oveja Negra, 1976) 229.

30. Antonio Skármeta, in Deniss Reale, "Entrevista con Antonio Skármeta." *KO-EYU Latinoamericano*, (La Paz, Bolivia), 20 (1981): 39.

31. Mempo Giardinelli, in Teresa Mendes-Faith, "Entrevista con Mempo Giardinelli," *Discurso Literario* 5.2 (1988): 318.

32. Mempo Giardinelli, "Variaciones sobre la postmodernidad o ¿Qué es eso del posboom latinoamericano," *Puro Cuento* (Buenos Aires) 23 (1990): 30.

33. Mempo Giradinelli, "Fichero," *Nuevo Texto Crítico* 5 (1990): 187.

34. In Gwen Kirkpatrick, "Entrevista con Teresa Porzecanski." *Discurso Literario* 5.2 (1988): 306.

35. Montevideo: Marcha, 1969.

36. Buenos Aires: Hispamérica, 1976.

37. Madrid: Orígenes, 1986.

38. Mexico City: Katún, 1983.

39. Jaques Leenhardt, "La estructura ensayistica de la novela latinoamericana," *Más allá del Boom*, ed. Viñas 137–38.

40. Andreas Huyssen, *After the Great Divide: Modernism, Mass Culture, Postmodernism* (Bloomington: Indiana UP, 1986) 16.

41. Earle, "Back to the Center" 23.

42. Juan Armando Epple, "El contexto histórico-generacional de la literatura de Antonio Skármeta," *Del cuerpo a las palabras*, ed. Cáceras 101–15.

43. Angel Rama, ed., *Novísimos narradores hispanoamericanos en marcha* (Mexico City: Marcha, 1981). The updated version of the introduction appears in Angel Rama, *La novela latinoameriacana, 1920–80* (Bogotá: Instituto Colombiano de Cultura, 1982) 455–94.

44. Epple, "El contexto histórico-generacional" 108.

45. José Agustín, "Contemporary Mexican Fiction," *Three Lectures: Literature and Censorship in Latin America Today*, U of Denver Occasional Papers 1 (Denver: U of Denver, Dept. of Foreign Languages and Literatures, 1978) 23.

46. Donald L. Shaw, "'La Cenicienta de San Francisco' by Antonio Skármeta," *Revista de Estudios Hispánicos* 22 (1987): 89–99.

47. Angel Rama, "Más allá del la ciudad letrada," *Espejo de Escritores*, ed. Reina Roffé (Hanover NH: Ediciones del Norte, 1985) 208–10.

48. Angel Rama,"Los contestatarios del poder," *La novela latinoamericana 1920–1980* (Bogotá: Instituto Colombiano de Cultura, 1982) 466.

49. Julio Cortázar, "Modelos para desarmar," *Espejo de escritores*, ed. Roffé 60–61.

50. Rama, "Los contestarios del poder" 490.

51. González Echevarría, "Severo Sarduy, the Boom and the Post-Boom"; and *La ruta de Severo Sarduy* (Hanover, NH: Ediciones del Norte, 1987) especially 243–53.

52. Ronald Christ, "Interview with José Donoso," *Partisan Review* 49 (1982): 41.

53. Philip Swanson, "Structure and Meaning in *La misteriosa desaparición de la marquesita de Loria*," *Bulletin of Hispanic Studies* 58 (1986): 247–56; "Donoso and the Post-Boom," *Contemporary Literature* 28 (1987): 520–29; and *José Donoso: The Boom and Beyond* (Liverpool: Cairns, 1988).

54. Swanson, "Donoso and the Post-Boom" 527.

55. Raymond L. Williams, "The Boom Twenty Years Later: An Interview with Mario Vargas Llosa." *Latin American Literary Review* 15.29 (1986): 201, 202.

56. González Echeverría, *La ruta de Severo Sarduy* 249.

57. Duncan, *Voices, Visions and a New Reality* 5.

58. Foster, *Alternate Voices*, chap. 1; René Jara and Hernán Vidal, *Testimonio y literatura* (Minneapolis: Institute for the Study of Ideologies and Literature, 1986); Elzbieta Sklodowska, *Testimonio hispanoamericano: Historia, teoría, poética* (New York: Lang, 1992).

59. Gutiérrez Mouat, "La narrativa latinoamericana del Post-Boom 8–9.

## CHAPTER 2. THE TRANSITION

1. Elsa Dehennin, "A propósito del realismo de Mario Benedetti," *Revista Iberoamericana* 160–61 (1992): 1079, 1084.

2. Eileen Zietz, *La crítica, el exilio y más allá en las novelas de Mario Benedetti* (Montevideo: Amesur, 1986).

3. Mario Benedetti, "El escritor y la crítica en el contexto del subdesarrollo." *Casa de las Américas* 107 (1978): 3–21. Later included in *El recurso del supremo patriarca* (Mexico City: Nueva Imagen, 1979) 33–67. Additional page numbers given in the text are from the 1978 publication.

4. Mario Benedetti, *El escritor latinoamericano y la revolución posible* (Buenos Aires: Alfa Argentina, 1974) 95. Page references are to this edition.

5. Mario Benedetti, *Gracias por el fuego* (Montevideo: Alfa, 1972) 206.

6. David William Foster, *Alternate Voices in the Contemporary Latin American Narrative* (Columbia: Missouri UP, 1985) 2.

7. David Viñas, *De Sarmiento a Cortázar* (Buenos Aires: Siglo Veinte, 1971) 84, 89.

8. David Viñas, "Después de Cortázar: Historia y privatización," *Cuadernos Hispanoamericanos* 234 (1969): 734–39.

9. Diógenes Fajardo, *La novelística de David Viñas* (Lawrence: Kansas UP, 1981) 28.

10. Angela Dellepiane, "La novela argentina desde 1950 hasta 1965," *Revista Iberoamericana* 66 (1968): 281.

11. In David Viñas et al., *Más Allá del Boom* (Buenos Aires: Folios, 1984) 16.

12. Gustavo Sainz, *Gustavo Sainz* (Mexico City: Empresas Editoriales, 1966) 34.

13. Juan Carlos Tealdi, *Borges y Viñas* (Madrid, Orígenes: 1983) 102.

14. Julio Cortázar, "El escritor y su quehacer en América Latina," *El País Semanal* 17 October 1982: 81.

15. Julio Cortázar, "La literatura latinoamericana a la luz de la historia contemporánea," *INTI* 10–11 (1979–80): 15.

16. For Puig see for instance Jonathan Tittler, *Manuel Puig* (New York: Twayne, 1993) and for Sarduy, Roberto González Echevarría, *La ruta de Severo Sarduy* (Hanover, NH: Ediciones del Norte, 1987) 243–53.

17. Fredric Jameson, foreword, *The Post-Modern Condition: A Report on Knowledge*, by Jean-François Lyotard (Minneapolis: Minnesota UP, 1988) viii.

18. Jacques Derrida, *Writing and Difference* (Chicago: U of Chicago P, 1980) 292.

19. Tittler, *Manuel Puig* 53.

20. Mario Vargas Llosa, "The Latin American Novel Today" *Books Abroad* 44 (1970): 7–16; Emir Rodríguez Monegal, "The New Latin American Novel," *Books Abroad* 44 (1970): 45–50.

21. Fredric Jameson, "Third World Literature in the Era of Multinational Capitalism," *Social Text* 15 (1986): 82; Linda Hutcheon, *The Politics of Postmodernism* (London: Routledge, 1989) 8, 47; Lucille Kerr, *Suspended Fictions* (Urbana: Illinois UP, 1987) 5, 24.

22. Tittler, *Manuel Puig* vii; Pamela Bacarisse, *Impossible Choices* (Calgary: U of Calgary P; Cardiff: U of Wales P, 1993) 149.

23. Fredric Jameson, "Postmodernism; or, The Cultural Logic of Late Capitalism," *New Left Review* 146 (1984): 54–55.

24. Hutcheon, *The Politics of Postmodernism* 44.

25. Jean Franco, "Memoria, narración y repetición: La narrativa hispanoamericana en la época de la cultura de masas," *Más allá del Boom*, ed. Viñas 122–23.

26. Tittler, *Manuel Puig* 9.

27. In Saul Sosnowski, "Manuel Puig, entrevista," *Hispamérica* 3 (1973): 73.

28. Marie-Lise Gazarian Gautier, "Manuel Puig," *Interviews with Latin American Writers* (Elmwood Park, IL: Dalkey Archive P, 1989) 229.

29. M. Osorio, "Entrevista con Manuel Puig," *Cuadernos Para el Diálogo* 231 (1977): 51, 53.

30. Kerr, *Suspended Fictions* 14.

31. Enrique Giordano, "*Boquitas pintadas*: recontextualización de la cultura popular," *Manuel Puig, montaje y alteridad del sujeto*, by Roberto Echevarren and Enrique Giordano (Santiago de Chile: Monografías del Maitén, 1986) 27.

32. Cit. Bella Josef without reference to a source in "Manuel Puig: Reflexión al nivel de la enunciación," *Nueva Narrativa Hispanoamericana* 4 (1974): 112.

33. Guillermo Yepes Boscán, "Asturias, un pretexto del mito." *Aportes* 8 (1968): 99–116; Nelson Osorio, "Lenguaje narrativo y estructura significativa de *El Señor Presidente*," *Escritura* (Caracas) 5–6 (1978): 99–156.

34. Manuel Puig interviewed by Reina Roffé in *Espejo de escritores*, ed. Reina Roffé (Hanover, NH: Ediciones del Norte, 1985) 131.

35. Jorgelina Corbatta, "Encuentros con Manuel Puig," *Revista Iberoamericana* 123–24 (1983): 611.

36. Roffé, *Espejo de escritores* 144.

37. Milagros Ezquerra in the discussion reproduced in *Manuel Puig*, ed. Juan Manuel García Ramos (Madrid: Cultura Hispánica, 1991) 52.

38. García Ramos, *Manuel Puig* 40.

39. Corbatta, "Encuentros con Manuel Puig" 609.

40. René Prieto, "In Fringe: The Role of French Criticism in the Fiction of Nicole Brossard and Severo Sarduy," *Do the Americas have a Common Literature?* ed. Gustavo Pérez Firmat (Durham: Duke UP, 1990) 270.

41. Echevarren and Giordano, *Manuel Puig* 73.

42. Roberto González Echevarría, "Sarduy, the Boom, and the Post-Boom," *Latin American Literary Review* 15.29 (1987): 57–72. See also María Acosta Cruz, "El regreso al Caribe de Severo Sarduy," *Hispanófila* 113 (1995): 69–80, which develops González Echevarría's approach to include *Cocuyo*.

43. Suzanne Jill Levine, preface to *Cobra*, by Severo Sarduy (New York: Dutton, 1975) vii.

44. Ada Teja, "Entrevista: Severo Sarduy," *Hispamérica* 61 (1992): 62.

45. Macedonio Fernández, *Museo de la novela de la Eterna* (Buenos Aires: Corregidor, 1975) 48.

46. Roberto González Echevarría, preface to *Maitreya*, by Severo Sarduy, trans. Suzanne Jill Levine (Hanover, NH: Ediciones del Norte, 1987) viii.

47. Oscar Montero, *The Name Game* (Chapel Hill: U of North Carolina P, 1988) 67.

48. José Agustín, *Three Lectures: Literature and Censorship in Latin America Today* (Denver: University of Denver, Department of Foreign Languages and Literatures, 1978) 9.

49. Severo Sarduy, *Escrito sobre un cuerpo* (Buenos Aires: Sudamericana, 1969) 25.

50. Adriana Méndez Rodenas, "Severo Sarduy: *Colibrí*," *Revista Iberoamericana* 130–31 (1985): 399.

51. Teja, "Entrevista: Severo Sarduy" 63.

52. Montero, *The Name Game* 47.

53. Teja, "Entrevista: Severo Sarduy" 60.

54. Agustín Cadena, "*Farabeuf*, el espacio como metáfora del tiempo," *Plural* (Mexico) 258 (1993): 51.

55. Alejandro Toledo and Daniel González Dueñas, "Entrevista," *Universidad de México* 484 (1991): 41.

56. Bucknell UP, 1994.

57. Enrico Marío Santí, "Textual Politics: Severo Sarduy." *Latin American Literary Review* 8.16 (1980): 158.

## CHAPTER 3. ISABEL ALLENDE

1. Julio Cortázar, "Algunos aspectos del cuento," *Casa de las Américas* 2.15–16 (1962–63): 3–4.

2. Adriana Méndez Rodenas, *Severo Sarduy: El neobarroco de la transgresión* (Mexico City: Universidad Autónoma, 1983) 63; Gustavo Guerrero, *La estrategia neo-barroca* (Barcelona: Ediciones del Mall, 1987) 53.

3. Gloria Gutiérrez, "Entrevista con Isabel Allende," *Realismo mágico, cosmos latinoamericano, teoría y práctica* (Bogotá: América Latina, 1991) 134.

4. Michael Moody, "Entrevista con Isabel Allende," *Discurso Literario* 4.1 (1986): 46; and see more comments in Margaret Munro-Clark, "An Inter-

view with Isabel Allende," *Antipodas* 6–7 (1994–95): 15–27.

5. Patricia Hart, *Narrative Magic in the Fiction of Isabel Allende* (London: Associated University Presses, 1989). On the specific issue of imitation of García Márquez, see Laurie Clancy, "Isabel Allende's Dialogue with García Márquez," *Antipodas* 6–7 (1994–95): 29–43.

6. Isabel Allende, "Sobre *La Casa de los Espíritus*," *Discurso Literario* 2.1 (1984): 69.

7. Isabel Allende, lecture on her work at the University of Virginia on 7 October 1987.

8. Hart, *Narrative Magic* 39.

9. Marie-Lise Gazarian Gautier, "Isabel Allende," *Interviews with Latin American Writers* (Elmwood Park, IL: Dalkey Archive P, 1989) 14.

10. Marjorie Agosín, "Isabel Allende: *La Casa de los Espíritus*," *Revista Interamericana de Bibliografía* 35 (1985): 448–58.

11. Isabel Allende, *La Casa de los Espíritus*, 22nd ed. (Barcelona: Plaza y Janés, 1986) 379.

12. Linda Hutcheon, "The Pastime of Past-Time: Fiction, History, Historiographic Metafiction," *Postmodern Genres*, ed. Marjorie Perloff (Norman: U of Oklahoma P, 1989) 55.

13. Marcel Coddou, *Para leer a Isabel Allende* (Concepción: LAR, 1988) 48.

14. Hart, *Narrative Magic* 93.

15. Cit. Hart, *Narrative Magic* 123 from an interview by Allende with Vera Janach published in *El Mundo* (Puerto Rico) in March 1985.

16. Coddou, *Para leer a Isabel Allende* 104.

17. Ana María Barrenechea, "La crisis del contrato mimético en los textos contemporáneos," *Revista Iberoamericana* 118–19 (1982): 377–81 (a crucial article for understanding the differences between the peak of the Boom and the Post-Boom); Guerrero, *La estrategia neo-barroca* 111–27, "El personaje y sus discursos."

18. Virginia Invernizzi, "The Novels of Isabel Allende: A Reevaluation of Genre," diss. U of Virginia, 1991.

19. Sharon Magnarelli, *The Lost Rib* (London: Associated UP, 1985) 191.

20. Marjorie Agosín, "Interview with Isabel Allende," *Imagine* l.2 (1984): 53–55.

21. Philip Swanson, *José Donoso: The Boom and Beyond*. Liverpool: Cairns, 1988, 69.

22. Gazarian Gautier, "Isabel Allende" 16. "An Interview with Isabel Allende." *Contemporary Literature* 33.4 (1991).

23. María I. Lagos Pope, "*De amor y de sombra*," *Latin American Literary Review* 15.29 (1987): 211.

24. Juan Manuel Marcos, "El género popular como meta-estructura textual del Post-Boom latinoamericano." *Revista Monográfica* 5.1–2 (1988): 270.

25. Kamta Panjabi, "Tránsito Soto: From Periphery to Power," *Critical Approaches to Isabel Allende's Novels*, ed. Sonia Riquelme Rojas and Edna Aguirre Rehbein (New York: Lang, 1991) 11–12.

26. Isabel Allende, *De amor y de sombra*, 8th ed. (Barcelona: Plaza y Janés, 1986) 141.

27. Gabriela Mora, "Las novelas de Isabel Allende y el papel de la mujer como ciudadana," *Ideologies and Literature* 2.1 (1987): 53–61; Monique J. Lemaitre, "Deseo, incesto y represión en *De amor y de sombra* de Isabel Allende," *Critical Approaches*, ed. Riquelme Rojas and Aguirre Rehbein, especially 105.

28. Lagos-Pope, "*De amor y de sombra*" 211–12.

29. "Optimist": cit. Hart, *Narrative Magic* 123. "Despair": Isabel Allende, "Por qué y para quien escribo," *Araucaria de Chile* (Madrid) 41 (1988): 123. "Aim": cit. Coddou, *Para leer a Isabel Allende* 106. "Love": Gazarian Gautier, *Interviews* 16.

30. Virginia Invernizzi and Melissa Pope, "A Parallel: Silent History in Novels," *Iris* 19 (1988): 28.

31. Beatriz Hernández-Gómez, "*De amor y de sombra*: Un juego de oposiciones," *Quaderni di Letterature Iberiche e Iberoamericane* 5 (1986): 59.

32. Susan de Carvalho, "Escrituras y escritoras: The Artist Protagonist of Isabel Allende," *Discurso Literario* 10.1 (1992): 64–65.

33. Ellen Friedman, "Where Are the Missing Contents? (Post) Modernism, Gender and the Canon," *PMLA* 108 (1993): 240–52.

34. Riquelme Rojas and Aguirre Rehbein, *Critical Approaches* 195.

35. Elyse Crystall, "An Interview with Isabel Allende," *Contemporary Literature* 33.4 (1992): 588.

36. Wolfgang Karrer, "Transformism and Transvestism in *Eva Luna*," *Critical Approaches*, ed. Riquelme Rojas and Aguirre Rehbein 161.

37. Isabel Allende, *Eva Luna*, 3rd ed. (Barcelona: Plaza y Janés, 1987) 244.

38. Pilar Rotella, "Allende's *Eva Luna* and the Picaresque tradition," in *Critical Approaches*, ed. Riquelme Rojas and Aguirre Rehbein 131.

39. Miguel Alfonso, "*Eva Luna*: El folletín: ¿Tránsito a la novela total?" *Araucaria de Chile* (Madrid) 41 (1988): 166.

40. Gazarian Gautier, *Interviews* 16.

41. Marcelo Coddou, "Dimensión paródica de *Eva Luna*" in *Critical Approaches*, ed. Riquelme Rojas and Aguirre Rehbein 139–49; María Montserrat Alas-Brun, "*Bolero*, el *kitsch* en *Eva Luna*," *Antipodas* 5–6 (1994–95): 45–54; Edna Aguirre Rehbein, "The Act/Art of Writing in *Eva Luna*," *Antipodas* 5–6 (1994–95): 179–90; de Carvalho, "Escrituras y escritoras," 59–67.

42. Isabel Allende, *El Plan Infinito* (Buenos Aires: Sudamericana, 1991) 196.

43. Ernesto Sábato, *El escritor y sus fantasmas*, 3rd ed. (Buenos Aires: Aguilar, 1967) 37.

44. See Donald L. Shaw, "Notes on the Presentation of Sexuality in the Modern Spanish American Novel," *Bulletin of Hispanic Studies* 59 (1982): 275–82; and "More Notes on the Presentation of Sexuality in the Modern Spanish American Novel," *Carnal Knowledge*, ed. Pamela Bacarisse (Pittsburgh: Tres Rios, [1993]) 113–27.

45. See Moody, "Entrevista con Isabel Allende" 51.

46. John Rodden, "The Responsibility to Tell You," *Kenyon Review* 13.1 (1991): 117, 119.

## CHAPTER 4. ANTONIO SKÁRMETA

1. For a fuller treatment of this author, see my *Antonio Skármeta and the Post-Boom* (Hanover NH: Ediciones del Norte, 1994), on which this chapter is based.

2. See my article "'La Cenicienta en San Francisco' by Antonio Skármeta," *Revista de Estudios Hispánicos* 21.2 (1987): 89–99.

3. Ciro Bianchi Rossi, "Skármeta, la huella de la época," *Cuba Internacional* 16.177 (1984): 55.

4. Veronica Cortínez, "Polifonía: Entrevista a Isabel Allende y Antonio Skármeta," *Revista Chilena de Literatura* 32 (1988): 81.

5. Ariel Dorfman, "¿Volar?" *Revista Chilena de Literatura* 1 (1970): 74; and see my article "Skármeta and Sexuality," *Paunch* 65–66 (1991): 11–29.

6. Menene Gras Balaguer, "Entrevista con Antonio Skármeta," *Insula* 478 (1986): 14.

7. Carlos Rincón, "Entrevista con Antonio Skármeta," *Caribe* (Caracas) 4 January 1976 (pages unnumbered).

8. "Foro" (unsigned interview), *Parapara* (Caracas) 7 (1983): 37.

9. Raúl Silva Cáceres, "Elementos para una poética de lo cotidiano en la obra de Antonio Skármeta," *Del cuerpo a las palabras: La narrativa de Antonio Skármeta*, ed. Raúl Silva Cáceres (Madrid: LAR, 1982) 16.

10. Antonio Skármeta, "Tendencias en la más nueva narrativa hispanoamericana," *Enciclopedia Labor*, vol. 9, *Avances del Saber* (Barcelona: Labor, 1975) 754; and "La novísima generación: Varias características y un límite," *Revista de Literatura Hispanoamericana* (Maracaibo, Universidad de Zulia) 10 (1976): 10. A French version of this second article appeared in *Europe* (Paris) 570 (1976): 191–98.

11. See my article: "The structure of Antonio Skármeta's *Soñé que la nieve ardía*," *Paradise Lost or Gained?* ed. Fernando Alegría and Jorge Ruffinelli (Houston: Arte Público, 1990) 145–50.

12. Antonio Skármeta, *No pasó nada* (Santiago de Chile: Pehuén, 1985) 20.

13. Grinor Rojo, "El tema del viaje y del aprendizaje en *No pasó nada*," *Del cuerpo a las palabras*, ed. Silva Cáceres 69–80.

14. María Elena Wood, "Antonio Skármeta" (interview), *Caras* (Santiago de Chile) 4 (15 June 1983): 56.

15. Ariel Dorfman, "La derrota de la distancia: La obra de Antonio Skármeta," *Del cuerpo a las palabras*, ed. Silva Cáceres 85.

16. Victoria Verlichak, "Del entusiasmo a la insurrección," *Unomasuno*, (Mexico City) (3 July 1982): 4.

17. Gras Balaguer, "Entrevista con Antonio Skármeta" 14.

18. Elzbieta Sklodowska, *La parodia en la nueva novela hispanoamericana*, Purdue University Monographs (Amsterdam: Benjamins, 1991) 35–43 etc.; and Seymour Menton, *Latin America's New Historical Novel* (Austin: U of Texas P, 1993) 64–80 etc.

19. For more on this alluring topic, see my articles mentioned in chapter 3, note 38 and my "Skármeta and Sexuality," mentioned in note 5 above.

20. Antonio Skármeta, *Ardiente paciencia* (Hanover, NH: Ediciones del Norte, 1985) iii.

21. Gras Balaguer, "Entrevista con Antonio Skármeta."

22. Antonio Skármeta, *Match Ball* (Buenos Aires: Sudamericana, 1989) 60.

23. See my article "La metáfora del abismo en *Sobre héroes y tumbas* de Sábato," *Actas del X Congreso de la Asociación Internacional de Hispanistas*, ed. Antonio Villanova, vol. 4 (Barcelona: Promociones y Publicaciones Universitarias, 1992) 985–91.

24. Andrea Pagni, "Entrevista con Antonio Skármeta." *Discurso Literario* 5.1 (1985): 66.

25. Horacio Xaubet, *Entrevista con Antonio Skármeta*, Washington U Occasional Paper (St. Louis: Washington U, 1988) 13.

## CHAPTER 5. LUISA VALENZUELA

1. For a discussion of these see my article "Which Was the First Novel of the Boom?" *Modern Language Review* 89 (1994): 360–71, and the last chapter of my *Nueva narrativa hispanoamericana*, 5th ed. (Madrid: Cátedra, 1992).

2. See Pamela Bacarisse, "An Interview with Manuel Puig," *Carnal Knowledge*, ed. Pamela Bacarisse (Pittsburgh, Tres Ríos, 1993) 129.

3. Sharon Magnarelli, *Reflections/Refractions: Reading Luisa Valenzuela* (New York: Lang, 1988) 211.

4. Z. Nelly Martínez, *El silencio que habla: Aproximación a la obra de Luisa Valenzuela* (Buenos Aires: Corregidor, 1994) 53–54.

5. Magnarelli, *Reflections* 7.

6. Magnarelli, *Reflections* 7.

7. Magnarelli, *Reflections* 207.

8. Luisa Valenzuela, "Little Manifesto," *Review of Contemporary Fiction* 6.3 (1986): 20–21.

9. Luisa Valenzuela in Marie-Lise Gazarian Gautier, *Interviews with Latin American Writers* (Elmwood Park, IL: Dalkey Archive, 1989) 314.

10. See Luisa Valenzuela, "So-Called Latin American Writing," *Critical Theory, Cultural Politics and Latin American Narrative*, ed. Steven Bell (Notre Dame: U of Notre Dame P, 1993) 209–21. The reference is to p. 214.

11. Valenzuela, "So-Called Latin American Writing" 213; Gazarian Gautier, *Interviews* 304.

12. See her interview, "Luisa Valenzuela," in Evelyn Picón Garfield, *Women's Voices from Latin America* (Detroit: Wayne State UP, 1985) 150, 153.

13. Gazarian Gautier, *Interviews* 298, 308.

14. The quotations come from, respectively, Picón Garfield, "Luisa Valenzuela," 154, 158; Magnarelli, *Reflections* 207; Gazarian Gautier, *Interviews* 300; and Valenzuela, "So-Called Latin American Writing" 218.

15. Magnarelli, *Reflections* 49.

16. Picón Garfield, "Luisa Valenzuela," 147.

17. Valenzuela, *Los heréticos* 29.

18. Dorothy Mull and Elsa de Angulo, "An Afternoon with Luisa Valenzuela," *Hispania* 69 (1986): 351.

19. Martínez, *El silencio que habla* 65.

20. Magdalena García Pinto, *Women Writers of Latin America: Intimate Histories* (Austin: U of Texas P, 1988) 216.

21. Luisa Valenzuela, "Dangerous Words," *Review of Contemporary Fiction* 6.3 (1986) 9.

22. Ana Fores, "Valenzuela's *Cat-o-Nine Deaths*," *Review of Contemporary Fiction* 6.3 (1986): 39–47.

23. Diane Marting, "Female Sexuality in Selected Stories by Luisa Valenzuela," *Review of Contemporary Fiction* 6.3 (1986): 48.

24. Juanamaría Cordones-Cook, *Poética de la transgresión en la novelística de Luisa Valenzuela* (New York: Lang, 1991) 24.

25. Martínez, *El silencio que habla* 38.

26. García Pinto, *Women Writers* 197, 200.

27. Luisa Valenzuela, *Open Door* (San Francisco: North Point, 1988) ix.

28. Luisa Valenzuela, "A Legacy of Poets and Cannibals," first published in the *New York Times Book Review* 16 March, 1986: 34 and reproduced in Doris Meyer, *Lives on the Line: The Testimony of Contemporary Latin American Authors* (Berkeley: California UP, 1988) 292–97.

29. Gazarian Gautier, *Interviews* 299–300.

30. Magnarelli, *Reflections* 49.

31. Luisa Valenzuela, *Como en la guerra* (Buenos Aires: Sudamericana, 1977) 92.

32. See, for example, Emily Hicks, "That which Resists: The Code of the Real in Luisa Valenzuela's *He Who Searches*," *Review of Contemporary Fiction* 6.3 (1986): 55–61; Margo Glantz, "Luisa Valenzuela's *He Who Searches*," *Review of Contemporary Fiction* 6.3 (1986): 52–65; Guillermo Maci, "The Symbolic, The Imaginary and the Real in Luisa Valenzuela's *He Who Searches*," *Review of Contemporary Fiction* 6.3 (1986): 67–77; Magnarelli, *Reflections* 77–98; Cordones-Cook, *Poética*, 31–45.

33. The English translation appears in *Strange Things Happen Here* (New York: Harcourt, Brace, Jovanovich, 1979). "Page Zero" is not the only omission from the Argentine edition. Cf pp. 52, 100, 150, and 162–63 of the Argentine edition (Buenos Aires: Sudamericana, 1977) and pp. 125, 135–37, 191, and 200 of the American one, respectively.

34. Montserrat Ordoñez, "Máscaras de espejos, un juego especular," *Revista Iberoamericana* 132–33 (1985): 516.

35. Magnarelli, *Reflections* 79.

36. Cordones-Cook, *Poética* 33.

37. Hicks, "That which Resists the Code" 51; Maci, "The Symbolic" 69; Magnarelli, *Reflections* 96.

38. Valenzuela, *Como en la guerra* 125.

39. Meyer, *Lives on the Line* 294.

40. Luisa Valenzuela, *Cambio de armas* (Hanover, NH: Ediciones del Norte, 1982) 9.

41. Luisa Valenzuela, *Novela negra con argentinos* (Barcelona: Plaza y Janés, 1990) 135.

42. Magnarelli, *Reflections* 189.

43. Joanne Saltz, "Luisa Valenzuela's *Cambio de armas*: Rhetoric of Politics," *Confluencia* (Colorado) 3.1 (1987): 63.

44. Gabriela Mora, "Las novelas de Isabel Allende y el papel de la mujer como ciudadana," *Ideologies and Literature* 2.1 (1987): 53–61.

45. Martínez, *El silencio que habla* 164.

46. María I. Lagos Pope, "Mujer y política en *Cambio de armas* de Luisa Valenzuela," *Hispamérica* 46–47 (1987): 81.

47. But see the argument for greater complexity advanced by Diane E. Marting in "Gender and Metaphoricity in Luisa Valenzuela's 'I'm Your Horse in the Night," *World Literature Today* 69.4 (1995) (Luisa Valenzuela Number): 702–8, with a critique of the present author's view of Valenzuela as a Post-Boom writer.

48. Cordones-Cook, *Poética* 56; Martínez, *El silencio que habla* 178–79.

49. Gazarian Gautier, *Interviews* 316.

50. Barbara Pauler Fulks, "A Reading of Luisa Valenzuela's Short Story 'La palabra asesino,'" *Monographic Review* 4 (1988): 179–88. See my "The Narrative Strategy of 'La palabra asesino,'" *Antipodas* 6–7 (1994–95): 173–81.

51. Debra A. Castillo in chapter 3 (pp. 96–136) of her *Talking Back* (Ithaca: Cornell UP, 1992); see also Willy O. Muñoz, "El lenguaje hémbrico en 'Cambio de armas,'" *Antipodas* 6–7 (1994–95): 183–89.

52. Rosemary Geisdorfer Feal, "The Politics of 'Wargasm': Sexuality, Domination and Female Subversion in Luisa Valenzuela's *Cambio de armas*," *Structures of Power*, ed. Terry J. Peavler and Peter Standish (Albany: State U of New York P, 1996) 162.

53. Valenzuela, "Legacy" 293.

54. Luisa Valenzuela, *Cola de lagartija*, 2nd ed. (Buenos Aires: Bruguera, 1983) 7.

55. See Gwendolyn Diaz, "Postmodernismo y teoría del caos en *Cola de lagartija* de Luisa Valenzuela," *Letras Femeninas*, número extraordinario (1994): 97–105. It is not enough to float the idea that chaos theory may include the postulate of a mysterious order. The whole notion of chaos theory is incompatible with Valenzuela's stated aim.

56. Cordones-Cook, *Poética* 80.

57. Bruce G. Gartner, "Un regodeo en el asco: Dismembered Bodies in Luisa Valenzuela's *The Lizard's Tail*," *Indiana Journal of Hispanic Literature* 2.2 (1994): 205.

58. Valenzuela, *Open Door* ix.

59. Ordoñez, "Máscaras" 518.

60. Z. Nelly Martínez, "Luisa Valenzuela's 'Where the Eagles Dwell': From Fragmentation to Holism," *Review of Contemporary Fiction* 6.3 (1986): 109–15.

61. Luisa Valenzuela, *Donde viven las águilas* (Buenos Aires: Celtia, 1983) 44.

62. Evelyn Picón Garfield, "Interview with Luisa Valenzuela," *Review of Contemporary Fiction* 6.3 (1983): 29.

63. Valenzuela, *Novela negra con argentinos* 134.

64. Alyce Cook, "Narrative Technique in Selected Fictional Works of Luisa Valenzuela," diss., U of Virginia, 1995, 235.

65. This aspect of the novel is explored by Catherine Perricone in "Valenzuela's *Novela negra con argentinos*: A Metafictional Game." *Romance Notes* 36 (1996): 237–42. I feel that she overestimates the importance of the ludic and purely literary elements in the novel.

66. Magnarelli, "The New Novel/A New Novel: Spider's Webs and Detectives in Luisa Valenzuela's *Black Novel (with Argentines),*" *Studies in Twentieth Century Literature* 19 (1995): 49.

67. Magnarelli, "New Novel," 54–55.

68. See the following, all from *World Literature Today* 69.4 (1995) (Luisa Valenzuela Number): María Inés Lagos, "Displaced Subjects: Valenzuela and the Metropolis" 726–32; Lucille Kerr, "Novels and 'Noir' in New York" 733–39; and Juanamaría Cordones-Cook, "*Novela negra con argentinos*: The Desire to Know" 745–51. Richard A. Young, "Detective novels and Argentinians in Luisa Valenzuela's *Novela negra con argentinos*," *Antípodas* 6–7 (1994–95): 191–203 studies the form in relation to the political content.

69. Julio Cortázar in Oscar Collazos, *Literatura en la revolución y revolución en la literatura* (Mexico: Siglo XXI, 1971) 69–70.

70. See Juanamaría Cordones-Cook, "Luisa Valenzuela habla sobre *Novela negra con argentinos* y *Realidad nacional desde la cama*," *Letras Femeninas* 18 (1992): 119–26.

71. Luisa Valenzuela, *Realidad nacional desde la cama* (Buenos Aires: Grupo Editor Latinoamericano, 1990) 26.

72. But see, in *World Literature Today* 69.4 (1995), the articles by Z. Nelly Martínez, "Dangerous Messianisms: The World According to Valenzuela" 697–701; and Ricardo Gutiérrez Mouat, "Luisa Valenzuela's Literal Writing" 709–16, for more, especially on the religious theme in *Simetrías*.

73. Gwendolyn Díaz, "Politics of the Body in Luisa Valenzuela's *Cambio de armas* and *Simetrías*," *World Literature Today* 69.4 (1995): 751–56.

74. Martínez, *El silencio que habla* 184.

75. Valenzuela, *Cambio de armas* 78, 80.

76. Valenzuela, *Novela negra* 191–92.

## CHAPTER 6. ROSARIO FERRÉ

1. But see Margarite Fernández Olmos, "Constructing Heroines: Rosario Ferré's *Cuentos infantiles* and Feminine Instruments of Change," *The Lion and the Unicorn* 10 (1986): 83–94. There is a Spanish version in her *Sobre la literatura puertorriqueña de aquí y de allá: Aproximaciones feministas* (Santo Domingo: Alfa y Omega, 1989) 55–71.

2. Magdalena García Pinto, *Women Writers of Latin America* (Austin: U of Texas P, 1988) 97.

3. Rosario Ferré, *El acomodador* (Mexico City: Fondo de Cultura Económica, 1986) 71.

4. San Juan, PR: Cultural, 1990.

5. Rosario Ferré, *El árbol y sus sombras* (Mexico City: Sersa; Silver Spring, MD: Literal Books, 1992) 11.

6. Cit. Rosario Ferré, *Cortázar, el romántico en su observatorio* (San Juan: Cultural, 1990) 14.

7. Rosario Ferré, *Sitio a Eros* 2nd ed. (Mexico City: Mortiz, 1986) 16.

8. According to Carmen Rivera, she was most instrumental in "opening the doors for the feminist movement on the island" [of Puerto Rico]. "Rosario Ferré," *Dictionary of Literary Biography*, vol. 145 (Detroit: Bruccoli Clark Layman, 1994) 130. More recently, in a series of essays in *El coloquio de las perras* (Mexico City: Sersa; Silver Spring, MD: Literal Books, 1992), she has returned to the strongly feminist stance of some of her earlier criticism.

9. Jean Franco, "Going Public: Rehabilitating the Private," *On Edge*, ed. George Yudice (Minneapolis: U of Minnesota P, 1992) 74–75.

10. Ferré, *Sitio a Eros* 22.

11. Ferré, *Sitio a Eros* 194.

12. Ferré, *Sitio a Eros* 20, 21.

13. Wolfgang Binder, "Entrevista con Rosario Ferré," *La Torre* 8.30 (1994): 242.

14. Rosario Ferré, *El acomodador* 31.

15. Yvette López, "'La muñeca menor': Ceremonias y transformaciones en un cuento de Rosario Ferré," *Explicación de Textos Literarios* 11.1 (1982–83): 49–58.

16. This is the view of Diana Vélez, kindly communicated to me in a letter.

17. Rivera, "Rosario Ferré" 132.

18. Lee Skinner, "Pandora's Log: Charting the Evolving Literary Project of Rosario Ferré," *Revista de Estudios Hispánicos* 29 (1995): 463.

19. Ferré, *Cortázar* 111.

20. Garcia Pinto, *Women Writers* 98.

21. Julio Cortázar, "Algunos aspectos del cuento," *Casa de las Américas* 2.15–16 (1962–63): 4. This crucially important essay is also included in Cortázar's *La casilla de los Morelli* (Barcelona: Tusquets, 1981).

22. Rosario Ferré, *Papeles de Pandora*, 3rd. ed. (Mexico City: Mortiz, 1987) 48.

23. However, Juan Escalera Ortiz in a cogent analysis, "Perspectiva del cuento 'Mercedes Benz 220 SL,'" *Revista/ Review Interamericana* (Puerto Rico) 12 (1982): 407–17, makes the important point that, while Ferré endorses the viewpoint of the young couple, she is careful to show that the girl is able to cope with her lover's death only by a process of illusion. She, too, is alienated from reality in the end.

24. María I. Lagos-Pope, "Sumisión y rebeldía: El doble o la representación de la alienación femenina en narraciones de Marta Brunet y Rosario Ferré," *Revista Iberoamericana* 132–33 (1985): 745.

25. Rosario Méndez-Panedas develops this point very cogently in "'Cuando las mujeres quieren a los hombres': El doble como una metáfora de un mundo intra-textual," *Symposium* 48 (1995): 311–17.

26. María M. Solá, "Para que lean el sexo, para que sientan el texto, escribimos también con el cuerpo," introduction to her anthology *Aquí cuentan las mujeres* (Pío Piedras: Huracán, 1990) 22. See, in this connection, Ferré's own essay on the story, "¿Por qué quiere Isabel a los hombres? *El coloquio de las perras* 77–80.

27. Gustavo Sainz, *Obsesivos días circulares* (Mexico City: Mortiz, 1979) 203.

28. *Sic* in the first edition, but this is clearly a slip and has been corrected in the English translation, "Sleeping Beauty," *The Youngest Doll* (Lincoln: U of Nebraska P, 1991) 89–90, where the letters are dated late May 1973. This translation (by Ferré herself along with Diana Vélez) also reveals a number of significant changes and suppressions with respect to the original text that merit serious attention.

29. Aída Apter-Cragnolino, "El cuento de hadas y la Bildungsroman: Modelo y subversión en 'La bella durmiente' de Rosario Ferré," *Chasqui* 20.2 (1991): 5.

30. Diana L. Vélez, "Power and the Text: Rebellion in Rosario Ferré's *Papeles de Pandora*," *Journal of the Mid-Western MLA* 17.1 (1984): 71.

31. Ferré, *Sitio a Eros* 18.

32. García Pinto, *Women Writers* 82.

33. Binder, "Entrevista con Rosario Ferré" 247.

34. Rosario Ferré, *Maldito amor* (Mexico City: Mortiz, 1986) 17, 18. Carmen Pérez Marín in her useful article on the novella, "De la épica a la novela: La recuperación de la voz en *Maldito amor* de Rosario Ferré," *Letras Femeninas* 20 (1994): 35–43, points out (p. 39) that Ubaldino is deliberately modeled on the Puerto Rican patriot and politician José de Diego (1866–1918).

35. Skinner ("Pandora's Log" p. 465) is surely wrong to present this fiction as a serious "historical project." To do so is to overlook an important aspect of Ferré's irony with regard to Hermenegildo.

36. Cit. Carmen Vega Carney, "El amor como discurso político en Ana Lydia Vega y Rosario Ferré," *Letras Femeninas* 17.1–2 (1991): 81.

37. Mexico City: Mortiz, 1992.

38. Jean Franco, foreword, *The Youngest Doll*, by Rosario Ferré (note 28 above) xii.

39. Cit. Susan Minot, introduction, *Summer*, by Edith Wharton (New York: Bantam Books, 1993) viii.

40. Skinner's remark ("Pandora's Log" p. 468) that "Her new writing is one which continually pulls itself to pieces" and postulate that after her early work Ferré becomes increasingly concerned with techniques that displace the narrative persona and problematize the author's role are most percipient. But in my view the resulting ambiguity does not seriously compromise her position as a Post-Boom writer.

## CHAPTER 7. GUSTAVO SAINZ

1. Emir Rodríguez Monegal "Gustavo Sainz," *El arte de narrar* (Caracas: Monte Avila, 1968) 263.

2. Gustavo Sainz, "Carlos Fuentes: A Permanent Bedazzlement," *World Literature Today* 57.4 (1983) (Carlos Fuentes issue): 568–72.

3. Gustavo Sainz, *Gustavo Sainz* (Mexico City: Empresas Editoriales, 1966) 34–35.

4. Gustavo Sainz, *A la salud de la serpiente* (Mexico City: Grijalbo, 1988) 21.

5. Sainz, *A la salud* 54.

6. José Agustín, "Contemporary Mexican Fiction, *Three Lectures: Literature and Censorship in Latin America Today,* U of Denver Occasional Papers 1 (Denver: University of Denver, Dept. of Foreign Languages and Literatures, 1978) 23.

7. Sainz, *Gustavo Sainz* 5.

8. Sainz, "Carlos Fuentes" 569.

9. Rodríguez Monegal, "Gustavo Sainz" 257.

10. Sainz, *Gustavo Sainz* 6.

11. Lanin A. Gyurko, "Reality and Fantasy in *Gazapo,*" *Revista de Estudios Hispánicos* 8 (1974): 142, 143, 145.

12. Rodríguez Monegal, "Gustavo Sainz" 259.

13. Gyurko, "Reality and Fantasy" 127.

14. James W. Brown, "*Gazapo,* modelo para armar," *Nueva Narrativa Hispanoamericana,* 3.2 (1973): 243.

15. Rodríguez Monegal, "Gustavo Sainz" 258.

16. Gyurko, "Reality and Fantasy" 130.

17. Rodríguez Monegal, "Gustavo Sainz" 256.

18. Sainz, *A la salud* 274.

19. Rodríguez Monegal, "Gustavo Sainz" 262.

20. Gabriel García Márquez, *Crónica de una muerte anunciada* (Bogotá: Oveja Negra, 1981) 13.

21. David Decker, "*Obsesivos días circulares*: Avatares del voyeur," *Texto Crítico* 9 (1978): 95.

22. John P. Dwyer, "Cuates agazapados y otros temas: unas palabras con Gustavo Sainz," *Revista Iberoamericana* 90 (1975): 86.

23. Margo Glantz, "Onda y Escritura en México: Jóvenes de 20 a 33," *Repeticiones* (Xalapa: Vera Cruz UP, 1979) 104.

24. Gustavo Sainz, *La Princesa del Palacio de Hierro,* 6th ed. (Mexico City: Ediciones del Océano, 1982) 81.

25. Philip Swanson, "Only Joking? Gustavo Sainz and *La Princesa del Palacio de Hierro*: Funniness, Identity and the Post-Boom," *Studies in Twentieth Century Literature* 19 (1995): 101–15. The quotations are from pp. 105, 108, and 110, respectively. Reprinted as chapter 7 (pp. 114–27) of his *The New Novel in Latin America* (Manchester: Manchester UP, 1995).

26. Julie Jones, "The Dynamics of the City: Gustavo Sainz's *La Princesa del Palacio de Hierro,*" *Chasqui* 14 (1982): 18.

27. The quotations are from, respectively, Sainz, *La Princesa* 84 and Rodríguez Monegal, "Gustavo Sainz" 261.

28. The date of publication of *Compadre Lobo* is not clear. According to the second edition (Mexico City: Grijalbo, 1977), the novel was copyrighted in 1975. Page references are to this second edition.

29. Gustavo Sainz, *Fantasmas aztecas* (Mexico City: Grijalbo, 1982) 174.
30. Gustavo Sainz, *Paseo en trapecio* (Mexico City: Edivisión, 1985) 28.
31. Jacobo Sefamí, "Vertiginosidad del fuego: *Muchacho en llamas* de Gustavo Sainz," *Revista Canadiense de Estudios Hispánicos* 15 (1990): 130.
32. Gustavo Sainz, *Muchacho en llamas* (Mexico City: Grijalbo, 1988) 29.
33. Luis H. Peña, "La nostalgia precoz: *Gazapo*," *Escritura en escisión* (Xalapa: Vera Cruz UP, 1990) 82.
34. Joel Hancock, in "Re-Defining Autobiography: Gustavo Sainz's *A la salud de la serpiente.*" *Revista de Estudios Hispánicos* 29 (1995) 139–52, heavily emphasizes the autobiographical element. While many of his remarks are insightful, this approach obscures the novel's importance as a Post-Boom text. Read alongside Skármeta's "Al fin y al cabo," for instance, it can be seen at once to contain a massive amount of material that, though diffuse and at times perversely self-contradictory, essentially confirms Skármeta's opinions.
35. Margo Glantz, "Onda y Escritura en Mexico: Jóvenes de 20 a 33," in the book of the same name (Mexico City: Siglo XXI, 1971) and reprinted, along with "Narrativa jóven de Mexico" and "La Onda diez años después: ¿epitafio o revaloración?" in her *Repeticiones* (89–113, 77–88 and 115–129 respectively). Also useful in this connection are: J. Ann Duncan, *Voices, Visions and a New Reality: Mexican Fiction since 1970* (Pittsburgh: U of Pittsburgh P, 1986); chapter 2 ("Mexican Postmodernities" pp. 21–42) of Raymond L. Williams's *The Postmodern Novel in Latin America* (New York: St. Martin's, 1995); and Cynthia Steele, *Politics, Gender and the Mexican Novel 1968–1988* (Austin: U of Texas P, 1992).

## CHAPTER 8. CONCLUSION:
## POST-BOOM AND POSTMODERNISM

1. George Yudice, "¿Puede hablarse de postmodernidad en América Latina?" *Revista de Crítica Literaria Latinoamericana* 15.29 (1989): 118.
2. Santiago Colás, *Postmodernity in Latin America: The Argentine Paradigm* (Durham: Duke UP, 1994); Raymond L. Williams, *The Postmodern Novel in Latin America* (New York: St Martin's, 1995); Doris Sommers and George Yudice, "Latin American Literature from the 'Boom' On," *Postmodern Fiction*, ed. Larry McCaffery (Westport: Greenwood, 1986) 189–214.
3. Cf. George Yudice, "Postmodernism on the Perifery," *South Atlantic Quarterly* 92.3 (1993): 555; George Yudice, introduction, *On Edge: The Crisis of Contemporary Latin American Culture*, ed. George Yudice (Minneapolis: U of Minnesota P, 1992) xii.
4. Néstor García Canclini, "Memory and Innovation in the Theory of Art," *South Atlantic Quarterly* 92.3 (1993): 428.
5. Yudice, *On Edge* 4.
6. Colás, *Postmodernity in Latin America* ix.
7. Colás, *Postmodernity in Latin America* 25, 114.
8. *South Atlantic Quarterly* 453–59, 461–71.
9. R. L. Williams, "Preface to *The Boom in Retrospect*," *Latin American Literary Review* 15.29 (1987): 8.

10. Williams, *Postmodern Novel* 10.

11. Williams, *Postmodern Novel* 9.

12. Williams, *Postmodern Novel* 14.

13. J. S. Brushwood, "Two Views of the Boom: North and South," *Latin American Literary Review* 15.26 (1987): 22.

14. Roberto González Echevarría, "Sarduy, the Boom and the Post-Boom, *Latin American Literary Review* 15.26 (1987): 70.

15. González Echevarría, "Sarduy, the Boom and the Post-Boom" 70.

16. Ihab Hassan, "Discussion after Terry Eagleton's Paper," *Criticism in the Twilight Zone: Postmodern Perspectives on Literature and Politics*, Danuta Zadworna-Fjellestad, ed. (Stockholm: Alonquist and Wiksell, 1990) 32.

17. Fredric Jameson to Douglas Keller in the latter's *Postmodernism, Jameson, Critique* (Washington: Maison Neuve, 1989) 50, 69.

18. *Social Text* 15 (1986): 65, 66, 69, and 82.

19. See, in this connection, Aijaz Ahmad, "Jameson's Rhetoric of Otherness and the 'National Allegory,'" *Social Text* 17 (1987): 3–25 and Jameson's "A Brief Response," *Social Text* 17 (1987): 26–27.

20. Martin Hopenhayn, "Postmodernism and Neoliberalism in Latin America," *Boundary 2* 20.3 (1993): 97.

21. Cornel West, "Black Culture and Postmodernism," *Modernism/Postmodernism*, ed. Peter Brooker (London: Longmans, 1992) 217, 218, 222.

22. Peter Brooker, "Introduction," *Modernism/Postmodernism*, ed. Peter Brooker (London: Longmans, 1992) 13.

23. Laura García-Moreno, "Situating Knowledges: Latin American Readings of Postmodernism," *Diacritics* 25.1 (1995): 63, 68.

24. John Beverley and José Oviedo, "Introduction to the Postmodernism Debate in Latin America," *Boundary 2* 20.3 (1993): 14.

25. Raymond L. Williams, "What is Modernism?" *The Politics of Modernism*, ed. Raymond Williams (London: Verso, 1989) 31–35; Fredric Jameson, *Aesthetics and Politics*, 2nd ed. (London: Verso, 1980) 211.

26. György Lukács, *The Meaning of Contemporary Realism* (London: Merlin, 1963) 25. The attempt, notably on the part of Brian McHale in *Postmodernist Fiction* (London: Methuen, 1987) 51–53 and elsewhere in the book to associate the Boom writers with postmodernism seems only to reveal the inadequacy of his definition of the movement and of his reading of the writers in question. Characteristically McHale associates postmodernism with "denying external objective reality" (p. 220)!

27. Umberto Eco, *Reflections on* The Name of the Rose (London: Secker and Warburg, 1985) 65.

28. Linda Hutcheon, *The Politics of Postmodernism* (London: Routledge, 1989) 34.

29. Hutcheon, *The Politics of Modernism* 116, 66.

30. Hutcheon, *The Politics of Modernism* 143.

31. Colás, *Postmodernity in Latin America* 18.

32. Colás, *Postmodernity in Latin America* 172.

33. Simon During, "Postmodernism or Postcolonialism," *Landfall* 39 (1985): 366–80; Helen Tiffin, "Post-Colonialism, Post-Modernism and the

Rehabilitation of Post-Colonial History," *Journal of Commonwealth Literature* 23.1 (1988): 169–81; Diana Palaversich, "Eduardo Galeano: Entre el postmodernismo y el postcolonialismo," *IJHL*, 1.2 (1993): 11–24. See also on this hot topic: Kwane A. Appiah, "Is the Post- in Post-Modernism the Post- in Postcolonial?" *Critical Enquiry* 17 (1991): 336–57; Neil Larson, "Forward," *Border Writing*, by D. E. Hicks (Minneapolis: U of Minnesota P, 1991, xi–xxi; Benita Parry, "Problems in Current Theories of Colonial Discourse," *Oxford Literary Review* 91.2 (1988): 27–58.

    34. García-Moreno, "Situating Knowledges" 65.

    35. For more theoretical considerations connected with applying the notion of postcolonialism to aspects of Spanish American culture, see Walter Mignolo, "La razón postcolonial: Herencias coloniales y teorías postcoloniales," *Revista Chilena de Literatura* 49 (1995): 91–114; Fernando de Toro, "Latin American Postmodern/Postcolonial Positionalities," *World Literature Today* 69 (1995): 35–40.

    36. Geeta Kapur, "When was Modernism in Indian/Third World Art?" *South Atlantic Quarterly* 92.3 (1993): 474.

# BIBLIOGRAPHY

Acosta Cruz, María. "El regreso al caribe de Severo Sarduy." *Hispanófila* 113 (1995): 69–80.

Agosín, Marjorie. "Interview with Isabel Allende." *Imagine* 1.2 (1984): 49–56.

———. "Isabel Allende: *La Casa de los Espíritus*." *Revista Interamericana de Bibliografía* 35 (1985): 448–58.

Agustín, José. *Three Lectures: Literature and Censorship in Latin America Today*. U of Denver Occasional Papers 1. Denver: U of Denver, Dept. of Foreign Languages and Literatures, 1978.

Ahmad, Aijaz. "Jameson's Rhetoric of Otherness and the 'National Allegory.'" *Social Text* 17 (1987): 3–25.

Alegría Fernando, "Isabel Allende: Somos una generación marcada por el exilio." *Nuevo Texto Crítico* 4.8 (1991): 73–90.

Alfonso, Miguel. "*Eva Luna*: El folletín: ¿Tránsito a la novela total?" *Araucaria de Chile* (Madrid) 41 (1988): 165–72.

Allende, Isabel. *La casa de los Espíritus*. 22nd ed. Barcelona: Plaza y Janés, 1986.

———. *Cuentos de Eva Luna*. Buenos Aires: Sudamericana, 1990.

———. *De amor y de sombra*. 8th ed. Barcelona: Plaza y Janés, 1986.

———. *Eva Luna*. 3rd ed. Barcelona: Plaza y Janés, 1987.

———. "La magia de las palabras." *Revista Iberoamericana* 132.3 (1985): 447–52.

———. "Mis raíces están en los libros que escribo." *Cambio 16* (Madrid), no. 1048 (22 December 1991): 120–21.

———. *El plan infinito*. Buenos Aires: Sudamericana, 1991.

———. "Por qué y para quién escribo." *Araucaria de Chile* (Madrid) 41 (1988): 155–62.

———. "Sobre *La casa de los Espíritus*." *Discurso Literario* 2.1 (1984): 64–71.

Alonso, Carlos. *The Spanish American Regional Novel*. Cambridge: Cambridge UP, 1990.

Appiah, Kwame A. "Is the Post- in Post-Modernism the Post- in Post-Colonial?" *Critical Enquiry* 17 (1991): 336–57.

Apter-Cragnolino, Aida. "El cuento de hadas y la Bildungsroman: Modelo y subversión en 'La bella durmiente' de Rosario Ferré." *Chasqui* 20.2 (1991): 3–9.

Bacarisse, Pamela, ed. *Carnal Knowledge*. Pittsburgh: Tres Ríos, 1993.

———. *Impossible Choices*. Calgary: U of Calgary P; Cardiff: U of Wales P, 1993.

Barrenechea, Ana María. "La crisis del contrato mimético en los textos contemporáneos." *Revista Iberoamericana* 118–19 (1982): 377–81.

Bell, Steven, ed. *Critical Theory, Cultural Politics and Latin American Narrative*. U of Notre Dame P, 1993.

Benedetti, Mario. *El escritor latinoamerican y la revolución posible*. Buenos Aires: Alfa Argentina, 1974.

——. "El escritor y la crítica en el contexto del subdesarrollo." *Casa de las Américas* 107 (1978): 3–21.

——. *Gracias por el fuego*. Montevideo: Alfa, 1972.

Beverley, John, and Oviedo, José. "Introduction to the Postmodernism Debate in Latin America." *Boundary 2* 20.3 (1993): 1–17.

Bianchi Rossi, Ciro. "Skármeta, la huella de una época." *Cuba Internacional* 16.177 (1984): 50–55.

Binder, Wolfgang. "Entrevista con Rosario Ferré." *La Torre* 8.30 (1994): 239–53.

Brooker, Peter, ed. *Modernism/Postmodernism*. London: Longmans, 1992.

Brown, James W. "*Gazapo*, modelo para armar." *Nueva Narrativa Hispanoamericana* 3.2 (1973): 237–44.

Cadena, Agustín, "*Farabeuf*, el espacio como metáfora del tiempo." *Plural* (Mexico) 258 (1993): 50–56.

Carpentier, Alejo. *La novela hispanoamericana en vísperas de un nuevo siglo y otros ensayos*. 2nd ed. Mexico City: Siglo XXI, 1981.

Castillo, Debra. *Talking Back*. Ithaca: Cornell UP, 1992.

Christ, Ronald. "Interview with José Donoso." *Partisan Review* 49 (1982): 23–44.

Coddou, Marcelo. *Para leer a Isabel Allende*. Concepción: LAR, 1988.

Colás, Santiago. *Postmodernity in Latin America: The Argentine Paradigm*. Durham: Duke UP, 1994.

Collazos, Oscar. *Literatura en la revolución y revolución en la literatura*. 2nd ed. Mexico City: Siglo XXI, 1971.

Cook, Alyce. "Narrative Technique in Selected works of Luisa Valenzuela." Diss. U of Virginia, 1995.

Corbatta, Jorgelina. "Encuentros con Manuel Puig." *Revista Iberoamericana* 123–24 (1983): 591–620.

Cordones-Cook, Juanamaría. "Luisa Valenzuela habla sobre *Novela negra con argentinos* y *Realidad nacional desde la cama*." *Letras Femeninas* 18 (1992): 119–26.

——. "*Novela negra con argentinos*: The Desire to Know." *World Literature Today* 69.4 (1995): 733–39.

——. *Poética de la transgresión en la novelística de Luisa Valenzuela*. New York: Lang, 1991.

Cortázar, Julio. "Algunos aspectos del cuento." *Casa de las Américas* 2.15–16 (1962–63): 3–14.

——. "El escritor y su quehacer en América Latina." *El País Semanal* 17 October 1982: 81.

——. "La literatura latinoamericana a la luz de la historia contemporánea." *INTI* 10–11 (1979–80): 11–20.

——. "La literatura latinoamericana de nuestro tiempo." *Argentina: Años de alambrados culturales*. Ed. Saúl Yurkievich. Buenos Aires: Muchnik, 1984. 108–20.

Cortínez, Verónica. "Polifonía: entrevista a Isabel Allende y Antonio Skármeta." *Revista Chilena de Literatura* 32 (1988): 79–89.

Crystall, Elyse et al. "An Interview with Isabel Allende. "*Contemporary Literature* 33.4 (1991): 585–600.

De Carvalho, Susan. "Escrituras y escritoras: The Artist Protagonist of Isabel Allende." *Discurso Literario* 10.1 (1992): 59–67.

Decker, David. "*Obsesivos días circulares*: Avatares del Voyeur." *Texto Crítico* 9 (1978): 95–116.

Dehenin, Elsa. "A propósito del realismo de Mario Benedetti." *Revista Iberoamericana* 160–61 (1992): 1077–90.

Dellepiane, Angela. "La novela argentina desde 1950 hasta 1965." *Revista Iberoamericana* 66 (1968): 237–82.

Derrida, Jacques. *Writing and Difference*. Chicago: U of Chicago P, 1978.

De Toro, Fernando. "Latin American Postmodern/Postcolonial Positionalities." *World literature Today* 69 (1995): 35–40.

Diaz, Gwendolyn. "Politics of the Body in Luisa Valenzuela's *Cambio de armas* and *Simetrías*." *World Literature Today* 69.4 (1995): 751–56.

———. "Postmodernismo y teoría del caos en *Cola de lagartija* de Luisa Valenzuela." *Letras Femeninas*, número extraordinario (1994): 97–105.

Dorfman, Ariel. "¿Volar?" *Revista Chilena de Literatura* 1 (1970): 59–78.

Duncan, J. Ann. *Voices, Visions and a New Reality: Mexican Fiction since 1970*. Pittsburgh: U of Pittsburgh P, 1986.

During, Simon. "Postmodernism or Postcolonialism." *Landfall* 39 (1985): 366–80.

Dwyer, John P. "Cuates agazapados y otros temas: Unas palabras con Gustavo Sainz." *Revista iberoamericana* 90 (1975): 85–89.

Earle, Peter G. "Back to the Center: Hispanic American Fiction Today." *Hispanic Review* 58 (1990): 19–35.

Echevarren, Roberto, and Giordano, Enrique. *Manuel Puig, montaje y alteridad del sujeto*. Santiago de Chile: Monografías de Maitén, 1986.

Eco, Umberto. *Reflections on* The Name of the Rose. London: Secker and Warburg, 1985.

Escalera Ortiz, Juan. "Perspectiva del cuento 'Mercedes Benz 220SL.'" *Revista/Review Interamericana* (Puerto Rico) 12 (1982): 407–17.

Escobar, Ticio. "The Furtive Avant-Gardes." *South Atlantic Quarterly* 92.3 (1993): 461–71.

Fajardo, Diógenes. *La novelística de David Viñas*. Lawrence: Kansas UP, 1981.

Fernández, Macedonio. *Museo de la novela de la Eterna*. Buenos Aires: Corregidor, 1975.

Fernández Olmos, Margarite. *Sobre la literatura puertorriqueña de aquí y de allá: Aproximaciones femeninas*. Santo Domingo: Alfa y Omega, 1989.

Ferré, Rosario. *El acomodador*. Mexico City: Fondo de Cultura Económica, 1986.

———. *El árbol y su sombra*, Mexico City: Sersa; Silver Spring, MD: Literal Books, 1992.

———. *El coloquio de las perras*. Mexico City: Sersa; Silver Spring, MD: Literal Books, 1992.

———. *Cortázar: El romántico en su observatorio*. San Juan, PR: Cultural, 1990.

———. *Las dos Venecias*. Mexico City: Mortiz, 1992.

———. *Fábulas de la garza desangrada*. Mexico City: Mortiz, 1982.

———. *Maldito amor*. Mexico City: Mortiz, 1986.

———. *Papeles de Pandora*. 3rd ed. Mexico City: Mortiz, 1987.

———. *Sitio a Eros*. 2nd ed. Mexico City: Mortiz, 1986.

Fores, Ana. "Valenzuela's *Cat-o-Nine Deaths*." *Review of Contemporary Fiction* 6.3 (1986): 39–47.

Foster, David William. *Alternate Voices in Contemporary Latin American Narrative*. Columbus: Missouri UP, 1985.

Friedman, Ellen. "Where Are the Mising Contents? (Post) Modernism, Gender and the Canon." *PMLA* 108 (1993): 240–52.

Fuentes, Carlos. *La nueva novela hispanoamericana*. Mexico City: Mortiz, 1969.

Fulks, Barbara P. "A Reading of Luisa Valenzuela's Short Story 'La palabra asesino.'" *Monographic Review* 4 (1988): 179–88.

García Canclini, Néstor. "Memory and Invention in the Theory of Art." *South Atlantic Quarterly* 92.3 (1993): 423–43.

García Márquez, Gabriel. *Crónica de una muerte anunciada*. Bogotá: Oveja Negra, 1981.

———. *La soledad de América Latina*. Bogotá: Corporación Editorial Universitaria de Colombia, 1983.

García-Moreno, Laura. "Situating Knowledges: Latin American Readings of Postmodernism." *Diacritics* 25.1 (1995): 63–81.

García Pinto, Magdalena. *Women Writers of Latin America: Intimate Histories*. Austin: U of Texas P, 1988.

García Ramos, Juan Manuel, ed. *Manuel Puig*. Madrid: Cultura Hispánica, 1991.

Gartner, Bruce D. "Un regodeo en el asco: Dismembered Bodies in Luisa Valenzuela's *The Lizard's Tail*." *Indiana Journal of Hispanic Literature* 2.2 (1994): 203–25.

Gazarian Gautier, Marie-Lise. *Interviews with Latin American Writers*. Elmwood Park, IL: The Dalkey Archive P, 1989.

Giardinelli, Mempo. "Fichero." *Nuevo Texto Crítico* 5 (1990): 185–88.

———. "Un retorno a la espontaneidad." *Clarín* (Buenos Aires) Suplemento Cultura y Nación, 2 January 1986: 2.

———. "Variaciones sobre la postmodernidad o ¿Qué es eso del posboom latinoamericano?" *Puro Cuento* (Buenos Aires) 23 (1990): 30–33.

Glantz, Margo. "Luisa Valenzuela's *He Who Searches*." *Review of Contemporary Fiction* 6.3 (1986): 52–65.

———. *Repeticiones*. Xalapa: Vera Cruz UP, 1979.

González Echeverría, Roberto. *Myth and Archive*. Cambridge: Cambridge UP, 1990.

———. *La ruta de Severo Sarduy*. Hanover, NH: Ediciones del Norte, 1987.

———. "Sarduy, the Boom, and the Post-Boom." *Latin American Literary Review* 15.2 (1987): 57–72.

Gras Balaguer, Menene. "Entrevista con Antonio Skármeta." *Insula* 478 (1986): 1, 14.

Guerrero, Gustavo. *La estrategia neo-barroca*. Barcelona: Ediciones del Mall, 1987.

Gutiérrez, Gloria. *Realismo mágico, cosmos latinoamericano, teoría y práctica*. Bogotá: América Latina, 1991.

Gutiérrez Mouat, Ricardo. "Luisa Valenzuela's Literal Writing." *World Literature Today* 69.4 (1995): 709–16.

———. "La narrativa latinoamericana del Post-Boom." *Revista Interamericana de Bibliografía* 38 (1988): 3–10.

Gyurko, Lanin A. "Reality and Fantasy in *Gazapo*." *Revista de Estudios Hispánicos* 8 (1974): 117–45.

Hancock, Joel. "Redefining Autobiography: Gustavo Sainz's *A la salud de la serpiente*." *Revista de Estudios Hispánicos* 29 (1995): 139–52.

Hart, Patricia. *Narrative Magic in the Fiction of Isabel Allende*. London: Associated UP, 1989.

Hernández-Gómez, Beatriz. "*De amor y de sombra*: Un juego de oposiciones." *Quaderni di Letterature Iberiche e Iberoamericane* 5 (1986): 41–63.

Hicks, Emily. *Border Writing*. Minneapolis: Minnesota UP, 1991.

———. "That which Resists: The Code of the Real in Luisa Valenzuela's *He Who Searches*." *Review of Contemporary Fiction* 6.3 (1986): 55–61.

Hintz, Suzanne S. *Rosario Ferré, A Search for Identity*. New York: Peter Lang, 1995.

Hopenhayn, Martin. "Postmodernism and Neoliberalism in Latin America." *Boundary 2* 20.3 (1993): 93–109.

Hutcheon, Linda. *The Politics of Postmodernism*. London: Routledge, 1989.

Huyssen, Andreas. *After the Great Divide: Modernism, Mass Culture, Postmodernism*. Bloomington: Indiana UP, 1986.

Invernizzi, Virginia. "The Novels of Isabel Allende: A Reevaluation of Genre." Diss. University of Virginia, 1991.

Invernizzi, Virginia, and Pope, Melissa. "A Parallel: Silent History in Novels." *Iris* 19 (1988): 25–29.

Jameson, Fredric. *Aesthetics and Politics*. 2nd ed. London: Verso, 1980.

———. "A Brief Reply." *Social Text* 17 (1987): 26–27.

———. "Postmodernism; or, the Cultural Logic of Late Capitalism." *New Left Review* 15 (1984): 53–92.

———. "Third World Literature in the Era of Multinational Capitalism" *Social Text* 15 (1986): 65–88.

Jara, René, and Vidal, Hernán. *Testimonio y literatura*. Minneapolis: Institute for the Study of Ideologies and Literature, 1986.

Jitrik, Noé. *El no existente caballero*. Buenos Aires: Megalópolis, 1975.

Jones, Shannon, and Prillaman, Bill. "Interview with Isabel Allende." *Virginia Advocate* (campus magazine, University of Virginia) 3.2 (1987): 11–13.

Jones, Julie. "The Dynamics of the City. Gustavo Sainz's *La Princesa del Palacio de Hierro*." *Chasqui* 12 (1982): 14–23.

Josef, Bella. "Manuel Puig: Reflexión al nivel de la enunciación." *Nueva Narrativa Hispanoamericana* 4 (1974): 111–16.

Kapur, Geeta. "When was Modernism in Indian/Third World Art?" *South Atlantic Quarterly* 92.3 (1993): 473–514.

Keller, Douglas. *Postmodernism. Jameson. Critique.* Washington: Maison Neuve, 1989.

Kerr, Lucille. *Suspended Fictions.* Urbana: Illinois UP, 1987.

Kirkpatrick, Gwen. "Entrevista con Teresa Porzecanski." *Discurso Literario* 5.2 (1988): 305–10.

Lagos-Pope, María I. "*De amor y de sombra.*" *Latin American Literary Review* 15.29 (1987): 205–13.

———. "Displaced Subjects: Valenzuela and the Metropolis." *World Literature Today* 69.4 (1995): 726–32.

———. "Mujer y política en *Cambio de armas* de Luisa Valenzuela." *Hispamérica* 46–47 (1987): 71–83.

———. "Sumisión y rebeldía: El doble o la representación de la alienación femenina en narraciones de Marta Brunet y Rosario Ferré." *Revista Iberoamericana* 132–33 (1985): 731–49.

López, Yvette. "'La muñeca menor': Ceremonias y transformaciones en un cuento de Rosario Ferré." *Explicación de Textos Literarios* 11.1 (1982–83): 49–58.

Lukacs, George. *The Meaning of Contemporary Realism.* London: Merlin, 1963.

Lyotard, Jean-François. *The Post-Modern Condition: A Report on Knowledge.* Minneapolis: U of Minnesota P, 1988.

Maci, Guillermo. "The Symbolic, the Imaginary and the Real in Luisa Valenzuela's *He Who Searches.*" *Review of Contemporary Fiction* 6.3 (1986): 67–77.

Magnarelli, Sharon. *The Lost Rib.* London: Associated UP, 1985.

———. *Reflections/Refractions: Reading Luisa Valenzuela.* New York: Lang, 1988.

———. "The New Novel/A New Novel: Spider's Webs and Detectives in Luisa Valenzuela's *Black Novel (with Agentines).*" *Studies in Twentieth Century Literature* 19 (1995): 43–60.

Marcos, Juan Manuel. *De García Márquez al Post-Boom.* Madrid: Orígenes, 1986.

———. "El género popular como meta-estructura textual del Post-Boom latinoamericano." *Revista Monográfica* 5.1–2 (1988): 268–78.

———. *Roa Bastos, precursor del Post-Boom.* Mexico City: Katún, 1983.

Martin, Gerald. *Journeys through the Labyrinth.* London: Verso, 1989.

Martínez, Z. Nelly. "Dangerous Messianisms: The World According to Valenzuela." *World Literature Today* 69.4 (1995): 697–701.

———. "Luisa Valenzuela's 'Where the Eagles Dwell': From Fragmentism to Holism." *Review of Contemporary Fiction* 6.3 (1983): 109–15.

———. *El silencio que habla: Aproximación a la obra de Luisa Valenzuela.* Buenos Aires: Corregidor, 1994.

Marting, Diane. "Female Sexuality in Selected Stories by Luisa Valenzuela." *Review of Contemporary Fiction* 6.3 (1986): 48–54.

———. "Gender and Metaphoricity in Luisa Valenzuela's 'I'm Your Horse in the Night.'" *World Literature Today* 69.4 (1995): 702–8.

McCaffery, Larry, ed. *Postmodern Fiction*. Westport: Greenwood, 1986.

McHale, Brian. *Postmodernist Fiction*. London: Methuen, 1987.

Mejía Duque, Jaime. *Literatura y realidad*. Medellín: Oveja Negra, 1976.

Méndes-Faith, Teresa. "Entrevista con Mempo Giardinelli." *Discurso Literario* 5.2 (1988): 313–21.

Méndez-Panedas, Rosario. "'Cuando las mujeres quieren a los hombres': El doble como una metáfora de un mundo intra-textual." *Symposium* 48 (1995): 311–17.

Méndez Rodenas, Adriana. "Severo Sarduy: *Colibri*." *Revista Iberoamericana* 130–31 (1985): 399–401.

———. *Severo Sarduy: El neobarroco de la transgresión*. Mexico City: Universidad Autónoma, 1983.

Menton, Seymour. *Latin America's New Historical Novel*. Austin: U of Texas P, 1993.

Meyer, Doris. *Lives on the Line: The testimony of Contemporary Latin American Authors*. Berkeley: California UP, 1988.

Mignolo, Walter. "La razón postcolonial: Herencias coloniales y teorías postcoloniales." *Revista Chilena de Literatura* 49 (1995): 91–104.

Montero, Oscar. *The Name Game*. Chapel Hill: U of North Carolina P, 1988.

Moody, Michael. "Entrevista con Isabel Allende." *Discurso Literario* 4.1 (1986): 41–53.

Mora, Gabriela. "Las novelas de Isabel Allende y el papel de la mujer como ciudadana." *Ideologies and Literature* 2.1 (1987): 53–61.

Mull, Dorothy, and de Angulo, Elsa. "An Afternoon with Luisa Valenzuela." *Hispania* 69 (1986): 350–52.

Ordoñez, Montserrat. "Máscaras de espejos, un juego especular." *Revista Iberoamericana* 132/33 (1985): 511–19.

Osorio, M. "Entrevista con Manuel Puig." *Cuadernos Para el Diálogo*, 231 (1977): 51–58.

Osorio, Nelson. "Lenguaje narrativo y estructura significative de *El Señor Presidente*." *Escritura* (Caracas) 5–6 (1978): 99–156.

Pagni, Andrea. "Entrevista con Antonio Skármeta." *Discurso Literario* 5.1 (1985): 59–73.

Palaversich, Diana. "Eduardo Galiano: Entre el postmodernismo y el postcolonialismo." 1.2 *IJHL* (1993): 11–24.

Parry, Benita. "Problems in Current Theories of Colonial Discourse." *Oxford Literary Review* 91.2 (1988): 27–58.

Peavler, Terry, and Peter Standish, eds. *Structures of Power*. Albany: State U of New York P, 1996.

Pellón, Gustavo. "Ideology and Structure in Giardinelli's *Santo oficio de la memoria*." *Studies in Twentieth Century Literature*. 19.1 (1995): 81–99.

Peña, Luis H. *Escritura en excisión*. Xalapa: Vera Cruz UP, 1990.

Pérez Firmat, Gustavo. *Do the Americas Have a Comon Literature?* Durham: Duke UP, 1990.

Pérez Marín, Carmen. "De la épica a la novela: La recuperación de la voz en *Maldito amor* de Rosario Ferré." *Letras Femeninas* 20 (1994): 35–43.

Perloff, Marjorie, ed. *Postmodern Genres*. Norman: U of Oklahoma P, 1989.

Perricone, Catherine. "Valenzuela's *Novela negra con argentinos:* A Metafictional Game." *Romance Notes* 36 (1996): 237–42.

Picón Garfield, Evelyn. "Interview with Luisa Valenzuela." *Review of Contemporary Fiction* 6.3 (1983): 25–30.

———. *Women's Voices from Latin America*. Detroit: Wayne State UP, 1985.

Rama, Angel. *La novela latinoamericana 1920–1980*. Bogotá: Instituto Colombiano de Cultura, 1982.

Reale, Deniss. "Entrevista con Antonio Skármeta." *KO-EYU* (La Paz, Bolivia) 20 (1981): 39–40.

Richards, Nelly. "The Latin American Problematic of Theoretical-Cultural Transference: Postmodern Appropriations and Counterappropriations." *South Atlantic Quarterly* 9.2–3 (1993): 453–59.

Rincón, Carlos. "Entrevista con Antonio Skármeta." *Caribe* (Caracas) 4 January 1976: pages unnumbered.

Riquelme Rojas, Sonia, and Edna Aguirre Rehbein, eds. *Critical Approaches to Isabel Allende's Novels*. New York: Lang, 1991.

Rivera, Carmen. "Rosario Ferré," *Dictionary of Literary Biography*. Vol. 145 (1994): 130–37. Detroit: Bruccoli Clark Layman.

Rodden, John. "The Responsability to Tell You: An Interview with Isabel Allende." *Kenyon Review* 13.1 (1991): 113–23.

Rodríguez Monegal, Emir. *El arte de narrar*, Caracas: Monte Avila, 1968.

———. "The New Latin American Novel." *Books Abroad* 44 (1970): 45–50.

Roffé, Reina, ed. *Espejo de escritores*. Hanover NH: Ediciones del Norte, 1985.

Ross, Peter. "The Politician as Novelist." *Antipodas* 3 (1991): 165–75.

Ruffinelli, Jorge. "Antonio Skármeta, la embriaguez vital." *Crítica en Marcha*. Montevideo: Premio, 1979. 132–45.

Rumold, Inca. "Independencia cultural de Latinoamérica." *Plural* (Mexico) 241 (1991): 18–23.

Sábato, Ernesto. *El escritor y sus fantasmas*. 3rd ed. Buenos Aires: Aguilar, 1967.

Sainz, Gustavo. *A la salud de la serpiente*. Mexico City: Grijalbo, 1988.

———. "Carlos Fuentes: A Permanent Bedazzlement." *World Literature Today* 57.4 (1983): 568–72.

———. *Compadre Lobo*. 2nd ed. Mexico City: Grijalbo, 1977.

———. *Fantasmas aztecas*. Mexico City: Grijalbo, 1982.

———. *Gazapo*. 9th ed. Mexico City: Mortiz, 1978.

———. *Gustavo Sainz*. Mexico City: Empresas Editoriales, 1966.

———. *Muchacho en llamas*. Mexico City: Grijalbo, 1988.

———. *Obsesivos días circulares*. Mexico City: Mortiz, 1979.

———. *Paseo en Trapecio*. Mexico City: Edivisión, 1985.

———. *La Princesa del Palacio de Hierro*. 6th ed. Mexico City: Ediciones del Océano, 1982.

———. *Retablo de inmoderaciones y heresiarcas*. Mexico City: Mortiz, 1992.

Saltz, Joanne. "Luisa Valenzuela's *Cambio de armas*: Rhetoric of Politics." *Confluencia* (Colorado) 3.1 (1987): 61–66.

Santí, Enrico Mario. "Textual Politics: Severo Sarduy." *Latin American Literary Review*. 8.16 (1980): 152–60.

Sarduy, Severo. *Cobra*. Buenos Aires: Sudamericana, 1975.

———. *Escrito sobre un cuerpo*. Buenos Aires: Sudamericana, 1969.

———. *Maitreya*. Trans. Suzanne Jill Levine. Hanover NH: Ediciones del Norte, 1987.

Sefamí, Jacobo. "Vertiginosidad del fuego: *Muchacho en llamas de Gustavo Sainz*." *Revista Canadiense de Estudios Hispánicos* 15 (1990): 130–39.

Shaw, Donald L. *Antonio Skármeta and the Post-Boom*. Hanover NH: Ediciones del Norte, 1994.

———. "'La Cencicienta en San Francisco' by Antonio Skármeta." *Revista de Estudios Hispánicos* 21 (1987): 89–99.

———. "La metáfora del abismo en *Sobre héroes y tumbas* de Sábato." *Actas del X Congreso Internacional de Hispanistas,* vol. 4. Ed. Antonio de Villanova. Barcelona: Promociones y Publicaciones Universitarias, 1992. 985–91.

———. "More Notes on the Presentation of Sexuality in the Modern Spanish American Novel." *Carnal Knowledge*. Ed. Pamela Bacarisse. Pittsburgh: Tres Ríos, [1993?]: 113–27.

———. "Notes on the Presentation of Sexuality in the Modern Spanish American Novel." *Bulletin of Hispanic Studies* 59 (1982): 275–82.

———. *Nueva narrativa hispanoamericana*. 5th ed. Madrid: Cátedra, 1992.

———, ed. *The Post-Boom in Spanish American Fiction. Studies in Twentieth Century Literature* (Special Issue) 19:1 (1995).

———. "Skármeta and Sexuality." *Paunch* 65–66 (1991): 11–29.

———. "The Structure of Antonio Skármeta's *Soñé que la nieve ardía*." *Paradise Lost or Gained?* Ed. Fernando Alegría and Jorge Ruffinelli. Houston: Arte Público, 1990: 145–50.

———. "Towards a Description of the Post-Boom." *Bulletin of Hispanic Studies* 66 (1989): 87–94.

———. "Which Was the First Novel of the Boom?" *Modern Language Review* 89 (1994): 360–71.

Silva Cáceres, Raúl. *Del cuerpo a las palabras: La narrativa de Antonio Skármeta*. Madrid: LAR, 1983.

Skármeta, Antonio. "Al fin y al cabo es su propia vida la cosa más cercana que cada escritor tiene para echar mano." *Del cuerpo a las palabras: la narrativa de Antonio Skármeta*. Ed. Raúl Silva Cáceres. Madrid: LAR (1983): 131–47.

———. *Ardiente paciencia*. Hanover, NH: Ediciones del Norte, 1985.

———. *Desnudo en el tejado*. Havana: Casa de las Américas, 1969.

———. *El entusiasmo,* Santiago de Chile: Zig-Zag, 1967.

———. *La insurrección*. Hanover NH: Ediciones del Norte, 1982.

———. *Match Ball*. Buenos Aires: Sudamericana, 1989.

———. *No pasó nada*. Santiago de Chile: Pehuén, 1985.

———. "La novísima generación: varias características y un límite." *Revista de Literatura Hispanoamericana* 10 (1976): 9–18.

———. *Soñé que la nieve ardía,* Barcelona: Planeta, 1975.

———. "Suprerrealidad e hiperrealidad en los cuentos de Juan Rulfo." *Spanien und Lateinamerika*. Ed. Carlos Segoviano and José M. Navarro. Nuremberg: Deutscher Spanisch-Lehrer Verlag, 2 (1984): 779–92.

——. "Tendencias en la más nueva narrativa hispanomericana." *Avances del saber*, vol. 9 of *Enciclopedia Labor*. Barcelona: Labor (1975): 753–71.

——. *Tiro Libre*. Buenos Aires: Siglo XXI, 1973.

Skinner, Lee. "Pandora's Log: Charting the Literay Project of Rosario Ferré." *Revista de Estudios Hispánicos* 29 (1995): 461–76.

Sklodowska, Elzbieta. *La parodia en la nueva novela hispanoamericana*. (Purdue University Monographs) Amsterdam: Benjamins, 1991.

——. *Testimonio hispanoamericano: Historia, teoría, poética*. New York: Lang, 1992.

Solá, María M. *Aquí cuentan las mujeres*. Río Piedras: Huracán, 1990.

Sosnowski, Saúl. "Manuel Puig, entrevista." *Hispamérica* 3 (1973): 69–80.

Steele, Cynthia. *Politics, Gender and the Mexican Novel 1968–1988*. Austin: U of Texas P, 1992.

Stone, Kenton. *Utopia Undone: The Fall of Uruguay in the Novels of Carlos Martínez Moreno*. Lewisburg: Bucknell UP, 1994.

Swanson, Philip. "Conclusion: After the Boom." *Landmarks in Modern Latin American Fiction*. London: Routledge, 1990. 222–45.

——. "Donoso and the Post-Boom." *Contemporary Literature* 28 (1987): 520–29.

——. *José Donoso: The Boom and Beyond*. Liverpool: Cairns, 1988.

——. *The New Novel in Latin America*. Manchester: Manchester UP, 1995.

——. "Structure and Meaning in *La misteriosa desaparición de la marquesita de Loria*." *Bulletin of Hispanic Studies* 58 (1986): 247–56.

Tealdi, Juan Carlos. *Borges y Viñas*. Madrid: Orígenes, 1983.

Teja, Ada. "Entrevista: Severo Sarduy." *Hispamérica* 61 (1992): 54–64.

Tiffin, Helen. "Post-Colonialism, Postmodernism and the Rehabilitation of Post-Colonial History." *Journal of Commonwealth Literature* 23.1 (1988): 169–81.

Tittler, Johnathan. *Manuel Puig*. New York: Twayne, 1993.

Toledo, Alejandro, and Daniel González Dueñas. "Entrevista." *Universidad de México* 484 (1991): 37–41.

Valenzuela, Luisa. *Aquí pasan cosas raras*. Buenos Aires: Ediciones de la Flor, 1975.

——. *Cambio de armas*, Hanover NH: Ediciones del Norte, 1982.

——. *Cola de lagartija*. 2nd ed. Buenos Aires: Bruguera, 1983.

——. *Como en la guerra*. Buenos Aires: Sudamericana, 1977.

——. "Dangerous Words." *Review of Contemporary Fiction* 6.3 (1986): 9–12.

——. *Donde viven las águilas*. Buenos Aires: Celtia, 1983.

——. *El gato eficaz*. Mexico City: Mortiz, 1972.

——. *Hay que sonreír*. Buenos Aires: Américalee, 1966.

——. *Los heréticos*. Buenos Aires: Paidós, 1967.

——. "A Legacy of Poets and Cannibals." *New York Times Book Review* 16 March 1986: 34.

——. "Little Manifesto." *Review of Contemporary Fiction* 6.3 (1986): 20–21.

——. *Novela negra con argentinos*. Barcelona: Plaza y Janés, 1990.

———. *Open Door*. San Francisco: North Point, 1988.

———. *Realidad nacional desde la cama*. Buenos Aires: Grupo Editorial Latinoamericano, 1990.

———. *Simetrías*. Buenos Aires: Sudamericana, 1993.

Vargas Llosa, Mario. "The Latin American Novel Today." *Books Abroad* 44 (1970): 7–16.

Vega Carney, Carmen. "El amor como discurso político en Ana Lydia Vega y Rosario Ferré." *Letras Femeninas* 17.1–2 (1991): 77–87.

Vélez, Diana L. "Power and the Text: Rebellion in Rosario Ferré's *Papeles de Pandora*." *Journal of the Mid-Western MLA* 17.1 (1984): 70–80.

Verlichak, Victoria. "Del entusiasmo a la insurrección." *Unomasuno* (Mexico City) (3 July 1982): 4.

Vidal, Hernán. *Literatura hispanoamericana e ideología liberal: surgimiento y crisis*. Buenos Aires: Hispamérica, 1976.

Viereck, Roberto. "De la tradición a las formas: entrevista a Roberto Piglia." *Revista Chilena de Literatura* 40 (1992): 129–38.

Viñas, David. *De Sarmiento a Cortázar*. Buenos Aires: Siglo Viente, 1971.

———. "Después de Cortázar: Historia y privatización." *Cuadernos Hispanoamericanos* 234 (1969): 734–39.

——— et al. *Más allá del Boom*. Buenos Aires: Folios, 1984.

Wharton, Edith. *Summer*. New York: Bamtam, 1993.

Williams, Raymond. *The Politics of Modernism*. London: Verso, 1989.

Williams, Raymond L. "The Boom Twenty Years Later: An Interview with Mario Vargas Llosa," *Latin American Literary Review* 15.29 (1987): 201–6.

———. *The Postmodern Novel in Latin America*. New York: St Martin's, 1995.

Wood, Maria Elena. "Antonio Skármeta." *Caras* (Santiago de Chile) 4 (15 June 1983): 54–56.

Xaubet, Horacio. *Entrevista con Antonio Skármeta*. Washington U Occasional Paper. St. Louis: Washington U, 1988.

Yepes Boscán, Guillermo, "Asturias, un pretexto del mito." *Aportes* 8 (1968): 99–116.

Yudice, George. "Postmodernism on the Periphery." *South Atlantic Quarterly* 92.3 (1993): 543–56.

———. "¿Puede hablarse de postmodernidad en América Latina?" *Revista de Crítica Literaria Latinoamericana* 15.29 (1989): 105–28.

Yudice, George, ed. *On Edge: The Crisis of Contemporary Latin American Culture*. Minneapolis: U of Minesota P, 1992.

Zadworna-Fjellestad, Danuta. *Criticism in the Twilight Zone: Postmodern Perspectives on Literature and Politics*. Stockholm: Alonquist and Wiksell, 1990.

Zietz, Eileen. *La crítica, el exilio y el más allá en las novelas de Mario Benedetti*. Montevideo: Amesur, 1986.

# INDEX